O DE PANAMÁ
P OF PANAMA

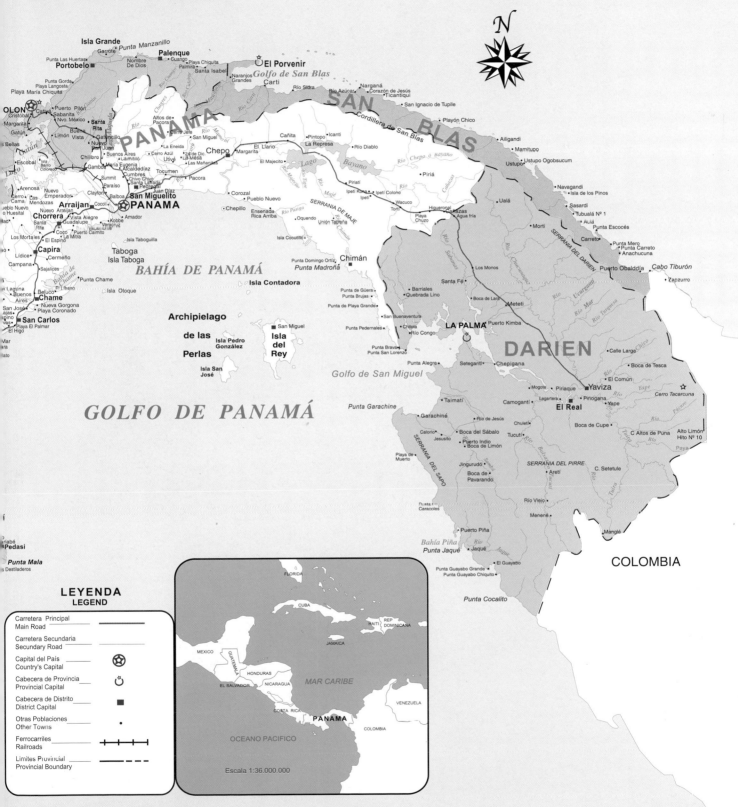

N

PANAMA

Isla Grande
Punta Manzanillo
Garrote
Palenque
Punta Las Huertas
Nombre De Dios
Cuango
Portobelo
Playa Chiquita
Santa Isabel
Palmira
El Porvenir
Punta Gorda
Playa Langosta
Naranjos Grandes
Golfo de San Blas
Playa María Chiquita
Cartí
Narganá
Río Sidra
Corazón de Jesús
SAN
Río Azúcar
Ticantiquí
OLON
Puerto Pilón
San Ignacio de Tupile
Cristóbal
Sabanita
Nvo. México
Santa Rita
Altos de Pacora
Cerro Jefe
Cordillera de San Blas
Playón Chico
BLAS
Margarita
Buena Vista
Ailigandí
Limón
Cañita
Pintopo
Icanti
Mamitupo
Gatún
Nuevo
Chilibre
La Eneida
San Miguel
Ustupo Ogobsucum
Bellas
Cerro Azúl
El Llano
La Represa
Río Diablo
Gamboa
Buenos Aires
Chepo
Margarita
Piriatí
Piriá
Navagandí
Isla de los Pinos
Escobal
Summit
María Eugenia
Alcaldedíaz
El Majecito
Lago
Ipetí Kuná
Ipetí Colono
U$ala
Sasardi
Arenosa
Cumbres
Tocumen
Pacora
Ipetí
Wacuco
Tubualá Nº 1
Nuevo Emperador
Santa Librada
Pedregal
Juan Díaz
Bayano
Tortí
Morti
Aula
Paraíso
Clayton
San Miguelito
Corozal
SERRANÍA DE MAJE
Higueronal
Punta Escocés
PANAMA
Pueblo Nuevo
Ensenada Rica Arriba
Playa Chuzo
Carreto
Arraiján
Vista Alegre
Balboa
Cocolí
Chepillo
Oquendo
Agua fría
Punta Mero
Chorrera
Guadalupe
Amador
Unión Tableña
Punta Carreto
Coco
La Mitra
Anachucuna
Los Mortales
El Espino
Isla Taboguilla
Isla Cocotillo
Los Monos
Puerto Obaldía
Cabo Tiburón
Lídice
Cerro Azúl
Taboga
Isla Taboga
SERRANÍA DEL DARIEN
Zapzurro
Campana
Sajalices
Punta Domingo Ortiz
Chimán
Santa Fé
Capira
Cerreño
Punta Madroña
Barriales
Río Chucunaque
Chame
Nueva Gorgona
Isla Otoque
Quebrada Lino
Calle Larga
Buenos Aires
Playa Coronado
Punta de Güera
Boca de Lara
Boca de Tesca
San José
San Carlos
Punta Brujas
Meteti
El Común
Playa El Palmar
El Higo
Punta de Playa Grande
San Buenaventura
LA PALMA
Puerto Kimba
DARIEN
BAHÍA DE PANAMÁ
Isla Contadora
Punta Pedernales
Chitola
Río Congo
Archipiélago de las Perlas
San Miguel
Isla Pedro González
Punta Brava
Punta San Lorenzo
Punta Alegre
Setegantí
Chepigana
Isla del Rey
Golfo de San Miguel
Mogote
Piriaque
Yaviza
Cerro Tacarcuna
Isla San José
Camoganti
Lagartera
Pinogana
Río Yape
El Real
Yape
GOLFO DE PANAMÁ
Punta Garachine
Taimatí
Chuletí
SERRANÍA DEL PIRRE
C Altos de Púna
Alto Limón Hito Nº 10
Garachiné
Río de Jesús
Boca de Cupe
Calorio
Boca del Sábalo
Tucutí
Paya
Jesusito
Puerto Indio
SERRANÍA DEL SAPO
Boca de Limón
Playa de Muerto
Jingurudó
SERRANÍA DEL PIRRE
Areti
C. Setetule
Boca de Pavarando
Río Viejo
Menené
Manglé
Bahía Piña
Puerto Piña
Punta Jaqué
Jaqué
El Guayabo
Pedasí
Punta Guayabo Grande
COLOMBIA
Punta Mala
Punta Guayabo Chiquito
Destiladeros
Punta Cocalito

FLORIDA
CUBA
HAITÍ
REP. DOMINICANA
MEXICO
JAMAICA
GUATEMALA
HONDURAS
MAR CARIBE
EL SALVADOR
NICARAGUA
VENEZUELA
COSTA RICA
PANAMA
COLOMBIA
OCEANO PACIFICO

Escala 1:36.000.000

Panama Now

PORTRAIT OF THE NATION

FOCUS

PANAMA NOW
Portrait of the Nation
Reference Book of the Republic

PANAMA HOY
Retrato de la nación
Obra de referencia de la República

PREFACE

"Panama Now" is a yearbook in content but published every few years. It is also related to the coffee- table genre. However you care to consider the book, it is, as its sub-title describes it, a portrait of the Panamanian nation.

This is the fifth edition of Panama Now which has become a standard reference work, a top seller at bookstores and news stands throughout the Republic and sought-after by investors, scholars and travellers; not to mention Panamanians who want to keep at hand concise information about all aspects of the Republic's affairs or send a copy to associates, friends or family abroad. The book is also published in a Spanish language edition called "Panama Hoy".

The chapters in the book are the work of Panamanian journalists, foreign correspondents and experts in various fields. Talented photographers, national and foreign, have contributed their work for the outstanding sections of pictures and many companies and institutions have submitted "profiles" which add another dimension in showing the strength of Panama's economy and social structure. It all adds up to an attractive book which reflects the exciting times in which we live.

This edition is special because it commemorates the centenary of the Republic. It spanned a time in which the world has seen the greatest technological and cultural advances in history and Panama has been in the vanguard. The year the country gained its independence from Colombia (1903), the Wright Brothers invented the airplane, an invention which, approximately 10 years later, was already delivering mail between Panama City and Colón. The construction of one of the greatest engineering projects of the 20th century –the Panama Canal—helped eradicate deadly diseases from the Isthmus years before many North American. cities had improved their own sanitation standards.

Back in a time when inter-cultural communications were still limited to the privileged few, and decades before the United Nations was created, Panama was experiencing one of the greatest sociological experiments of all times: North Americans, Europeans, Hispanics, Jews, West Indians, Asians and East Indians –all of whom arrived to dig the Canal—learned to work and live with each other. Not only did the experiment work, but created a colorful population of all shades of skin color and religious beliefs. Today, Panamanians are proud of living in the most cosmopolitan, safe, and prosperous country in the region.

Published in 2002 by Focus Publications (Int), S.A in separate Spanish and English editions.

Editor: Kenneth J. Jones
Associate Editor: Roberta G. Jones

Authors
Michele Labrut: Panama Canal, Financial Center, Economy, Reverted Areas, Ship Registry.
Dennis Smith: Telecommunications, City of Knowledge, Casco Viejo, Investment incentives
    The Panamanian Corporation.
Theodore James: Ports.
Gabriel Leonard: Tourism.
Roxanna Cain: Panama's Century.
Samuel Villamonte: Panama Statistics
Kenneth J. Jones: Air Transport.
Georgina de Alba: Smithsonian Institute.
Madelag: A stroll through the Old City.

Translators and editorial assistants
Gabriel Leonard
Maribel Corcó
Samuel Villamonte

Consulting editors, Spanish edition
Israel Arguedas
Gabriel Leonard
Samuel Villamonte

Design and illustration:
Verónica Villanueva
María Luisa Gutiérrez

Typesetting and formatting:
Gisela Abrego
Beatríz Pino

Frontispiece photo
Carlos Girón, Courtesy of "El Panama America"

Printed by: Printer Colombiana, Bogota

Focus Publications (Int), S.A.
P.O. Box: 6-3287, El Dorado, Panama Republic of Panama
Tel.: (507) 225-6638. Fax: (507) 225-0466
focusint@sinfo.net
www.focuspublicationsint.com

972.87
P191pan Panama now/; compilado por Kenneth Jones; traducción de Gabriel Leonard; ilustrador
        Verónica Villanueva -- 5a. ed.– Panamá: Focus Publications Int.
        2002.
            256.: il; 28 cm.
            ISBN 9962-5514-4-7
            1. HISTORIA – PANAMA   2. GOBIERNO – PANAMA
            3. TURISMO – PANAMA   4. ECONOMIA – PANAMA
            OTROS TEMAS.

Contents

This is Panama

A brief introduction to this fascinating country, the pathway between two oceans, with its mountains, jungles and vibrant economy

Panama occupies a narrow isthmus of 77,000 square kilometers,which links North and Central America with the countries of the South. The highway across the narrowest part is only 100 kilometers long... a bather could take a dip in the Atlantic, get in his car and be swimming in the Pacific in less than an hour and a half.

The topography of Panama is rugged and mountainous. A mountain chain travels lengthwise across the country and rises to a height of over 3,000 meters in the west, where it is a prolongation of the high mountains of Costa Rica. Panama's most towering peak is Volcan Barú, an extinct volcano in the western province of Chiriqui, at 3,475 meters. The mountain chain descends in uneven fashion down to the metropolitan area where the Canal is carved through hills about 100 meters high. To the east of the city the mountains gradually ascend again until reaching 2,000 meters before penetrating the Colombian frontier and eventually joining the cordillera of the Andes.

Panama is different from other countries of Central America because of the absence of active volcanoes. Volcan Barú has been inactive for a very long time and although the experts indicate that the isthmus of Panama, in common with the rest of the Central American isthmus, and the greater part of the Pacific coast of South and North America is in an area classified as "suffering frequent seismic disturbances", until now these disturbances have affected primarily the western area (provinces of Chiriquí and Bocas del Toro), and only been felt very mildly in the central or "metropolitan" region.

The tropical area

Panama is located within the world's torrid or tropical zone, between 7 and 9 degrees of northern latitude and 77 and 83 degrees of western latitude. A large part of the territory is (or was) covered with dense tropical forests bathed with heavy rains during the eight months that comprise the rainy or "winter" season from May to December.

As a tropical country, Panama enjoys (suffers!) a hot climate. The temperature in Panama fluctuates around 22 to 31 degrees centigrade nearly all the year. Temperatures are higher in July and August in step with the northern summer. In the highest areas of the country the average temperature is about 19 degrees.

Apart from its privileged geographical position, Panama has among its principal resources an abundance of water. Some 150 rivers empty along the Atlantic Coast. Among the most important are the Changuinola (140 kms.), the Indio (99 kms.), and the Chagres (92 kms.). About 350 rivers flow into the Pacific. The most important are the Bayano (280 kms.), the Chucunaque (242 kms.), and the Tuira (230 kms.).

In the jungle areas of Panama there is an extraordinary variety of insects, birds, reptiles and mammals. Marine life is extremely abundant and varied along the coasts of both oceans. Also there is a great diversity of trees, shrubs, grass and plants throughout the isthmus.

Civilizations and the tropics

Panama never developed large indigenous civilizations. Even so, the pre-Columbian inheritance of Panama is as rich as that of other Latin American countries. Archaeological evidence traces civilizations on the isthmus going back 11,000 years. In spite of the traumatic effect of the Spanish conquest and colonization on these indigenous people, there exist at present several important groups in Panama, among which are the Guaymies, the Kunas and the Chocoes.

In his fourth and last voyage, Columbus made landfall on the isthmus. The first exploration of Panama during the colonial era was by Rodrigo Galvan de Bastidas, who sailed from Cádiz around the end of 1500.

The first colony was established in 1503 by Vasco Núñez de Balboa, who had accompanied Bastidas. Núñez de Balboa crossed the dense jungle and discovered the Pacific Ocean, a monumental feat that immediately established the strategic importance of Panama. Nothing remains today of the site of the original colony, destroyed by the Indians and the jungle. It was followed by Portobelo, named by Columbus who was impressed by the beauty of the place.

After the discovery of the Southern Sea by Núñez de Balboa, who was beheaded in 1519 by order of the Governor, Pedro Arias Dávila, a land route was established from Portobelo to the site of the first City of Panama on the coast of the Pacific. This route, known as the Cruces Trail, acquired supreme importance for the Spanish crown, since it opened the route toward the gold of the Incas. The decadence of Spain and her relative weakness compared to England and other European powers led to changes in the original route of the Peruvian gold (which was later carried around Cape Horn to avoid the attention of Caribbean pirates) so from 1730 onwards the importance of Panama waned.

During the following years the Isthmians pursued agriculture and cattle-raising, especially in the peaceful coastal regions of the central provinces and Chiriqui. There the descendants of the Europeans were mixed with the Indians and blacks and established communities with their own distinctive culture and own folklore.

In spite of the bad times, the Isthmians stayed loyal to the Spanish crown until 1821, when independence was declared. Panama opted then to be joined to the "Great Colombia" of Bolivar. But the political strife and the constant civil wars that afflicted Colombia motivated the Isthmians to attempt a separation from Colombia as early as the year 1840.

With the signing of the Mallarino / Bidlack treaty in 1846 began the first phase of Panama's relationship with the United States, which was then protecting Colombia from English colonial aspirations, in exchange for free traffic for its citizens across the isthmus. The construction of the Trans-Isthmian Railroad in 1855, and the large banana plantations established in the province of Bocas del Toro at the end of the century helped to forge ties between Panama and the United States.

In the beginning of the 20th century the failure of a French attempt to build a Canal across the isthmus of Panama coincided with aspirations of the United States to find a convenient route between its coasts. The rejection of a treaty between Colombia and the U.S. for the construction of the Canal was the spark that fired a new separatist movement in Panama, one which had the enthusiastic support of Washington.

A new treaty permitted the construction of the Panama Canal from 1904 to 1914, an event which decisively marked the direction of the economic and social development of Panama. The metropolitan region, which comprises the coastal cities of Panama and Colón and their suburban areas, have enjoyed since then an intensive phase of economic and population growth. As a result, Panama has developed a sophisticated international trade center, a financial center, and supplies many other services of an international nature which have given Panama a relatively high per capita income. Also modern industry has been developed, though relatively less sophisticated than the services sector, partly because industry has been traditionally aimed mainly at the limited national market. The commercial evolution of the countryside has been slower.

Panama's Century

From the birth of the nation in 1903, Panama's progress has been hand in hand and sometimes eyeball to eyeball with the United States — but it was a largely peaceful century with a happy ending

The history of Panama can be characterized by two main elements - an aversion to violence and a century-long, love-hate relationship with the United States that ended officially on December 31, 1999, with the U.S. handover of the Panama Canal to Panama in accordance with treaties signed in 1977 between U.S. President Jimmy Carter and Panama strongman General Omar Torrijos.

Unlike its Central American neighbors, which throughout the century have lived the horror of civil and inter-country wars, Panama participated in only one war, a border dispute with Costa Rica.

Links with Spain and Colombia

Panama had been part of the Spanish Empire since the discovery of America in the 1600s, and remained bound to Spain until declaring independence in 1821 when most other Latin American countries did the same. Panama immediately decided voluntarily to join a loose confederacy of nations led by the legendary Simon Bolivar that was called the Gran Colombia. It was difficult for Bolivar to maintain his dream of Latin American unity, however. This was mostly because of the enormous geographical difficulties posed by the Andes mountain range, which made traveling through his possessions a matter of months. By the time he arrived in one capital to solve a problem, it had already changed or been solved, and his attention was drawn elsewhere, finally making the situation untenable. There were also great cultural differences between confederacy members, and eventually it fell apart. Much to Panama's credit, the only Bolivarian Congress of the confederacy was held in this city on June 22, 1826. Bolivar envisioned Panama as the center of this peaceful, progressive union. But Bolivar's powerful generals in South America betrayed him, and the dream came to an end with Bolivar's depression and death in 1830. Once the confederacy fell apart, Panama remained part of Colombia as a province or "department" for 82 years. Years of neglect by its distant capital, Bogota, and impoverished conditions in the department disillusioned citizens.

Relations with United States begin

For Panama the 20th century was marked by its relations with the United States. Sometimes for good, sometimes for bad, there was a strong attraction between the two countries: one large and powerful, the other small, but with enormous value to the United States —and this was not only between the two governments, but between

Presidents of Panama

These reproductions are from the oil paintings hanging in the Yellow Room of the presidential Palace of the Herons. Here are nearly all the Panamanians who, for short periods or complete terms, have filled the post of President. During the Republic's 100 years, Panama has had struggles, intrigues, achievements and triumphs. But always her chief executives have kept the national flag flying with pride.

The images on these pages were supplied by the State Office of Communication at the Presidency. No photos were available for the following presidents: Bolivar Urrutia 1968-1969, Arturo Sucre 1969-1972, Gerardo Gonzalez, 1976, Manuel Solis Palma 1988-1989 and Francisco Rodriguez 1989.

Manuel Amador Guerrero
1904 - 1908

José De Obaldía
1907
1908 - 1910

Carlos A. Mendoza
1910

Federico Boyd
1910

Pablo Arosemena
1910-1912

Rodolfo Chiari
1912 / 1923
1924 - 1928

Belisario Porras
1912 - 1916
1918 - 1920 / 1920 - 1924

Ramón M. Valdés
1916 - 1918

Ciro Luis Urriola
1918

Pedro A. Díaz
1918

Ernesto T. Lefevre
1920

Tomás Gabriel Duque
1928

Florencio H. Arosemena
1928 - 1931

Harmodio Arias
1931
1932 - 1936

Ricardo J. Alfaro
1931 - 1932

Domingo D. Arosemena
1933
1948 - 1949

Juan D. Arosemena
1936 - 1939

Ezequiel F. Jaén
1939

Augusto S. Boyd
1939 - 1940

Arnulfo Arias Madrid
1940 - 1941
1949 - 1951 / 1968

José Pezet
1941

Ernesto Jaén Guardia
1941

Ricardo A. de la Guardia
1941 - 1945

Enrique A. Jiménez
1945 - 1948

Daniel Chanis
1949

Roberto F. Chiari
1949
1960 - 1964

Alcibiades Arosemena
1951 - 1952

José A. Remón Cantera
1952 - 1955

José Ramón Guizado
1953 / 1955

Ricardo M. Arias Espinosa
1954
1955 - 1956

Ernesto de la Guardia
1956 - 1960

Sergio González R.
1961 - 1962

José D. Bazán
1962

Bernardino G. Ruiz
1963

Marcos Aurelio Robles
1964 - 1968

Max Del Valle
1967

José María Pinilla
1968 - 1969

Gral. Omar Torrijos
1972 - 1978

Demetrio B. Lakas
1969 - 1978

Aristides Royo
1978 - 1982

Ricardo De La Espriella
1982 - 1984

Jorge Illueca
1984

Nicolás Ardito Barletta
1984 - 1985

Eric Arturo Del Valle
1985 - 1988

Guillermo Endara
1989 - 1994

Guillermo Ford
1994

Ernesto Pérez Balladares
1994 - 1999

Tomás Altamirano Duque
1995

Mireya Moscoso
1999 -

the two peoples. Americans who came to Panama were fascinated by the tropical surroundings and fun-loving people and many stayed long after their official duties finished, often marrying black-haired beauties and making Panama their permanent home.

One of the first events that began to forge Panama's national personality as well as its unique relationship with the United States was the construction by U.S. financiers of the Panama Railroad in the 1850s. The railroad offered gold rushers a safe route across the 50-mile Isthmus of Panama. Indeed, because of Indian attacks on travellers crossing the U.S. continent, it was safer to travel from the East to the West Coast by sailing south to Panama's Atlantic coast. Here they booked passage on a Panama Railroad car, traveling the 50-mile route across the isthmus in some two hours, and disembarked on the Pacific side to board steamers to seek their fortune in California.

The arrival of American railroad men and of the thousands of travellers through the cities of Panama and Colon who stopped at the haberdashery for a new suit, found good fare at a restaurant, lodged at the local hotel, and enjoyed the night life of the admittedly muddy and insect-ridden cities, began to instill in city dwellers a cosmopolitan air. The West Indians remaining in town from the foiled French canal construction effort spoke fluent English so communication was easy. Wares began to be imported from as far as the Far East to meet the travellers' whimsical shopping needs. Indian merchants settled in the towns to cater to them. Persian carpets and bronze goblets were available in increasingly sophisticated stores, and Chinese laundry men who had settled in Panama, arriving from San Francisco, took in travellers' wash and allowed them to board their steamers looking impeccable for their northernward voyages to prosperity.

Construction of the American railroad through Panama was the first serious connection between the two cultures. It later even played a role in Panama's independence from Colombia in 1903, when railroad men, friendly with the cause and leaders of the independence movement managed to hold Colombian troops on the Atlantic side of the railway while independence was completed in the Pacific capital city of Panama. Here was a deep   friendship in the making.

Panama's Independence and the move to build the Canal

Had it not been for U.S. President Theodore Roosevelt's stubbornness in building an interoceanic canal to expand U.S. sea power, Panama may not have seen statehood. Roosevelt began negotiations for the Canal construction with Colombia, of which Panama was still a province at the time. However, these failed after the Colombian congress rejected the treaty as unsatisfactory. This was August 12, 1903. But Roosevelt was determined to have his canal. So immediately an overture was made to a group of Panamanian patriots who had long felt they had much to gain from independence. They were offered help in achieving independence in return for a treaty that would permit construction of a U.S. canal through their territory and $10,000,000 in hard cash to get the fledgling republic on its feet. The rebel group, mostly from the upper, educated class, accepted the offer and preparations began for a secret revolt against the motherland. To close the deal, the rights of the old French canal company were purchased for $40 million. The purchase of the French holdings in Panama was the largest real estate transaction in history until then.

A Shrewd Frenchman

A treaty would have to be drawn up for the canal construction, and for this the Panamanian rebels unwisely placed their trust in the cunning Frenchman, Philippe Buneau Varilla. Varilla had served as chief engineer for the French Canal construction effort, and had much to gain from a deal with the Americans that would help regain some of the millions lost by the bankrupt canal company as well as his own holdings in it if the United States agreed to purchase the French Canal rights.

The Panamanian revolutionaries appointed Buneau Varilla as plenipotentiary minister and sent him to Washington to negotiate. Soon realizing their mistake, the Panamanian revolutionaries despatched three plenipotentiary ministers by steamer to New York. The treaty was so advantageous to both the United States and Buneau Varilla, that the latter found a way to delay the three Panamanian diplomats in the Waldorf Astoria Hotel in New York until after the Hay-Buneau Varilla Treaty was signed, stamped, and sealed on November 18, 1903.

Under the treaties, the United States purchased all rights and properties of the old French canal company in

Panama for $40 million, a true fortune for the day. Second, and more ominously, Buneau Varilla granted the United States a 10-mile wide, 50-mile long strip of land in Panama to be used "as if sovereign" and "in perpetuity." According to Buneau Varilla himself, when the revolutionary leader and later first President of Panama, Manuel Amador Guerrero, heard the terms of the treaty, he looked as though he was about to faint. But as the story would be told later in Panama, the Panamanians in Washington had been by stages incredulous, indignant, and then livid with rage. One rebel leader is said to have hit Bunau Varilla across the face on the quay.

In Panamanian schools, children soon learn to identify Bunau Varilla as the man who sold Panama "down the river"

The unfavorable terms of the treaty constituted a thorn in the side of relations between the United States and Panama that would not begin to be solved until 1964, when riots led to 23 Panamanian dead and several U.S. wounded. Panama's President Roberto F. Chiari broke off diplomatic relations with the United States, and U.S. President Lyndon B. Johnson, realizing the seriousness of the matter, issued instructions for the beginning of earnest negotiations to replace the 1903 treaty. This finally came to fruition after 13 years of thorny, difficult negotiations that ended on September 7, 1977, with the signing of the Torrijos-Carter Treaties. The treaties promised full transfer of the Canal to Panama and the full withdrawal of U.S. military bases and troops from Panama within a 20-year term. In essence, it ended the clause of "perpetuity" of the 1903 treaty and permitted improved relations between the two countries. When one says "treaties" versus "treaty" that is because at the last moment the United States added a second treaty called the Neutrality Treaty that grants the United States the unilateral right to intervene in Panama if it deems the Canal is in imminent danger of being closed or otherwise seriously threatened. That was a second thorn in the side of Panamanians, but they had to accept it if they wanted the Torrijos-Carter Treaty signed, so they did.

The Building of the Panama Canal

Preparing for the gargantuan construction work that would be the Panama Canal, Panama's sleepy cities, especially Panama City, which was the capital, and Colon, the second major city, located on the Atlantic side, began to wake to the hubbub of activity as Americans, West Indians, and even Indians, Spaniards, and Greeks began to disembark at the quays along with tractors, cranes, steel, lumber and every conceivable implement one could imagine necessary both to build the largest-ever civil engineering work the world had known and also the complementary works: housing for employees, storehouses, schoolhouses for employees' children, not to mention swimming pools, clubs, and of course, grocery stores.

On March 4, 1904, with absolutely no ceremony, U.S. Lieutenant Mark Brooke received from French officials the keys to the French hospitals, marking the official transfer of the French installations to the United States and the beginning of the U.S. construction period.

The construction of the Canal, accomplished between 1904 and 1914, required the removal of gargantuan amounts of dirt and rock, cost the lives of 26,000 men, including those killed during the French construction effort the century before, but resulted in one of the greatest engineering feats of all time. More than 800,000 vessels have transited the waterway from more than 88 nations since its construction, carrying everything from coal and steel, iron ore, oil, automobiles, and containerized cargo. Passengers traveling on more than 300 cruise ships per year continue to marvel at its lush surrounding vegetation that contrasts sharply with the nuts and bolts and enormous structures that make possible a rapid, trouble-free transit even after 85 years of service.

After World War II and the launching of the U.S. aircraft carrier fleets in the Atlantic and Pacific, the Canal's importance became more commercial than military, Some 16 percent of commerce destined to or from U.S. ports continues to use the waterway and 4 percent of total world commerce travels through this ocean passage.

The growth of a country

Panama, like many Latin American countries, was and perhaps still is a country not so much of political ideals as of caudillos, or charismatic leaders. The first of these was Dr. Belisario Porras, who served the first of his three terms in office in 1912. He was considered a great Liberal leader. The political traditions of Panama's Colombian past - Liberalism against Conservatism - prevailed. Under Porras, government institutions were organized. But U.S. influence overpowered Panama, and in 1918, in violation of all constitutional order, the United

States, through the Governor of the Canal Zone, installed Dr. Porras back in power for a second term over his legal contender who had won the election. Fortunately, Porras was popular among the Panamanian populace, because once again in 1920, under U.S. influence over the electoral outcome, Porras became president for a third time. His government platform included developing the provinces, which were devoid of roads. The interior of the country still remained almost under the same conditions of the Colonial days. But again Porras did good deeds, simplifying the electoral code to have general elections every four years rather than two. He also set into place an organized economic plan for the development of the entire country and for road construction.

The one violent episode in that era occurred in 1921, under Porras' administration when a border war broke out with Costa Rica, Panama's western neighbor. It was called the War of Coto, and consisted of Costa Rica invading part of western Panama on the basis of a 1900 U.S ruling called the White Ruling. The Panamanians faced some 2,000 Costa Rican troops, mostly with weapons retrieved from President Porras' basement in the Presidential Palace. Again the United States intervened, this time on the side of the Costa Ricans, and Panama was forced to accept a humiliating ultimatum issued by U.S. President Harding and to lose a battle which was not to be solved until 1941.

President Porras' most visible work in Panama City is the Santo Tomas Hospital, considered a white elephant in its day and today the most important charity hospital in the country. So that one may gain an idea, the entire Republic of Panama in 1920 had a population of 449,098. The province of Panama had a population of 98,035. Colon Province had 45,151 inhabitants, and the southwesterly province of Los Santos 34,638. It is evident that whatever politicking went on in that era, it was small-town stuff.

Arnulfo Arias

Some elderly —and not so elderly— folks, especially in the provinces, still refer to Arnulfo Arias as "Doctor Arias." Admittedly a medical doctor by profession, the term was - and is - used more as a term of respect and admiration. Like Belisario Porras, he was president three times, though he never completed a full term in office. Although he was the second next great Panamanian caudillo, Arias' quirky personality and political passions always seemed to stir up trouble. To gain power for his political party, Accion Popular, for example, which was trying to seize power by force by assaulting the Police Headquarters and later the Presidency, Arias was able to enter the Presidency through a window he had left open the night before, and once inside, demanded the resignation of the incumbent president.

As president, despite his vociferous anti-Americanism, he liked and was well liked by U.S official representatives in Panama, albeit often only on the surface. It may have been a mixture of extremely charming diplomacy and the attraction of undeniable charismatic powers, and wining and dining the American ambassador in the exclusive Union Club.

His first term was served in 1940. His term had begun in the middle of World War II, and the United States asked permission to build new military bases in Panama. He accepted, under the condition that the United States commence earnest negotiations with Panama to revoke the insulting terms of the 1903 treaty. The United States agreed, but as soon as Arias departed Panama on a pleasure trip to Cuba, U.S. officials conspired with Panamanians unhappy with Arias' government and toppled him as soon as he returned. A government that had lasted but a year left as legacy the creation of the Social Security, today the most important social institution the country possesses. He became president the second time in 1949. Amid charges of corruption, riots broke out in Panama City, and in 1951 he was again toppled, this time by impeachment. His third term as president has to do with our next personage.

Omar Torrijos

Arias, like the the portraits of Omar Torrijos, the signatory of the 1977 treaty with the United States which handed over the Panama Canal to Panama on December 31,1999, still hangs in the homes of many Panamanian families, especially of humble extraction.

The story of Omar Torrijos began in 1952 with the creation of the Panama National Guard, similar in style to the U.S. National Guard. Its structure and organization received much support from the United States, in reaction to the Communist threat that loomed in many parts of the world. Its first commander was José Antonio

Remón Cantera, who later rose to become president, only to be assassinated, the act always remaining a mystery. Remón was the only president of Panama to meet such a fate.

Torrijos meantime was slowly rising though the ranks of the Guard under the protection of Commander Bolivar Vallarino. But once Vallarino retired, leadership became muddled in the National Guard, and political aspirations, which had already been there, came to the surface. Mostly of modest or middle class extraction, the officers and troops of the Guard, in common with much of Panama, were tired of decades of domination by the aristocratic, wealthy families of Panama who had held power since independence in 1903. They believed they had better ideas for governing the country - by now of some 1.5 million inhabitants and they decided they might just give it a try.

The story must take us back to Arnulfo Arias, who had just been elected to his third term in office on October 1, 1968. The guardsmen staged a military coup against him on October 11, sending Arias into exile into the Panama Canal Zone and declaring Torrijos as head of state. Thus began a military dictatorship that would last for 21 years. Torrijos was one of the colonels leading the coup, but his clever handling of both politics and people soon made him the "strongman" of Panama in 1969 until his mysterious death in a helicopter crash in 1981 in the mountains of Coclé Province.

In hindsight, very good and very bad things happened during Torrijos' dictatorship. He set out to modernize the country, both its infrastructure and institutions. He built hundreds of new schools and employed thousands of new teachers, improving education throughout the country.

The Banking Center was his creation. He opened up participation in government to the lower and middle classes, a phenomenon unknown until his day. To Torrijos one must attribute the birth of the middle class, today a thriving, important segment of Panama's society,

The ugly parts of every dictatorship were also present, from heavy press censorship, to unresolved disappearances of dissidents, to the milestone disappearance and presumed killing of Catholic priest Hector Gallego, who helped peasants operate a farm co-op in Veraguas Province. That murder is still unresolved, and it seriously tainted the Torrijos regime.

Despite all this, Torrijos had the clout to bring Panamanian masses to support him in the plebiscite called to approve or disapprove the treaty he had negotiated in Washington to once and for all repeal the odious Hay-Buneau Varilla Treaty of 1903. He won and the treaty was approved in Panama and in Washington. The treaties, called the Torrijos-Carter Treaties after their signatories, were signed in the headquarters of the Organization of American States in the presence of countless hemispheric leaders.

General Noriega

A sidebar on the Noriega years is called for. He became military dictator of Panama shortly after Torrijos' death which many believe ocurred in suspicious circumstances. Manuel Antonio Noriega had an impoverished, unhappy childhood. He did receive a military education, however, through help from a benefactor. He ruled the country through puppet presidents, and fear of his secret police tactics held the population at bay.

Resistance to Noriega's regime began to crystalize when he was accused of masterminding the killing and decapitation of former Deputy Health Minister and Nicaraguan guerrilla sympathizer Hugo Spadafora, a heroic and colorful medical doctor. The killing marked the beginning of Noriega's downfall.

The claim at the beginning of this chapter that Panamanians are characterized by nonviolence is shown by the fact that forcing Noriega from power was achieved in precisely that way (with final intervention of the United States). Panamanians from all segments of society took to the streets in the hundreds of thousands, armed with nothing more than white handkerchiefs to demand his ouster. The pressure was tremendous. The Church, student organizations, and countless civic organizations came together under the Cruzada Civilista or Civic Campaign. The banking sector was frozen.

The final straw was the presidential election in May 1989, in which the opponents of the political party he supported won by a landslide. Noriega voided the election.

Leaders of the Crusade went to the U.S. Congress to testify until formal drug trafficking charges were lodged. The final outcome, was the U.S. invasion to capture Noriega on December 20, 1989, and Noriega was taken away by U.S. forces as a prisoner of war. Noriega, formerly in the pay of the CIA, had built the Panama Defense Force into a formidable army, used to browbeat the civilian population, but puny in the face of a massive U.S onslaught.

Thousands cheered along the streets at the passing of U.S. forces, but intellectuals and nationalists continue to condemn the action to this day. If the aim was to capture one criminal, why invade an entire country? The issue continues to be debated to this day.

Return to democracy

Democracy in Panama was restored in December, 1989 when Guillermo Endara, who had won the popular elections annulled by Noriega earlier that year, took office in a U.S. military base, along with his two vice-presidents: Ricardo Arias Calderon and Guillermo Ford. The country, however, was bankrupt and war-torn, with an almost non-existent political framework following the abrupt removal of the 21-year-old military dictatorship.

A tight control of government expenditures was one of the main factors that allowed a prompt economic recovery. In a matter of months, most visible signs of the U.S. military action were erased. The strengthening of democratic institutions attracted foreign and local investment, and before the mid-1990s Panama boasted one of the highest economic growth rates in Latin America.

Panama City grew toward the skies as new banks, hotels and office buildings elongated the capital's skyline. Tourism, which had long been ignored by past governments despite the country's strong leisure potential, became fashionable, and new luxury cruise ports and lodging establishments of all sizes appeared throughout the country.

A new government institution, the Inter-oceanic Region Authority (ARI) was created to administrate the lands and U.S. military facilities that gradually returned to Panamanian hands as stated in the 1977 Panama Canal Treaties.

Democracy was consolidated in 1994, the year the most transparent elections in the nationís history were held. Ernesto Pérez Balladares, of the Democratic Revolutionary Party (founded by Omar Torrijos) became Panama's president, and began an aggressive campaign to steer the country toward globalization by privatizing a number of government entities. Balladares also launched a series of public work projects that included the refurbishment of the Pan-American Highway and the construction of the Corredor Norte and Sur expressways in the capital.

Perhaps the fear of change in regards to Balladares' economic policy can be considered one of the factors that motivated a majority of Panamanians to vote against the PRD in the 1999 elections. Such a decision made more history than immediately meets the eye. On September 1 of that year, Mireya Moscoso, the widow of legendary 20th century-leader Arnulfo Arias, became the first female elected as President of the Republic of Panama. Four months later, on December 31, on the steps of the Panama Canal Administration Building in Balboa, Moscoso led the nation in reaching its most coveted dream: the complete withdrawal of U.S. troops from the Isthmus and the control transfer of the famous waterway from U.S. to Panamanian hands.

Moscoso, who led the country into the 21st century, presented the nation with a package of projects targeted at reducing poverty. She discontinued her predecessor's policy on privatization. This, however, did little to spare the country from the effects of a world-wide economic recession that inflated national unemployment rates to over 14%. Nevertheless, the nation's booming tourist industry, a strong maritime sector and a healthy banking system gave the economy a measure of stability.

Special personalities

History is the story of people, and although some do not fit the formal description of political or cultural mold, they certainly deserve mention. The four-time boxing champion of the world, Roberto "Mano de Piedra" Duran certainly fits this category. This writer, finding herself in a taxicab in New York City many years ago driven by a heavily-accented Russian, was having trouble establishing her country of origin. Finally he turned and grinned broadly: "Ah, Roberto Duran, Panama." And all was resolved. Other characters of our social history are the singer and actor Ruben Blades, and the record-breaking jockey, Laffit Pinckay, who was born in Panama, as well as baseball great, the pitcher Mariano Rivera. They all complement the greatness of this small but very special country.

Government and the Constitution

Here are the nuts and bolts of the working of the Republic, which vests power in the people under three powers of state and which will have no army

The Panamanian nation is organized as a sovereign and independent state, known as the Republic of Panama. The power is solely vested in the people and exercised by the state, which functions through the Executive, Legislative and Judicial branches, as is expressed in the first two articles of the Political Constitution of the Republic of Panama, which lays down the social, economic and political principles of the country.

To date, Panama has had four constitutions, introduced in the years 1904, 1941, 1946 and 1972. The latter was revised in 1983. A noteworthy constitutional amendment, voted by two successive assemblies in 1994, affirms that Panama will have no army, only bodies of specialized police.

The government of Panama is divided into a central government and "decentralized" government entities. The central government is led by the cabinet, which consists of the president, vice presidents and ministers of state under the direction of the president. Thus, the cabinet represents the three powers of the state: Executive, Legislative and Judicial. The Comptroller General's office and the Electoral Tribunal are also represented on the Cabinet.

Executive Branch
The Executive branch comprises the president, the vice-presidents and the ministers of state. The president and the first and second vice presidents are elected by direct popular vote, and the president chooses the ministers.

There are thirteen ministries: Ministry of the Presidency, Ministry of Government and Justice, Ministry of Foreign Relations, Ministry of Economy and Finance, Ministry of Commerce and Industry (MICI), Ministry of Agricultural Development (MIDA), Ministry of Public Works (MOP), Ministry of Education, Ministry of Health, Ministry of Labor and Job Development (MITRAB), Ministry of Housing (MIVI), Ministry of Canal Affairs, and Ministry of Youth, Children, Women and Family.

Legislative Branch
The Legislative Assembly is composed of members elected by popular vote from electoral districts at the same time as the presidential vote. These legislators serve for five years and may be reelected for one consecutive

period. The Legislative Assembly must approve the nominations that the president makes for ministers of state and high court judges. Among its functions are: to make, reform or repeal the nation's laws and regulations, approve or disapprove international treaties negotiated by the executive arm, approve the budget and establish or change political divisions. The Assembly is also charged with the responsibility of assisting the Executive branch to maintain a state of peace and it has the power to declare war.

Judicial Branch

The judiciary comprises the Supreme Court, subordinate tribunals and district and municipal courts. The Supreme Court consists of nine judges who serve a ten-year term. Among the functions of the Supreme Court is the enforcement of the constitution, dealing with criminal proceedings against functionaries of the state, and finding administrative solutions in labor disputes in government entities.

The Electoral Tribunal

The Electoral Tribunal is an autonomous institution charged with making and interpreting the electoral laws, and directing the electoral process. It consists of three judges, elected for ten years and one representative each from the Legislative Assembly, the Supreme Court and the Executive branch. The Electoral Tribunal also organizes the process of "cedulación" or provision of identity cards to all Panamanian citizens over 18 years of age.

The Office of the Governor

The Governor is the highest authority of each of the provinces. This position is named directly by the president.

Municipalities

The Municipalities are autonomous political community organizations established in all districts of the country. Each municipality has a municipal council of elected representatives. The role of the municipalities includes promoting development and social welfare of each community, execution of national laws, and the establishment and operation of works and services within the community.

Comptroller's Department

The General Comptroller's Department is another independent state entity with the responsibility of the nation's budget, its internal and external debt, of managing public funds and property, of rendering financial statements of public funds to the Executive Branch and of preparing national statistics.

Decentralized Entities

The decentralized institutions fall under the responsibility of a ministry and follow the policies of the Government. Some autonomous institutions are: National Mortgage Bank, National Bank, the Government Savings Bank, Social Security Organization, Regulatory Entity for Public Services, National Lottery, University of Panama, Technical University, and the Colon Free Zone.

Some semi-autonomous institutions are: Comptroller General's Department, Attorney General's Office, Tourist Bureau, Fair Trade and Customers Affairs Commission, Bank of Agricultural Development, Agricultural Research Institute, Agricultural Marketing Institute, Agricultural Insurance Institute, Autonomous Cooperatives Institute, Civil Aeronautics, National Maritime Authority, Institute for Special Skill Training, National Culture Institute, National Sports Institute, Scholarship Institute, National Aqueduct and Sewage System Institute, National Transport Authority and the Interoceanic Region Authority, which has the role of administering and commercializing the lands and facilities which passed to Panama's control as a result of the 1977 Treaty between Panama and the U.S. under which the U.S. handed over the Canal and quit its military bases.

Canal Authority

A special case is the Panama Canal Authority (ACP), created in the 14th Constitutional title to administer the Canal and its watershed. Due to its importance, it enjoys financial autonomy, has its own assets and the right to manage them; its three-year budget is not part of the State's general budget.

ACP's management is handled by an executive board of 11 members; one of them is nominated by the President, acts as Minister of State for Canal Affairs and presides over the board.

Foto: Jaiguer

Album of a bygone era

The photographs on the following pages are by Carlos Endara, a photographer and painter of renown in the early part of the 20th century. Born in Ecuador, Mr. Endara came to Panama as a young man, later studying photography in France. Upon his return to Panama, he opened the city's first photographic studio. These examples of his work have been selected at random from a collection of thousands of photographs, mostly on 8"x10" glass plates. Since the collection is not catalogued, no attempt has been made to present a historical sequence; the aim is to offer a vignette of the life of Panama in days gone by. The custodian of the majority of the collection is Mr. Ricardo López Arias (ricardolopez@racsa.co.cr). Dr. Harry Castro Stanziola assisted in the compilation of the captions.

Pedro J. Sosa Street; showing on the left a part of the Metropolitan Cathedral, in Panama City's Old Quarter or "Casco Viejo". The photo illustrates the distinctive balconies of the area, and ornamental palms brought from Cuba, to beautify the city by José Gabriel Duque, owner of the La Estrella newspaper, one of the oldest newspapers on the continent which was published in Spanish, English and French. The photo also shows a horse-drawn cart carrying a "pepote", a big barrel from which drinking water was sold. The barrels were filled from the famous spring at Chorrillo. At the end of the street is the office of Brandon Brothers, a former stockbroking firm associated with New York's Morgan & Morgan, and guardians of the funds sent by the US to guarantee Panama's separation from Colombia.

This was the first United States Legation in Panama, situated on Fourth Street and Central Avenue, San Felipe. The US was the first country that recognized Panama's separation from Colombia, ten days after the event. France followed on November 16, 1903 and later Denmark, Belgium, Nicaragua, Cuba, Costa Rica, Austria, Hungary, Russia, Japan, Great Britain, Italy, China, Norway, Sweden and Peru.

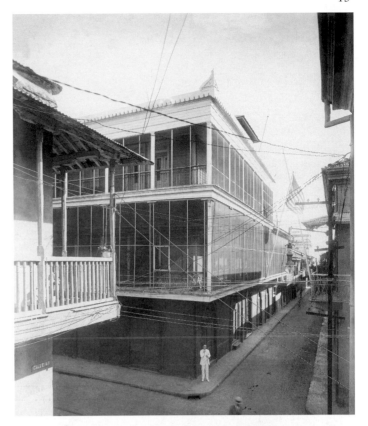

A meeting of the city's Council at the Town Hall or Municipal Palace. This building was built in the 17th century fronting Cathedral Plaza. The building has been modified on several occasions, but its appearance is much the same today.

Don Ricardo J.Alfaro and wife, Doña Amelia Lyons, in the living room of their house on First Street between Calle Estudiante and the present Avenue of the Martyrs. Born in 1882, Alfaro was a brilliant jurist and skilled diplomat who represented the country at many international summits and in many countries. He was also a linguist, professor, poet, writer and president from 1931 to 1932.

Bailey bridge over the La Villa river, which flows through the provinces of Herrera and Los Santos. It was popular to arrange trips to the country to enjoy the rivers and the countryside.

Avenida del Frente, the famous Front Street, the principal street in the early days of the city of Colon. Colon was founded on the island of Manzanillo as the Atlantic terminal of the Panama Railway. The building in the distance is the train station, and the street is lined with hotels, stores, houses and bars such as the famous Bilgray's Bar known by sailors around the world in Colon's former boisterous heyday as a port city.

Aerial View of Panama City from the sea in 1927. Shown are the suburbs of San Felipe, Chorrillo, La Exposición, Calidonia and Marañón. Neighborhoods like San Francisco, Betania, Marbella, Bella Vista and La Cresta had not yet been built or were barely started.

Juan Franco Racetrack, inaugurated on October 15, 1922 on a farm of the same name, in the district which today is Obarrio, The racetrack operated as a private company, the Club Hípico Nacional. It was here that President Jose Antonio Remon was assassinated. In 1956 it was closed when the present racetrack was inaugurated and named after President Remon. The Club Hipico Nacional was financed with a share offering of $50,000. Some of the original shareholders were Nicanor de Obarrio (125), Raul Espinosa (50), Enrique de la Guardia (30), Tomás Gabriel Duque (25), Carlos Muller (25), Moisés D. Cardoze (15), Angel de Castro (10), Manuel José Díaz (3), Anastasio Ruiz (3) and Federico Boyd (1). American citizens also bought shares.

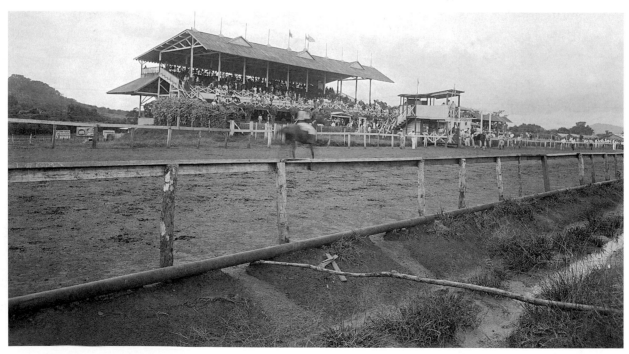

The stone-laying ceremony for the Gorgas Laboratory for Tropical Research, February 18, 1923. The laboratory was, and continues to be, dedicated to the research of tropical diseases. Shown is the three-times president Belisario Porras, Dr. Augusto Samuel Boyd and US guests among others.

Juana Dolores Paredes, later Mrs. Quezada, 1931 carnival queen. Carnival has been celebrated since 1906 with events and parades through the capital city; the renowned "matachines". People in the costumes of Spanish conquistadores, Indians and pirates and residents of the city met at the Plaza Peña Prieta to fight fake battles with much music and merriment . In 1919 carnival, was officially recognized.

Political cavalcade at Las Tablas during the 1920s, a popular custom in the isthmus. Organized to get supporters, they were also an excuse to show off elegant "caballos de paso". Music and fireworks were part of the show.

A party on the island of Taboga early in the century. This island is not only famous for its natural beauty and wealth of flowers and fruits, but for being, on November 14 1524, the starting point of Francisco Pizarro's first expedition of conquest to Peru. Taboga was also the headquarters of the Pacific Steamship Navigation Company and for many years a hub of activity as ships stopped to take on and unload supplies.

Hotel Central, built in 1855 between Central Avenue and Fifth Street, San Felipe. At right is shown the I.L. Maduro store, where they sold, among other goods, the famous Panama hats. In its heyday the hotel was a rendezvous for the important people of the town. The building still exists.

One of the sidewalks of the Santa Ana Plaza which had been a popular meeting place since the 19th century. It ranked with the Cathedral Plaza as the other half of the city's heart. At the left is the dome of the Variety Theater, built in 1906 to present vaudeville and all types of shows.

The Cecilia Theater, inaugurated in 1917, property of Manuel Espinosa Batista, where the first talkie, "The Jazz Singer" starring Al Jolson, was presented,. From 1914 there were movie theaters in Panama City and Colon, such as the Aurora, Broadway, Calidonia and Olimpia. Movies were also shown at the hotels Central and Metropole. General admission was 5 cents, and they showed many news features, most of them about First World War.

Dr. Belisario Porras receiving foreign diplomats and military brass in the Yellow Room of the Presidential Palace, or "Palace of the Herons", so named for the herons which have lived in the forecourt since the Palace was built. Above them are some of the portraits of former presidents. This photo was taken between 1920 and 1924 during Dr. Porras' third term.

Inauguration of the memorial to the Southern Sea's discoverer Vasco Núñez de Balboa, by President Belisario Porras, September 29, 1924. The statue was sculpted by two Spaniards, Mariano Benulliere and Miguel Blau. The statue was erected following correspondence between Belisario Porras and Spain's King Alfonso XIII.

Inauguration on December 24, 1923 of the French Plaza by Dr. Belisario Porras. The ceremony took place in front of Las Bovedas, the dungeons of the old city and headquarters of the former Chiriqui Garrison, on December 24, 1923. Attending the event were France's ambassador and a special military brigade which traveled from France for the occasion.

26

Students of one of the city's high school listening to a science lesson from the teacher.

Portrait of a typical rural family, in front of their house, with its well and water pump.

In 1826, Simón Bolívar ("El Libertador" the Liberator) summoned the countries of South America to the Anfictionic Congress of Latin American. His dream was to unite these countries into one, with its capital in Panama. His ambition was not realized, but 100 years later the Bolivarian Congress met in Panama, when a city square and a statue were dedicated to the great leader. The photo shows the crowds at the inauguration ceremony of Plaza Bolivar and statue on Avenida B between Third and Fourth Streets.

28

United Fruit Co. workers waiting to load bananas on the train. Banana cultivation in the republic was started at the end of the 19th century by German and American farmers. These farms merged in 1889 with the Boston Fruit Co. which later became the United Fruit Co. The prosperity of this transnational at the beginning of the 20th century was important to the development of the Bocas del Toro and Chiriqui provinces and attracted workers from Colombia, the West Indies and the rest of the country, including former Canal construction workers.

The deeper the Americans dug the Culebra Cut, the worse the catastrophic and life-threatening slides became. This photo below shows an overturned steam shovel in the slide on the east bank of May 29, 1913, shortly before the canal opened.

The SS Ancon arrives at Cristobal on September 2, 1909 with 1,500 laborers from Barbados.

Before the construction of the Bridge of the Americas in the sixties, vehicle and pedestrian traffic crossed the canal by way of the Thatcher Ferry.

The five photos at the end of this section were supplied by the Panama Canal Authority.

This photo, taken from Sosa Hill on May 18 1914, shows the townsite of Balboa and the Administration building under construction. It is interesting to note that the area on the left, now Albrook, was a swamp.

A graphic view from Naos Island looking north towards the shore, shows the construction of a breakwater which was later called The Causeway and is now part of the Amador tourist complex.

Panama's People and Provinces

The arrival of different cultures on the isthmus has created a complex ethnic mix distributed through nine very different provinces and three Indian reservations

The first political division in the Republic of Panama created the provinces of Panama and Veraguas in the year 1719. The Azuero and Chiriqui provinces were established with the annexation of Panama to Colombia. In 1885 the provinces of Coclé and Colón were created. In 1903, Bocas del Toro, formerly a district of Colón, was given the status of a province. The Indian reservations of Baru and San Blas were decreed in 1940 and the last change was made in 1946 when the province of Darién was created and the Azuero peninsula was divided into the provinces of Herrera and Los Santos. Nowadays, the Republic of Panama is divided into nine provinces, three Indian reservations and 75 districts which are subdivided into 594 "corregimientos" or localities.

The population of the Republic of Panama has increased from 336,742 in 1911 to 2.839 million at the last census in 2000. The greatest concentration of population is in Panama City which thrives on a broad plain, with a good climate. Apart from being the Pacific terminal of the Canal, the many economic activities of the city have attracted a strong migration from other parts of the country. Even though the population in Panama is small, the ethnic composition is complex and heterogeneous because of the influence of different cultures throughout the history of the isthmus. The Panamanian population is composed of the following ethnic groups:

Indigenous groups

Indigenous groups make up 5.3% of the total population of the republic. The most important Indian tribes on the isthmus are: The Kunas who are found on the islands of San Blas, and also in the jungle of Chucunaque and Bayano; the Ngobe Buglé (also known as Guaymíe) who live mainly in the mountainous areas of Bocas del Toro, Veraguas, and Chiriqui; the Emberá and Wounan (tribes of the Chocoes group) who live in the Darién jungle and the Teribe and Cricamola in the province of Bocas del Toro.

Afro-Colonial population

This group was brought by the Spanish from Africa in XVI century to work as slaves. Because of mistreatment by the Spanish many ran away and set up communities in the Bayano jungle and on the Caribbean coast, avoiding San Blas where they encountered the Kuna Indians. Nowadays their descendants are to be found in the Pacific areas They still retain a strong element of the Spanish culture to which they were exposed which produces a rich folklore.

Afro-West Indian Population

This group arrived on the isthmus from Jamaica, Martinique, and Trinidad to work on the construction of the Panama Canal. Their numbers decreased during the course of the First and Second World Wars. Their descendants can be found nowadays in Colón, Panama, Bocas del Toro and the former Canal Zone.

Mestizos

The most dominant group in the Republic is that of the mestizos, a mixture of the Spanish and Indian blood.

Other ethnic groups

Groups such as Chinese, East Indians, Europeans, Greeks and Americans also came during the Panama Canal construction and during succeeding years.

The Provinces and their characteristics

Panama

Population is mostly concentrated in the capital, Panama City. It was founded on January 21, 1673 by the Governor and Captain General Don Fernando de Cordoba y Mendoza. This province has the largest population of the country, estimated at 1.311 million inhabitants. Today it comprises the districts of San Carlos, Chamé, Capira, Chorrera, Arraijan, Taboga, Panama, San Miguelito, Chepo, Chiman and Balboa.

Colón

Its only city is Colón. It was officially founded on the island of Manzanilla during the railroad construction. The province is situated on the north coast with a population of 204,200 people, in the districts of Donoso, Chagres, Colón, Portobelo and Santa Isabel and the Indian reservation of San Blas. Colon City is the Atlantic terminal port of the Canal and the major employers of labour are the Canal, the ports and the Colón Free Zone, created in 1946 to reactivate the economy. Tourist attractions include the ruins of Portobelo and Fort San Lorenzo, Isla Grande, and Langosta beach.

Chiriquí, Valley of the Moon

Chiriquí is situated in the west, bordering on Costa Rica, with its capital being the city of David. It has a population of 368,800 people. Its districts are Barú, Renacimiento, San Felix, Bugaba, Boquerón, Alanje, Dolega, David, Boquete, Gualaca, San Lorenzo, Remedios and Tolé. Chiriquí is famous for its farm and cattle development. This province has fertile plains and cool mountain resorts like Volcán,Boquete and Cerro Punta. The Barú district has many banana plantations. Boquete is famous for coffee and citrus and popular as a tourist resort. Gualáca cultivates rice. Alanje, Boqueron, Remedios, San Felix and San Lorenzo are involved in cattle raising.

Los Santos, Guardian of Folklore

Los Santos is located on the Azuero Peninsula. Its capital is Las Tablas. It has an estimated population of 83,500 and in recent years has suffered a considerable decrease through migration to other provinces. Districts of the province are Los Santos, Guararé, Macaracas, Tonosí, Las Tablas, Pocrí, and Pedasí. Los Santos province is regarded as being the mecca of tradition and folklore which is enshrined in the carnival celebrations every year at Las Tablas. The main economic activities include: agriculture in Guararé and Pedasí; salt industry in Guararé; corn crops and cattle-raising in Pedasí and Tonosí; pig and chicken farming in Pocri.

Coclé

The capital of Coclé is Penonomé, so named after the legend of an Indian chief called Nomé. He was killed by the Spanish there and the name stems from the phrase "Aquí Penó Nomé" or "here Nomé suffered". Coclé is one of the central provinces and comprises the districts of Aguadulce, Natá, Olá, La Pintada, Penonomé and Antón. The principal economic activity is cattle and handicraft such as hats, purses, etc. In La Pintada, coffee is grown, and Aguadulce has extensive shrimp farms. In Antón, livestock and rice crops are the main activities. The population is approximately 202.500 people. The people of Coclé are proud of their cultural heritage and are conscious of regional solidarity.

Veraguas, the Republic's Granary

Birthplace of Urraca, a legendary Indian warrior, Veraguas is one of the central provinces, with its capital in

Santiago and districts of Las Palmas, Cañazas, Santa Fé, Calobre, San Francisco, La Mesa, Soná, Río de Jesús, Montijo, Santiago, and Atalaya. With a population of 209,100 people Veraguas is the only province with coasts on both oceans. The main economic activities of Veraguas include: coffee growing in Santa Fé, Calobre, and Cañazas; rice crops in La Mesa; tobacco in Las Palmas, livestock and agricultural business throughout the province and manufacturing straw hammocks.

Bocas del Toro, Province of Green Gold and Eco-Tourism

Its capital is also named Bocas del Toro, and the province has a population of approximately 132,291 inhabitants and three districts: Bocas del Toro, Chiriqui Grande, and Changuinola. It is also distinguished as the province with the most rain in the country, which is good for bananas, the "green gold", as well as cocoa, coconuts, plantains, oranges, and grapefruit. Recently Bocas del Toro has become a popular tourist destination.

Darién, Jungle Giant

The Darién province is largely jungle and its capital is La Palma. It is situated in the southeast of the isthmus. Its population is small (40,300) because of a need for roads but it is the most extensive province in the country. The Pan American Highway has recently been extended deep into the province as far as Yavisa. People are involved in farming, fishing and forestry.

Herrera

This smallest of the provinces is located in the Azuero peninsula. Its capital is the city of Chitré and its districts are Ocú, Santa María, Parita, Chitré, Las Minas, and Los Pozos. It has a population of 102,500. Its people are progressive and hard-working and have made Chitré the most important urban city in the Azuero peninsula. The main industries are the manufacturing of beverages, shoes, detergents, and leather products. There is also good farming, livestock and pig-raising, and also a good production of milk, cheese, and other by-products.

San Blas Indian reservation (Dule Nega)

This Indian reservation lies in the north east of the isthmus, on the coastal strip from San Blas Point to the border with Colombia; it also includes a beautiful archipelago of tiny islands inhabited by the Kuna Indians (32,446 inhabitants) who have their own type of government and also preserve their own culture. The Government administrator or "Intendente" works out of the island of El Porvenir. Great quantities of coconuts are grown and the "molas" which the women sew in reverse applique are a sought-after souvenir for tourists and cruise ship passengers who visit.

Ngobe Buglé

The creation of the Ngobe Buglé territory in the 1990s changed the map of the Republic, as it encompasses large segments of land formerly administrated by the provinces of Bocas del Toro, Chirquí and Veraguas.

Formerly known as Guaymie, this major subdivision of Native Americans comprises two cultural groups: the Ngobe and the Buglé, the members of which live in tiny hamlets scattered throughout the mountains of the Central Cordillera mountain range and work in agricultural activities, such as the banana and coffee plantations of the region.

The Ngobe Buglé are known for special handicrafts: the famous chaquiras —necklaces and bracelets made with tiny plastic beads—and the colorful female gowns, an attractive item for tourist women.

Considered the largest of Panama's indigenous groups (65.5% of local Native Americans), the Ngobe Buglé are also the country's fastest growing tribe. According to the 2000 Census, the group's population was estimated in 186,861 people.

The Emberá and Wounaan

Most of the members of this Native American group live in a special comarca (territory) in the heart of the Darién jungle. The group, however, is a relatively recent new-comer in Panama. They migrated to the Isthmus from the region of Chocó, in Colombia (hence their former name of Chocoes). Representing 10% of all Panamanian Indians, the Emberá and Wounaan (two related, but culturally different groups) make a living from agriculture, hunting and fishing. In 2000, their population stood at 29,367.

Panama's ports and cargo hub

**Already the largest port complex in Latin America, Panama,
has become one of the key cargo centers of the world**

Panama will soon become one of the key transshipment points in the world. Colon is already the largest port complex in Latin America, handling 1.3 million teus (twenty foot equivalent unit) per year, according to UN'S ECLA.

With its Canal linking the two greatest oceans, Panama has always been very aware of its advantage in having a unique geographical position, but making the most of this attribute and establishing the country as an important point for cargo handling has taken longer than it should. This was due to a number of factors beyond Panama's control. The first was the operation of the Panama Canal as a U.S. government agency.

With the opening of the Canal in 1914, the two major deep water ports of the country became Balboa, on the Pacific side of the Canal and Cristobal on the Atlantic side. The old Panama Canal Company, and later the Panama Canal Commission, looked upon these ports as simply adjuncts to the Canal itself, firstly for the convenience of Canal customers for servicing their ships, such as with coal and later bunker fuel and, secondly, as ports for the movement of cargo in and out of the Republic of Panama. The Canal Company did not look upon the ports as commercial operations which could be commercialized, modernized and expanded.

Meanwhile, the Colon Free Zone, on the Atlantic side of the Isthmus, founded in the 1940's, had grown into the biggest duty free zone in the western hemisphere despite the slow development of the ports.

After the signing of the Torrijos-Carter Canal Treaties and the handing over of the ports and the Panama Railroad in 1979, little changed. The succeeding military dictatorships and their civilian puppet governments clung to the ports and railroad and used them for giving jobs to their faithful for political ends. The railroad gradually ground to a halt for lack of funds and attention and the ports remained at virtually the same stage of development that had existed when they belonged to the Panama Canal Company.

It took the US military invasion of Panama in 1989, the destruction of the Panama Defense Force and the installation of the civilian government of Guillermo Endara Galimany to change the course of the ports.

Manzanillo International Terminal (MIT)

Under the Director General of the then Panama National Ports Authority(APN), Jerry Salazar, the Endara government gave a concession to Manzanillo International Terminal (MIT) to develop a private port operation adjacent to the Colon Free Zone.

The consortium comprised Motores Internacionales, S.A., a Colón Free Zone company specializing in the importation and sale of Russian-made vehicles, and Stevedoring Services of the Americas (SSA), of Seattle, Washington. In time, SSA bought out the share of Motores Internacionales.

MIT covers an area of 45 hectares. Another 51 hectares are available for future expansion. The port has ten container cranes in service. At present it has eight super post-Panamax container cranes and two Panamax container cranes. The port has 1,240 meters of continuous berths and a ro-ro facility.

As this port facility developed, its efficiency made it not only a strong competitor of other key ports such as Miami and Kingston, Jamaica, but also of the government-operated port of Cristobal. With a change of government in 1994, it was apparent to the incoming administration of Ernesto Perez Balladares that the government ports could not compete with MIT and plans were made to offer Balboa and Cristobal on concession to a private operator.

Colon Container Terminal (CCT)

Firstly, however, a concession contract was made by APN director, Dr.Hugo Torrijos, with the Evergreen group to construct another modern container terminal at Coco Solo, adjacent to the Manzanillo terminal. This port, known as Colon Container Terminal (CCT) provided Panama with another modern and highly-efficient operation. It has 612 meters of dock available with five Panamax container cranes and, in the first phase, covers an area of 25 hectares. This port has an additional area of 37 hectares in reserve for phases II, III and IV and will cover a total of 62 hectares. In the first quarter of 2002 it registered the highest growth rate of all container ports of 45.4 percent.

Panama Ports Company (PPC)

A bidding process on the ports of Balboa and Cristobal culminated with the international ports operator, Hutchison Whampoa, of Hong Kong, and Felixstowe, England, winning the process. Their Panama subsidiary, Panama Ports Company (PPC) totally reconstructed the Port of Balboa and has converted part of the Cristobal docks into a cruise ship terminal.

The old Pier 18, Balboa, part of the port complex built in the early 1900's at the time of construction of the Panama Canal, has now disappeared, replaced by a straight dock parallel to the Panama Canal, in its first phase, 350 meters long. It has general cargo berths of 1,466 meters in total length.

At the time of publication three super post-Panamax container cranes had already been installed on the completed section of the new structure. Eventually 12 super post-Panamax cranes will be installed and the complex will cover an area of 50 hectares.

Colon Port Terminal (CPT)

Located between Manzanillo International Terminal (MIT) and Colon Container Terminal (CCT), this port, which serves smaller coastal vessels and those trading to Central America, Colombia and the Caribbean, was also privatized during the past government. Its operators also have plans to modernize the facilities and install at least one container crane.

The Panama Canal Railway

The railway connecting the Atlantic and Pacific port terminals holds an historic place as the first trans-continental railroad link on the American continent. Built in the first half of the 19th Century, it was a popular method for "forty-niners" to cross the Isthmus on their way from the east coast of the United States to the gold rush in California. Before it was completely finished, some actually paid for the convenience of being allowed to walk along the line and the clearings between Colon and Panama City.

The railroad was a traditional link between the ports on both sides of the Isthmus and in its early years it carried cargo between the two oceans for the Pacific Steam Navigation Company (PSNC) which traded on the west coast of the Americas from Chile, in the south, to California, in the north.

The railway became part of the French canal building project and was eventually bought by the U.S.government along with the French rights for building the Panama Canal. It continued operating with subsidies from the Canal and the U.S. military until it was turned over to Panama in 1979. Without the continued support of the previous operators and because of neglect and overstaffing by Panama's military governments, its condition slowly declined.

However, the railway was seen as an important link between the various new terminals in the growing port system. As part of the privatization process under the Perez Balladares government it was offered under concession to private operators and bidding was won by Kansas City Southern Industries and Mi Jack Holdings of the U.S. The railway has now been reborn and has been re-named as the Panama Canal Railway Company, totally rebuilt, including new tracks and terminals. Double-deck container trains linking all of Panama's principal transshipment ports with a modern, fast and highly-efficient system complete the multi-modal transshipment opportunities offered by modern Panama. The railway was originally intended to carry cargo only, but as cruise ship calls in Panama's cruise terminals have grown, the railway has added modern coaches to its inventory of rolling stock with bubble-dome coaches for visitors to view the Panama Canal and travel through scenic jungle and lake areas along its route.

Cruise ship terminals

One of the first operational cruise ship terminals was Colon 2000, on the Atlantic coast of Panama. There are two other terminals —Gatun Yacht Club, which was refurbished to receive passengers off ships making a partial transit of the canal, and Pier 6, Cristobal, operated by Panama Ports Company. Another cruise ship terminal, the Fort Amador Resort and Marina, on the Pacific, is also receiving cruise ship calls. Calls by cruise ships on transcanal and Caribbean itineraries has grown rapidly because of the efforts of both the Panama Government Tourist Bureau (IPAT) and private operators and is showing indications of becoming another of the country's successful tourist developments.

Bunker Supply

The supply of bunker fuel to ships transiting the Panama Canal and calling at Panama ports is becoming a highly competitive activity again after many years in the doldrums. In the 1960s Panama was the major world supplier of maritime fuels after Rotterdam and Kuwait. A series of circumstances, including the world fuel crisis of the 70's and a poor internal fuel policy, which ignored the passing trade, lost Panama its position as a key supplier for many years.

When duty free petroleum zones were established at the Canal and at the trans-isthmian oil pipeline in the west of the country, near the border with Costa Rica, a slow, but positive change in this trade began again.

It took a dramatic turn when a consortium comprising Mobil Oil and the Alireza family, of Saudi Arabia, won a concession to use the former U.S. Naval Base of Rodman, on the west bank Pacific entrance of the Panama Canal, and a tank farm of 36 tanks at nearby Arraijan, connected to the docks. Since the amalgamation of Mobil with Exxon, this facility has been sold to the Libermann Group of Argentina and the Panamanian agricultural supply firm of Melo. They intend to continue upgrading the fuel facility and adding a bulk grain handling terminal.

Another major player, Almacenaje Petroliferos, S.A., has constructed a new maritime fuel supply center on the island of Taboguilla, at the Pacific entrance to the Panama Canal at a cost of U.S. $20-million. This company is a subsidiary of Catalana de Almacenaje Petroliferos, S.A., of Spain. The terminal is located less than two miles from the southern gateway of the Panama Canal on the Pacific Ocean. A number of smaller, but new and active suppliers have also been attracted to the market.

Braswell Shipyard Panama

Another very successful privatization project in the maritime sector is the Braswell Shipyard in Balboa under the administration of the Braswell family, who gained the concession to operate it. They also operate several other private drydocks in the United States.

The Braswell operation in Panama is a complex of three drydocks which reverted to Panama under the 1977 Panama Canal treaties. It was built at the same time as the Panama Canal, and its largest dock is the same dimension as the lock chambers on the Canal and can handle Panamax size vessels, the maximum size ship that can transit the Panama Canal. This dock is also the largest available on the Pacific coast of the American continent between Tierra del Fuego and Los Angeles, California.

The shipyard has sophisticated heavy industrial machinery and has carried out impressive repair and maintenance ranging from supply vessels and tugs, to cruise ships, container ships and tankers.

Panama Maritime Authority

With the rapid modernization and expansion of the ports, the government recognized that the country was growing in importance as a maritime nation. This led to the restructuring of the former Panama National Ports Authority (APN), incorporating the maritime-related departments scattered under various ministries were combined into one entity: the Panama Maritime Authority (AMP). This body is again under the directorship of Jerry Salazar, who has been actively involved in the shipping sector for more than 30 years. It incorporates the former Panama National Ports Authority (APN), the Consular and Shipping Department, the Panama Nautical School and the Maritime and Coastal Resources

The government of Mireya Moscoso, within its first 100 days, recognized the importance of the maritime sector by naming the Minister of the Canal to the post of chairman of the AMP Board and adding the Minister of the Presidency to the Board. This was obviously intended to keep the President of the Republic fully informed on activities in the maritime sector.

Maritime Sector Outlook

Panama presents a formidable complex of multimodal cargo movement options to world trade.

The effect of MIT, CCT and PPC is already being felt in the Caribbean and on the east coasts of South and Central America and as far north as the US and Canadian east coasts. A direct challenge to the Panama Canal for many years has been the U.S. mini landbridge - the rail connection between both coasts of the US. However, as the demand for cargo movement over this link has grown during the past decades, delivery time has often slowed down considerably because of congestion.

This was starkly demonstrated during the shut-out of US longshoremen by port operators in the last part of 2002, which resulted in massive cargo backlogs. Ship re-routing and transshipment through Panama's ports during and after this event will be reflected in the 2002 overall handling figures.

Despite a worldwide slump in cargo rates, a cyclical event, and the slowdown in the world economy during 2002, Panama's modernized cargo handling complex is expected to serve both as a "pressure valve" for the US mini-landbridge system as well as creating its own growing network of worldwide links.

In the first quarter of 2002, the overall growth of container movement in Panama's hub ports grew by 5.7 percent, and indications are that this trend will continue throughout the year and into 2003.

Shipping registry is world leader

Panama's fleet is still growing, getting younger and improving standards

Panama's lead as the country with the most shipping registered under her flag is impressive. The registry was established in 1925 when the government passed Law 8, creating an open registry for ships of all nations. It gained popularity after WWII and has been growing ever since.

With more than 10% of the world fleet and 10,157 vessels totalling 145.7 million gross tons according to Lloyd's Register at August 2002 in comparison with 10,091 and 142.7m at the end of 2001, Panama's commercial fleet is the world's largest register, over twice as big as its nearest rival Liberia which has something over 3,000 vessels.

New registrations during the first eight months of 2002 totaled 183 ships of which 108 were cargo ships and 44 oil tankers. The majority were relatively new ships; 179 of them were under 5 year old. A total of 291 vessels were registered in 2001 of which 285 were less than five years old.

New ship registrations are expected to accelerate once the impact of new legislation (Law No. 25 of June 3, 2002) begins to be felt. The new legislation modifies several articles of the existing law (Law No. 36 of 1995) granting attractive incentives to ship owners.

All vessels can join the registry whether they are cargo, passenger, dredges, barges or any other type. The law does not require that the owner be a national of Panama or an entity established in the Republic of Panama and offers fiscal incentives such as tax exemptions on earnings.

For many years, open registries had a very poor safety record but international and domestic pressure led Panama's government to modernize the registry and incorporate it into the International Maritime Organization (IMO), the London-based United Nations watchdog for the industry which, at the same time, sets standards for safety, maintenance and regulations.

The Panama Maritime Authority's directorate of Merchant Marine has made it easy to register vessels under Panama's flag. Applications must be filed by an attorney and presented in the Merchant Marine's offices in Panama or in any Panamanian consulate in the major shipping capitals of the world. Most law firms who belong to Panama's Maritime Law Association have offices in Asia, Europe and the U.S. and provide a personalized service worldwide to ship owners who want to use the registry. It is "the most competitive register of all", say

An evocative photograph of the facade of the Santuario Nacional, one of the principal city churches, juxtoposed with its modern neighbor — a steel and glass office block.

Photo: Jorge Quinzada Loo

Casco Viejo, Panama's old quarter, throbs with new life as restoration work on the ancient buildings continues. Sidewalk cafes are in vogue. The music of a jazz trumpeter on the patio of Las Bovedas Restaurant wafts out across the cobblestoned French Plaza.

Photos: Above and right, Jorge Quinzada Loo
Below left, María Luisa Gutiérrez

Easter time in Panama City and the city is ablaze with the glory of flowering trees. Cathedral Plaza, with its bandstand facing the old Hotel Central, is a colorful corner of the city. *Photo: Ester Zambrano*

Looking from the other side, the cathedral in a different but also typical setting... a rainy evening as worshippers attend a mass.
Photo: Jorge Quinzada Loo

A monument to Dr. Arnulfo Arias Madrid, one of the most charismatic political figures of Panama's century, now stands in the center of Balboa, at one time the Pacific side township of the U.S. Canal Zone. His widow is Mireya Moscoso, Panama's president (1999-2004).
Photo: Jorge Quinzada Loo

Right: This lamp from a lighthouse used on the old French Canal now reposes in the Panama Canal Museum at Cathedral Plaza, in San Felipe.

Panama's two oceans yield an abundance of seafood. Our photos show lobster and octopus, freshly caught and for sale at Panama City's Seafood Market, on Avenida Balboa, constructed as a gift by the Japanese Government. It is well-kept and a source of pride for the fishermen, vendors and customers. *Photos: Jorge Quinzada Loo*

Above: Panama City's night skyline from the bay.
Photo: Jorge Quinzada Loo

Right: A Guayacan tree in full bloom.
Photo: Jorge Quinzada Loo

Below: Panama City's "bus art", a custom that seems doomed as big modern buses replace the old "red devils".
Photo: Danny Lehman

Below right: A view of Paitilla residential district from Avenida Balboa and its ceramic art seawall. *Photo: María Luisa Gutiérrez*

Below left: Pigeons in Avenida Central, the city's famous shopping street, now a pedestrian precinct.

Below right: Homeward-bound with their purchases.
Photo: Jorge Quinzada Loo

Panama's latest tourist attraction: Amador, the Causeway, and its four islands. This photo, shot against the setting sun from a helicopter, shows the top of Flamenco Island in the foreground, below which lies the new Fort Amador Cruise Port and yacht basin flanked by Perico island. Then the Causeway crosses to Culebra and Naos Islands and on to mainland Amador and the Bridge of the Americas.
Photo: Tomás Munita

Panama Maritime Authority officials. The register offers quality mortgages, which are accepted by all international banks and a network of some 60 consulates around the world that can handle immediate transactions on behalf of Panama's government and register. Ship owners must meet all relevant safety requirements, comply with the ISM code and follow the rules of international conventions such as STCW, SOLAS, MARPOL and the ISO 9000 regulations and submit to regular inspections to eliminate substandard operations.

The Panama Maritime Authority has focused its efforts to improve safety standards and one of its primary goals is that users comply with the existing international maritime regulations, particularly the ISM code and the STCW implementation for a quality flag through annual state controlled inspections. The Authority is also undertaking a complete revision of the vessels registered under the Panamanian flag, in order to determine their technical and maritime safety conditions and labor regime. It is also increasing supervision of the authorised agencies that carry out statutory recognition and regulatory certification.

The new modifications to the incentive law cut registration fees to attract new buildings. One aim of the new law is to bring down the average age of the fleet which was around 16.5 years. Special discounts are given to groups of vessels: a 20 percent discount for groups of at least three vessels from 30,000 to 50,000 gross tons and 30 percent for groups exceeding 50,000 gt and up to 100,000gt. In addition, there would be a 25 percent discount on annual tax. The Director General of Merchant Marine can grant a 50% discount for the registration of one vessel with more than 100,000gt. Groups exceeding 100,000gt will receive 50 percent discounts on registration fees and 35 percent on annual tax. It will be at the Director of Merchant Marine's discretion to grant special discounts to groups representing at least fifteen vessels or with a tonnage superior to 150,000gt. New buildings, when registering in groups of a minimum of four vessels, will be offered additional discounts of up to 35 percent.

Tourism

A brief overview of Panama's tourism and leisure industry...
how it developed since the era of the Wright brothers

At the beginning of the twentieth century, when Panama gained independence from Colombia, the new republic could boast one of Central America's best regarded hotels: Hotel Central, which served however, not so much for tourism as for a socializing venue of the well-to-do, the élite of a city that housed no more than 10,000 souls back then.

The tourist industry for Panama was yet to be born. The reasons for this were simple: 1. International leisure travel was still reserved for the wealthy. 2. The country was completely unknown as a tourist destination. 3. The concept of tourism in the tropics, as we know it today, had not been developed (Strict Victorian and Edwardian beauty concepts scorned sun tans). 4. For those who knew anything about Panama, the Isthmus was nothing more than a swampy jungle infested with deadly, disease-carrying mosquitoes.

A lot of things have changed in a hundred years. The same year Panama became an independent republic (1903), the Wright brothers invented the airplane, which only 50 years later transformed the country into a major international hub. Roads also developed, linking the formerly maritime republic to the rest of Central and North America. The construction of the Panama Canal (1904-1914) fostered a huge sanitation campaign that forged one of the healthiest territories in the region. Many of those who came to dig the "Big Ditch", men and women from every corner of the earth, decided to stay. Their descendants now live in Central America's most modern, cosmopolitan and lively capital city –the southern rival of Miami.

Despite all these changes, one thing remains constant. The average 30-year-old, early-21st-century resident of, say, Minneapolis knows no more about Panama than his or her great-grandparents in 1903. Reasons? We'll cover that later in this chapter.

In the meanwhile, lets go back to the "Big Ditch". The Panama Canal was built during the "Golden Age" –a time in which the wealthy families of the world spent most of their spare time on great safaris, skiing in the Swiss Alps or enjoying long voyages to the Orient. The construction of an ocean-to-ocean waterway across the Isthmus of Panama brought not a few privileged folk to the country, most of whom, despite safety restrictions of the time, ventured out on many a safari, such as crocodile-hunting excursions to the province of Darien and to the swamp lands that once existed near the ruins of Old Panama.

The large civilian-military complex known as the Panama Canal Zone dominated most of the country's "tourist industry" during the first years of the republic. Most of the "tourists" of the time were family members visiting U.S. military personnel or civilian employees of the Panama Canal Company. Seeking to take advantage of this influx of foreigners, the government of Panama opened its first tourism department in the 1920s, although tourist infrastructure was almost non-existent. The Canal continued to be the country's main attraction and visitors often chose to lodge at Hotel Tivoli, within Canal Zone territory. The Canal Zone also boasted its own beaches, lakes, parks and other recreational facilities.

World War II created a lot of new activity around the strategic Panama Canal with the establishment of military bases elsewhere in the republic. U .S. military and civilian personnel started to discover the country's beaches, mountains, and the picturesque towns of the countryside. In the 1940s, and 50s Panamanian businessmen began a real estate development trend in coastal regions and mountains targeted at the American community on the Isthmus, which resulted in the appearance of weekend houses and a number of small hotels in the interior provinces –a phenomenon that also prompted the local middle class to enjoy weekend trips to the country.

Jazz, cabaret shows and good earnings

Big things also started to happen in Panama City shortly after World War II. The opening of luxurious El Panama Hotel, which made international news, prompted the arrival of large lodging facilities in the capital –a much needed commodity for the growing numbers of "jetsetters" needing to spend a night on the Isthmus before continuing their flight between North and South America. On the other hand, the main thoroughfares of Panama and Colón seemed to be always crowded by sailors and passenger ship travelers en route to far-away destinations. It was a time of Big Band Jazz, cabaret shows and good earnings at local stores.

By the 1970's, improvements in air travel had made overnight stays in Panama unnecessary, although the number of visitors actually increased with the establishment of an international banking center in Panama City. The country became the financial capital of Central America and business people constantly landed at Tocumen International Airport –one of the most modern of the region at the time— to participate in trade shows at state-of-the-art Atlapa Convention Center or close a deal in the Colón Free Zone.

The average stay of these "tourists" on the Isthmus was 2.5 days. For obvious reasons, the handful of local tour operators of the time sold packages including locations not far from the business cities: the beaches of the western province of Panama, the islands of Taboga and Contadora (Panama's best tourist offer at the time), and the San Blas archipelago. City tours focused on shopping (a long-time Panama City forte) and on the Panama Canal. This, of course, did little to help the slogan "Panama is a lot more than a canal", coined by the Panama Government Tourist Bureau (IPAT), which had entered the scene in the early 1960s and had launched programs to promote both national and international tourism.

The 1980s brought substantial changes in the Caribbean region regarding tourism. Yet, although cruise ships arrived en masse at places like Kingston, St. Croix or Nassau, luxury vessels largely ignored Panamanian ports, except for their constant transit of the Canal and for cruise callings in the San Blas islands —a fact that greatly benefitted the economy of the Kuna Indians, who were happy to sell their famous molas to fascinated visitors.

Spared from the natural disasters and civil wars that ravaged most of Central America during the decade, Panama started an ambitious program to transform a large percentage of its verdant forests (21% of the national territory) into national parks. Nevertheless, the term "eco-tourism" was still new, and the country was more pre-occupied with business concerns and did little to promote the nation's green wealth abroad.

The mid-to-late 80s were tough years for tourism in Panama. The Noriega dictatorship and the political and economic crisis of the time severely damaged the country's reputation abroad, especially in the United States, Panama's traditional source of visitors.

The "Roaring '90s"

The restoration of democracy in 1990 also revived the economy. Panama City, already cosmopolitan in nature, grew in size —this time upward. Many of the new high rises that appeared on the city's skyline were banks, which funded the construction of even more high rises: hotels.

A number of luxury lodging establishments, some of which were the new branches of international chains which had left Panama in the 1980s, (Marriott, Holiday Inn, etc.) opened during the mid-to-late 90s. The period was a time of record economic growth in Panama and many local and foreign experts predicted a boom in the tourist industry. Local visionaries, such as Mr. Herman Bern, not only stretched the city's skyline with the Miramar Hotel towers (the tallest structures in the republic), but also gave eco-tourism a more elegant meaning with Gamboa Rainforest Resort, the most ambitious project of its kind in Central America.

On the other hand, a local consortium promised to restore the luster of the country's cruise ship industry, which had dwindled three decades before. Built on a landfill on the shores of the city of Colón, on the Caribbean coast, "Colón 2,000", as it was named, was bound to become the best luxury vessel port on Central America's mainland.

Cruise ships also began to stay a day in Gatun Lake, passengers experiencing a canal transit up through the Gatun locks and taking tours from the Gatun Yacht Club. This was an initiative of the shipping agencie C. Fernie.

The interior provinces also experienced a measure of this optimism. The bed & breakfast, a lodging "institution" popular in northern countries, but unknown in Panama until then, appeared in idyllic country towns such as El Valle, and Boquete. As the Panamanian government improved roads to the beautiful coastal region of Costa Arriba in the province of Colón, and to the white water rapids of the province of Chiriquí, the Panama Government Tourist Bureau (IPAT) evaluated the country's rich folklore heritage and popular town and country festivals (including the famous pre-Lenten Carnival) as promotional "baits" for international markets.

In the skies, COPA, the country's privately-owned national airline, transformed its corporate image and changed its entire fleet, thanks to an association with U.S. carrier, Continental Airlines. The airline's expansion throughout the entire continent, coupled with the arrival of new carriers and other factors, contributed to a substantial increase in the number of visitors to Panama, which, by the end of the decade, was estimated at nearly half-a-million people per annum. Consequently, Tocumen International Airport, which at the beginning of the '90s was still regarded as one of the best in the region, had suddenly become too small.

The 1990s also brought a long-expected occurrence: the gradual withdrawal of U.S. military personnel from the Isthmus. Viewed from the point of view of a member of the industry in the first years of the 21st century, the control transfer of the Panama Canal from U.S. to Panamanian hands in 1999 proved to be a mixed blessing for the country's leisure sector. On the one hand, thousands of hectares of pristine forests –an eco-tourists' treasure— were finally available, prompting the development of tourist projects of all sizes (Gamboa Rainforest Resort, the Canopy Tower, etc.) Yet, the departure of the American troops and their families, which were fond of taking week-end trips to the countryside, negatively affected the occupancy of provincial hotels and resorts. The same happened with city hotels, which had always housed a large number of military personnel.

A new century

The first full year of the 21st century was a year of great contrasts for Panama's tourism industry. The year 2001 represented the first year of a world-wide economic recession that complicated matters for local hoteliers, already suffering the effects of the departure of U.S. troops from Panama. Nevertheless, 2001 brought great success for the country's cruise ship industry, which had officially returned to life the year before (experimental luxury vessel callings had actually started in 1997 as a joint project between the Panama Canal Commission, IPAT, and local tour operators). The "Colón 2000" cruise port and the Pier 6 terminal, both located on the Caribbean coast of the Isthmus, were the first facilities of their kind in the country, although a third facility, Fort Amador Resort & Marina, later became Panama's first cruise port on the Pacific coast.

The big "surprise of the century," in the leisure industry, nevertheless, was the sudden emergence of the province of Bocas del Toro —until recently considered merely a banana-producing territory— as the republic's most popular tourist attraction. With virtually no official promotion, the region's untouched natural environment, crystal-clear waters and its easy-going Caribbean lifestyle attracted increasing numbers of European visitors, many of whom became local hoteliers themselves.

Then came September 11, the first shock waves of which were obviously felt in the international travel industry. Yet, although the negative consequences of terrorism did not spare the Isthmus, the attacks prompted an interesting reaction: European travelers chose to visit places other than the United States and increasing numbers of U.S. tourists preferred to travel not far from their country. This was one of the factors behind the success of the Decameron beach resort complex in western Panama, which recorded a 60-100% occupancy during its second season –right after the events of September 11.

Looking ahead

The nation's large tracts of verdant forests, hundreds of islands, a folklore encompassing Spanish, Indian and African traditions, Native American nations living the same way their ancestors did 500 years ago, and a capital city which could be the envy of a similar-size metropolis in the U.S., can only confirm one fact: Panama is among the top countries in the region regarding diversity of attractions –far more diverse than Costa Rica, its popular neighbor to the west.

The lack of coordinated promotional programs is the obvious reason behind Panama's relative obscurity abroad, but things are changing. As this book went to the press, IPAT had invested US$10 million in a public relations/advertising campaign in Europe, Latin America and the United States, featuring ads on cable T.V., plus adverts and articles in prestigious international magazines. This, combined with the hosting of the Miss Universe pageant in Panama City in May of 2003, constitutes the first sign that the image of the country abroad is finally taking on a positive look.

On the other hand, despite the world economic crisis of the time, the building of major tourist infrastructure continues in 2003. Mr. Jean Feghali, the head of Grupo F, a Panamanian business conglomerate, is building and promoting Panama Canal Village, a large complex of hotels, high fashion stores, theme parks, cruise facilities and other attractions that promise to be the largest entertainment center south of Orlando.

Private trade organizations, such as the Panama Chamber of Tourism (CAMTUR) are working along with IPAT in training industry members, Indian communities, elementary-school children and university students in a wide range of areas. At the turn of the century, tourism is among the fastest growing fields of study at Panamanian universities.

The tourism boom predicted in the 1990's is still a few years away. Yet, one thing is certain. The country's leisure industry has come a long way in the last 100 years.

Selling off the former Canal Zone

Good use is being made of most the "reverted" land and facilities

The Interoceanic Region Economic Development Authority (ARI) was established in 1993 to administer lands, housing and projects in the "reverted areas" (name given to the former U.S. Canal Zone lands) and make sure that these resources would be utilized for the benefit of the people of Panama and to incorporate the former Canal Zone into the nation's development plan. The Interoceanic Region includes both commercial and environmentally sensitive areas and stretches from the Atlantic to the Pacific and covers about five percent of the total area of Panama. Thousands of buildings, recreation facilities and installations, including airports, houses, hangars, office buildings and power plants have been available for residential, commercial and industrial use. Although parts of those reverted areas had been gradually turned over to the government of Panama since the beginning of the Panama Canal Treaty implementation, some 925,868 acres and more than 4,000 buildings that constituted the former military bases were passed to Panamanian administration and under ARI's guardianship on December 31, 1999 when the Panama Canal was transferred to Panama.

The use of those reverted lands began in the early 1990s with the privatization of port activity and the construction of two major ports on the Atlantic side, Manzanillo International Terminal and Colon Container Terminal which have become the pillars of maritime business on the Atlantic coast. The port system also included privatization of both the ports of Cristobal and Balboa which has become a major container terminal on the Pacific coast, and the renovation of the trans-isthmian railway. ARI is developing the former US base of Fort Amador at the Pacific entrance of the Canal into a major tourist attraction. Investments in that sector represent over US$1bn and include a cruise port and marina. Hotels and tourist developments have been set up in other former US military bases, even in the infamous former School of the Americas now the Hotel Melia.

The ambitious "City of Knowledge" in the former Fort Clayton Army base has gathered a number of international universities, research centres and technology businesses in addition to a network of Internet related and software companies.

The jewel of ARI is the former Howard Air Force base, scheduled be put to international bid. The World Bank's International Finance Corporation has been advising the Authority on the use and promotion of this base which includes one of the largest commercial airports in Latin America. But the global recession, aggravated after the September 11 terrorists attacks in the US, has delayed the project, which had to wait until there were signs of economic recuperation in the US, Europe and Asia where companies from those regions had shown interest in participating. In addition to the airport itself which has a 2,591m long by 46m wide airstrip, there are four hangars and a total of over 600 buildings comprising some 300,000m2 of construction. The area of the eventual development is of approximately 1,500 hectares.

Panama has, on the Atlantic and Pacific ends of the Canal respectively, over 2,000 hectares (4,940 acres) and nearly 1,200 hectares (2,964 acres) available for investment. They constitute optimal real estate for commercial, port and maritime development and the more built-up areas have infrastructure and public utilities services. The areas of Coco Solo, Telfers Island on the Atlantic and Rodman as well as Farfan on the Pacific entrance of the Canal are available for investment in the maritime sector.

On the Atlantic side, the Fort Davis industrial zone is open for new businesses. A Panama-Taiwan joint venture was tried but failed and the area has returned completely to Panama. Companies can set up in the premises with all the benefits of an export-oriented and duty free processing zone. Areas near the Colon Free Zone, created in 1948, are also available to complement the activities of the world's second largest duty free zone that houses some 2,000 companies and 25 banks established within its walls.

ARI has sold most of the residential housing on former military bases to Panamanians attracted by the "green environment" of both Albrook and Fort Clayton.

The site of the former US Army jungle training centre at Fort Sherman, on the Pacific side of the Panama Canal, remains another coveted jewel in ARI's crown. Its jungle, mangrove and coral reef areas have been kept and protected and cover some 13,800 hectares which will be developed into environmental projects that will conserve flora and fauna. But the winning prize is without doubt Amador's aquarium and centre for biodiversity designed by the award-winner US architect Frank Gehry, estimated at US$ 40m. The project is in its blueprint phase with the beginning of construction expected for the end of 2003-2004.

The City of Knowledge

This imaginative concept, which occupies a barracks vacated by the U.S. Army has proved to be a winner. A steady flow of new companies and institutions is entering the "city"

Nowhere has the proverb "Necessity is the mother of invention", been so apt as in Panama during the era of the withdrawal of U.S. forces.

Planners contemplating the problem of what to do with the administrative and operational area of the huge Fort Clayton army base turned a daunting problem into a classic solution and invented a "City of Knowledge."

The ambitious City of Knowledge (Ciudad del Saber) project is defined as an international service center drawing together prestigious academic and cultural institutions, scientific research centers, and a technology park (Tecnoparque Internacional de Panama or TIP). The concept is that intellectuals, scientists and businesspersons work within their fields of expertise, while at the same time creating an interdependent, self-sustaining commercial park and university campus.

The center is located on 296 acres of what was the former Fort Clayton U.S. military base, on the bank of the Panama Canal, a few miles outside Panama City. The master plan of the City of Knowledge calls for the conversion of what once was a bustling military installation into a quiet, subtle and efficient campus complex and residential area.

Available on premises are 140 buildings (ninety-five percent of which are three-storied with basement) which are now being used for industrial and academic occupancy, including offices, laboratories, a central library, an auditorium, computer facilities, meeting halls, restaurants and shops, among others. Another 180 structures (including single-, duplex- and cuadraplex-designs) contain 371 housing units for the use of those choosing to live on-site in the "City". All buildings are for lease only. Industrial and residential tenants may decorate the interiors of their businesses, schools and homes as they wish, but every exterior must be painted the same stately off-white.

Currently, 172 acres of the City area are open space and a great deal of attention has been given to creating a "green-community" effect. The grounds are (or will be converted to) a pleasing, carefully maintained mixture of manicured lawns and sculpted gardens, bisected by unobtrusive walkways. No fencing is allowed without official approval and the current parking lots will not be enlarged, at least in the short term. Measures for beautifying anything that may not have bothered the soldiers but is potentially offensive to the more genteel eyes of the academics are under consideration, even to the point of disguising and standardizing utility poles.

By the time the U.S. military withdrew from Fort Clayton at the end of 1999, the City was already well planned. The autonomous, non-profit City of Knowledge Foundation was created in 1995. It features a Board of Trustees comprising representatives from the academic, business, labor, and government sectors. The board administers the City. UNESCO devised the project's strategic plan. Its feasibility study was conducted by the United States' Academy for Educational Development (AED), which stated in its findings that, "[As a result of the City of Knowledge] Panama is now in a position, because of its unique situation and resources, to create and demonstrate a 21st-century approach to educational, commercial and cultural interchange for the welfare of the region, the republic and its people." For the Technoparque segment of the City, the European Union assisted in project development and strategic-plan definition as well.

Seemingly endless arrays of possible participation categories within the City have been defined. A limited sample includes the arts, biology, business, climatology, ecotourism, ecology, environmental design, engineering, industry, IT, language, law, maritime projects, medicine and multimodal transportation. TIP welcomes such diversities as aquaculture, banking software, biodiversity, communications, data processing, multimedia and remote sensing.

For those companies and institutions wishing to participate, several generous exemptions have been granted. Fiscal incentives include: (1) exemption of all taxes, contributions, duties or import fees on all machinery, equipment, furniture, vehicles, appliances, or materials necessary for project development; (2) exemption of the Movable Property Transfer Tax (ITBM) on machinery, equipment, vehicles, appliances and materials necessary for project development; and, (3) exemption of any tax, duty, or lien imposed on the remittance of money abroad, when such remittance or transfer of funds takes place in relation to project purposes.

The Panamanian government will issue special visas to foreign staff entering the country with the purpose of participating in project development. This includes researchers, professors and technicians, their spouses and dependent children, and students.

Participating entities are allowed to lease sites and housing for an initial, renewable, 25-year period. Shops, restaurants and other services are offered concessions.

Membership in the City has grown steadily since the center's inception and includes some of the world's most prestigious institutions and corporations. As we go to press, academic programs are offered by over 20 universities and affiliated institutions, including the Canal Authority of Panama, the Smithsonian Tropical Research Institute (STRI), USAID, Cornell, Florida State University, McGill University, Texas A&M, and the University of Madrid. The TIP boasts over 25 IT-related businesses (both on-and offsite) including ADYCE, ADN, ALTEC, S.A., Arango Software, Aula Inteligente, BCEOM, Broadband Wireless Communications, Conservas Chiguirí, Core Laboratories, Corporate University, Cripto Data, Explora, Arts and Science Center, Futuro Forestal, Gate Computer, GEOINFO, Highlights of Ophthalmology, Image Corporation, Metro Call, Net Direct, PROSES, Telco Virtual, Telecarrier and Trainmar Panamá. The "Don Alberto" Business Incubator combines Graciliaria de Panamá, S.A., Aloe Panamá, S.A. Prime Tech Internationaland, Ingeniería de Confiabilidad, Top Art Multimedia, Twin Seas, Intercuentas, CoBuys.com, Win Soft Corp. and the Universidad Tecnológica de Panamá.

Panama's City of Knowledge is continually gaining in acceptance and international status. The International Development Bank has extended the City a $5.7 million credit line. UNICEF has a presence there. The International Human Development Corporation has signed an accord. The Global Development Learning Network is associated as well.

The facts speak for themselves. The City of Knowledge is proving to be one of Panama's most successful forays into the major international development scene.

The economy

Panama GDP is one of the highest in the region
and Panama fares better than its neighbors

Panama's strategic location has been the backbone of its service-oriented economy from as far back as the 17th century when the isthmus was famous for the Portobolo fairs held by the Spanish whose galleons arriving from Europe brought merchandise for the new territories prior to loading the gold and silver destined for the court of King Ferdinand. The construction of the Panama Canal and the unique monetary system based on the US dollar since 1904, have led the country to become an important international trading, banking and maritime center.

While Panama's neighbors in South and Central America battled to survive on-going crises during the past decade, the economy of Panama had sustained a relatively continuous growth, showing a performance higher than many other Latin American countries. Nevertheless, the global recession, combined with the tragic events of September 11th, have put some stress on the country's economy. According to government officials, Panama's gross domestic product per capita is one of the highest in the region with an estimated US$3,663 in 2001, though it reflects a general trend in the metropolitan area of Panama City and Colon where 75% of all economic activity is concentrated. Inequalities in income distribution remain a problem in rural areas.

The economy grew 0.3% in real terms in 2001, falling from 2.7% growth the year before and 3.2% in 1999. Although it was the lowest growth rate registered in a decade, the economic slowdown in the United States, which is Panama's main commercial partner, was the factor that affected a decrease in exports, particularly traditional products. By October 2002, the government announced a GDP growth of 0.8% during the first quarter and of 1% during the second quarter of the year and forecast an annual increase of 1%-1.5%.

The banking sector, which provides some 10,000 well-paid jobs, has now developed strong regulations in compliance with the Basle recommendations. It remained stable despite the global recession and problems in Latin American countries, with assets totaling US$38.08bn at the end of 2001. By July 2002, total assets had fallen by 9.2% to US$ 34.53m mostly because of the financial problems in Argentina which forced several banks of the center to reduce their exposure in that country. Deposits fell slightly to US$24.18m down from US$26.59m in December 2001, of which internal deposits accounted for US$13.08m and US$11.095m for external deposits. The number of banks dropped to 77 in March 2002. There were 82 at the end of 2000, 104 in 1998. The drop is as a result of mergers and acquisitions. However the Banking Superintendency had granted five additional new licences to Latin American banks in June 2002.

Miss Universe Justine Pasek, the first Panamanian to gain this honor, flanked by two other Panamanian beauties in their polleras, signs the book at a ceremony at the El Panama Hotel in Panama City.
Photo: Jorge Quinzada Loo

Famous orchestras and classical music ensembles visit Panama year round, especially during the season of the National Concert Association. This photo shows the National Theatre during a performance by the National Concert Symphony Orchestra and singers of the Bel Canto Foundation. *Photo: Jorge Quinzada Loo*

Horsemanship ranks high as a Panamanian pursuit. The horse population is high, from the spunky ponies of the cowboys of the interior provinces to high-stepping throughbreds on the showground of the Coronado Esquestrian club, shown in these pictures. Coronado is a leisure-living beach community on the Pacific coast a little over an hour from Panama City. The Coronado Club Suites Resort, one of Panama's finest resort hotels, is adjacent to the club. *Photos: Jorge Quinzada Loo*

Panama City's theaters are active, presenting plays, musicals and concerts. Photo above shows the exhuberance of a folklore show. *Photo: Danny Lehman*

Left: Lyrical singer Lizi Rodriguez singing at an operatic concert. *Photo: Jorge Quinzada Loo*

Right: Popular folk singer, Sandra Sandoval in action. *Photo: Tomas Munita*

A scene from a performance of "Fiddler on the Roof" with a Panamanian cast, directed by Bruce Quinn. *Photo: Tomas Munita*

The evangelical churches, such as this Assembly of God on Vía España in Panama City, seem to be capturing the attention of growing numbers of people seeking an outlet for their religious fervour and enjoying participation in the proceedings of the service. This church is a vast hall with a capacity for approximately 5,500 devotees.
Photos: Jorge Quinzada Loo

The government strategy

When elected to office in 1999, the government of Mireya Moscoso pledged to increase social spending, reduce the level of poverty in which some 40% of the population lived, and diminish unemployment. During the Legislative Assembly sessions of 2000 and 2001, Ms. Moscoso lost the majority at the Assembly making it difficult for her to promote a number of reforms presented by her government. However, in September 2002, she successfully regained control of the assembly through political maneuvers that brought over to her side two dissident deputies of the opposition Revolutionary Democratic party (PRD) who had broken from party ranks. This was significant in a critical year when presidential candidates began their political campaign for the presidential elections due in May 2004. It also gives President Moscoso the ability to approve laws and projects of reforms that had been delayed in the previous years.

Although Ms. Moscoso 's policies marked a change from her predecessor's economic policy and privatization programme, her government had renewed its commitment to abide by the agreements with the IMF, World Bank and WTO made by the former Revolutionary Democratic Party administration of Perez Balladares. The government signed a new standby agreement with the IMF in June 2000 which could not be completely fulfilled. An extension is likely to be approved before the end of this year. The IMF had recommended cutting fiscal deficit by 1% in 2000 and 0% in 2001 as well as structural adjustments to reform the social security system, adopt a tax reform and close two state-owned development and mortgage banks. The reforms were very unpopular and never made it to the Legislative Assembly mostly because the government did not have the majority to pass the legislation. However, the tax reform may be presented during the 2002-2003 Assembly session if a consensus is reached through the National Dialogue that includes political parties, business organizations and representatives of civic associations.

Some positive steps have been taken to reactivate the economy. The installation, in October 2001 of a National Dialogue, with ample participation of the sectors mentioned above, led to a law modifying the use of the Fondo Fiduciario (FFD, Trust Fund for Development set up with proceeds of privatization of public utilities). The bill establishes public debt ceilings and permits the use of former Canal Zone lands as payment for some public works projects. It also allows using some US$200m of the US$1.3bn fund for investment in public works that will generate employment and reactivate the economy. The fiscal accountability measures put a ceiling on total net public debt at 50% of GDP, net external public debt at 35% of GDP and fiscal deficit at 2% of GDP. These ceilings are to be achieved within the next 15 years.

After having passed a number of laws to curtail money laundering, Panama was removed in June 2001 from the OECD's Financial Action Task Force black list of countries suspected of not co-operating in the fight against drug trafficking. In February 2002 Panama began talks on a tax information treaty with the U.S. and the government has also signed a memorandum with the OECD to improve the transparency of its tax system and establish a system of exchange of information on tax issues by December 2005.

US economic assistance to Panama for 2003 rose to US$20.7m, up from $13.7m in 2002. The extra money will fund anti-drug trafficking activities, training for Panama's border police and programmes to strengthen democracy.

The United States effected a smooth transition of the Panama Canal to Panamanian control on December 31st, 1999. Since then, the Panama Canal Authority (ACP, Autoridad del Canal de Panama) the successor to US-Panamanian Panama Canal Commission, has been intent on transforming itself into a market-driven, profit-making administration. Widening of the Gaillard Cut, as part of a US$1bn modernization programme, was finished at the end of 2001, increasing Canal transit capacity by 20%.

The ACP announced a toll hike increase of 13% in two phases of 8% effective October 1st 2002 and 4.5% to come into effect July 1st, 2003. Canal users protested the increase as ill-timed when the shipping industry is going through its worst period in 20 years. The last toll increase of 15.7% was in 1996, in two phases effective in 1997 and 1998. Canal authorities also changed the toll pricing structure of "one-fits-all", in place since 1914, for a more customer-oriented structure of seven categories that will enable the ACP to "customize" their tariffs and services. The seven-category system includes container, passenger, dry bulk, liquid bulk, large bulk, and ro-ro and reefer ships.

To modernize the Canal to accommodate larger ships, the ACP is considering an estimated US$3bn-$5bn expansion project for which some 200 feasibility studies have been commissioned since 1998, the results of which will be ready by mid-2003. The 10-year project includes the eventual construction of a third set of larger locks to accommodate post-panamax vessels and a decision is expected to be announced by end of 2003.

Panama Canal officials will announce before the end of 2003 the Canal expansion plan at a cost estimated between US$3bn-5bn. Financing could be provided by increases of tolls and Global bond issuances and since the Canal Authority has no liability, it expects to receive an investment grade in order to go to the international market. The expansion will boost the economy and attract foreign companies and investments. It will also foster the maritime and port activity in creating a transshipment hub around the project.

Panama's economy is based primarily on well developed service-oriented sectors that represent nearly 75% of gross domestic product. Services include the Panama Canal, port activity, the ship registry, legal services, insurance, banking, tourism and the Colon Free Zone. The participation of manufacturing (7.5% of GDP in 2001) and agriculture (6.2% of GDP in 2001) has decreased since the entry of Panama in the WTO, as many industrial companies reconverted into distribution of imported goods.

The government has been active in bilateral and multilateral negotiations to sign free trade accords with Central American countries, Mexico and Chile. It had also initiated conversations with the United States and Taiwan. So far, Panama has concluded a bilateral free trade accord with El Salvador, pending ratification in both countries and expects to finish negotiations with all its regional neighbors by mid-2003.

Although Panama's GDP per capita is one of the highest in the region (US$3,663 in 2001) the figure does not reflect the differences in income distribution. According to a UN Development Programme (UNDP) report published in February, a total of 40.5% of the population live under the poverty line of which 14% are classified as being in "poverty" and 26.5% in "extreme poverty" . This is in spite of high per head social spending, one of the highest in Latin America. Unemployment has been rising. 13.3% at end-2000. In 1999 it was 11.3%, in 2000 it was 13-3% and it had risen to 14.4% by the end of 2001.

The administration of Mireya Moscoso implemented the promises she made of increasing social spending to benefit poor rural communities and raising tariffs to encourage agricultural production. The government wished to use the Trust Fund for Development (Fondo Fiduciario) to buy back external debt but was unable to reverse previous legislation which did not permit this policy.

However, the government successfully reopened the Global 2012 bond, issuing an extra US$150m of paper. The government reportedly plans to reopen other global bonds to raise a further US$260m when it deems market conditions to be right. It repaid an outstanding sum of US$341.6m on a Eurobond due in 2002 on schedule in February; an early repayment on the bond of US$158.4m had already been made in July 2001.In addition, it also began to buy its own global bonds. Although it is not a buyback of its debt, it will simply pay interest to itself. Those measures show that in spite of fiscal difficulties, investor sentiment towards Panama is generally positive.

The targets recommended by the IMF stand-by agreement that included tax and social security reforms and closure of two state development banks, were not met. The goal of reducing fiscal deficit to 0% at the end of 2001 could not be reached and the year ended with a 1.4% deficit, although the government ended the previous year at 0.8%, bettering the IMF target of 1%. It is likely that the 2002 fiscal deficit may reach 2%-2.5%.

From the Trust Fund for Development, the government will use some US$200m for public works which will boost employment in the regions where highways and road repairs are scheduled. Foreign investments in the former US military bases, now under the Interoceanic Region Authority (ARI, Autoridad de la Region Interoceanica) have lost some momentum because of the global recession. An international tender for the former Howard US Air Force Base had been postponed but is expected to be re-launched once market conditions improve. Until now, most of the major developments in the reverted areas had been approved under the previous administration. Investments since 1999 have been concentrated in the tourism sector, mainly in the beautiful area of Fort Amador where cruise port, shops and restaurants have created local and international tourist attractions.

Sectoral trends

Some sectors have performed and continue to perform well. The maritime, financial and telecommunication sectors have registered constant growth in the past years. The telecommunication sector will be liberalized in January 2003 and some 23 companies have requested licences to operate though it is likely that only a few of those companies will enter the market of international calls which seems the most profitable. Mobile telephone concessions held by Bellsouth and Cable & Wireless expire in 2007.

For the second consecutive year, in 2002, the US Embassy 's Country Guide noted the sectors with more potential for foreign investors as ports, maritime services, telecoms, tourism and non-traditional agricultural exports.

Global recession and the aftermath of the September 11th terrorist attacks were the primary contributors to economic slowdown in 2001 in sectors such as port activity, tourism and exports. Construction, a main source of employment, fell 9.7% in 2001 with the conclusions of major public works, following increases of 7.5% in 2000 and 16% in 1999. Delays in the tender of the US$90m second bridge over the Panama Canal and its access roads affected the completion targets, but this and the expansion of the ports of Balboa, Manzanillo International Terminal and Colon Container Port may reactivate the sector early next year. Some US$200m in public works mostly road maintenance and widening of the Inter-American highway from Santiago to David, were also imminent.

Panama's agriculture fell by 3.3% in 2001 down from a mere 0.1% growth a year earlier. Traditional products were badly hit by low international prices and economic contraction in the USA, their main buyer. Coffee, bananas and sugar exports fell by 30.7%, 17% and 6% respectively. Banana production's future is dim because high costs of production have lowered its competitiveness on international markets. The sectors that experienced highest growth were fisheries, 21.14%, cattle, 21.6% and melons, 35.5%. Shrimp exports increased after the industry recuperated from the white-spot virus. Panama was certified in May as complying with international regulations to protect sea turtles which should boost exports to the US in the next months.

Panama's total exports grew by 4.9% in 2001 to US$809.6m, up from US$771.4m in 2000. Mining, less than 0.5% of GDP, dropped 12.8% for the second straight year as the low world market discouraged mineral explorations. In June 2002, with financing from the IDB, the government began to review the legal framework of the mining industry. A new legislation is expected for next year.

Industrial activity decreased by 5.7% in 2001, after a fall of 1.5% in 2000 and further decline was forecast for 2002 as a consequence of the entry of Panama in the WTO and lack of competitiveness and markets for industrial products, but once the regional free-trade negotiations are concluded they will open new markets for Panamanian products, exports and services.

Port activity grew by 13.3% in 2001 and remains one of the strongest contributors to economic growth although the sector was badly affected in the last quarter of 2001 as world shipping declined strongly in the aftermath of the September 11th terrorist attacks. Container movement grew by 15.9% and in teus by 16.3%. The trend continued in the first half of 2002. The Panama Canal Authority saw a few less transits in fiscal year 2001 (October-September) down to 13,492 from 13,653 in 2000 but tolls income grew to US$579.5m from US$574.2m a year earlier. Cargo transported fell slightly to 193.1m long tons from 193.7m in 2000 with an increase of Panamax-vessels transits to 4,424, up from 4,359 in 2000.

Colon Free Zone activity suffered from slow demand from its main Latin American customers, Colombia, Ecuador, Venezuela. Imports fell 0.6% to US$4.6bn in 2001 while exports rose to US$5.3bn, up 1.4%, with net exports growing marginally to US$718m.

Tourist expenditures were up 8% in 2001 and the number of visitors increased by 5.9% to 519,000. The government had begun a US$10m advertising campaign in Europe, the US and Latin America that should foster the sector. Three cruise port terminals, Colon 2000, and Cristobal, on the Atlantic side and the new Fort Amador Cruise Port, on the Pacific side, welcomed over 150,000 visitors during the latest season. More cruise lines are putting Panama in their schedules. The Tourist Bureau (IPAT) signed an accord with the Miss Universe contest to hold the world competition in Panama in 2003. The international event is expected to focus world attention on the isthmus and boost the image of eco-tourism and the " less travelled path" Panama is advertising worldwide.

Privatizations

After privatization of the telecommunications and energy sectors in recent years the administration of Mireya Moscoso has said it will not proceed with the sale of the public water company IDAAN, as announced by the former government, and was opposed to further privatizations. An agreement was reached with the International

Monetary Fund to restructure IDAAN with a board of directors and more financial autonomy. Proceeds from legislation modifying the use of the Trust Fund for Development will help IDAAN to modernize the institution and installations.

Tocumen International Airport privatization was also put on hold but the government announced it would create a state corporation to administrate Tocumen airport with more autonomy. Airport users, including airlines, pilots and concessionaries were promised seats on the board of directors.

The only concession granted by the Moscoso government was Atlapa Convention Centre. Atlapa, after a number of delays for lack of international interest was finally put to tender in 2002 and a Brazilian-Panamanian consortium selected for the ten-year concession, starting in 2003. The center was built in the mid-eighties and will need complete refurbishing to accommodate the international conventions the new consortium plans to organize.

The Financial sector

Panama's strong banking sector is immune to regional turmoil and economic crisis and the Banking Superintendency earns praise from the IMF

Panama's strong financial sector comprises the flourishing international banking center, the stock exchange, insurance and re-insurance companies. Because of a unique monetary system and free circulation of the US dollar, as legal tender since a 1904 treaty with the USA, Panama has been able to create, during the past three decades, a banking center that has grown immune to the regional turmoil and economic crisis. Furthermore, recent legislative reforms have helped the center to be active in globalization and international competition.

The center's contribution to the national economy has increased substantially in recent years with aggressive consumer credit policies and loans to the private sector and the Colon Free Zone while playing an important role in developing sectors such as ports, maritime activity and tourism, mostly in the reverted areas.

In times of regional crises and economic slow-down, the banking center, the most important component of the financial sector, has benefited from the country's dollarized economy and stable interest rates, keeping its prominence as a safe haven for Latin American investors.

Created in 1970 through innovative legislation that encouraged foreign institutions through a system of three licences (general, international and of representation), the center was modernised in 1998 with the passage of Decree Law 9-1998 that created an autonomous Banking Superintendency. Banking secrecy is a strict rule of the banking activity and includes coded or numbered accounts for both nationals and foreigners.

The number of banks decreased from 104 in 1998 to about 80 in 2002 because of mergers and acquisitions domestically and worldwide as part of a global trend toward globalization. Of the 80 banks operating in Panama in 2002; 45 held general licences, including two state-owned institutions, 29 held international licences and six held representative licences. Four new banks, —two international and two with general-licences— were waiting approval of their licences while five European and South American banks had begun proceedings to join the center.

At the end of 2001 assets of the center were \$38.08bn. Total deposits were at \$26.5bn in December 2001.

Net annual profits rose by 1.9% to $486m, and foreign bank assets grew by 0.7% while domestic institutions' assets fell by 2.2%. However, by July 2002, Panama's banking centre total assets decreased by 9.2% to $34.53bn with total deposits down by 9.1% to $24.17bn of which internal deposits fell by 5.4% to $13.08bn and external deposits by 13.1% to $11.09bn, mostly because of the domestic slow down of the economy and the financial crisis in Argentina.

The process of consolidation, through mergers and acquisitions, was the leading factor of the centre's domestic reorganisation during the period of 2000 to 2002 with the merger of Banco del Istmo, in 2000 with Pribanco to form Primer Banco del Istmo (Banistmo). Banistmo, through its subsidiary Banco Mercantil del Istmo, acquired the Panamanian branch of Dutch bank ABN-Amro, and later the domestic bank Bancolat bringing Banistmo's total assets to around $4.5Bn, making it the third largest domestic bank. Banistmo also bought a majority stake in the largest financial institution of Honduras, Grupo Financiero El Ahorro Hondureno, through Banistmo's parent company Compania Nacional de Seguros (Conase). The acquisition will enable Banistmo to strengthen its banking and insurance business in the region.

Grupo Financiero Continental, owner of 100% of Banco Continental, merged with grupo BIPAN, owner of 100% of Banco Internacional de Panama, that will operate under the name of Banco Continental and will enjoy a strong fifth position with a capital of $1.7Bn and 21 branches. In early 2002, Banco Continental through its holding GFC, acquired a majority stake in Banco Aleman Platina which has representative offices in Mexico, Colombia and Central American countries.

Banco General acquired, in 2000, Banco Comercial de Panama (Bancomer), becoming the fourth largest financial group. Banco General is part of Empresas Generales de Inversiones with interests in banking, fishing, insurance and gasoline distribution with assets of $2.43bn.

In a transaction completed in 2000, HSBC-USA, the local unit of the UK-based global bank, acquired the Panamanian operations of JP Morgan Chase, a bank that had been present in Panama since the opening of the Panama Canal in 1914, with 11 full-service retail branches. The combined entity has become the largest commercial lender in Panama and the Colon Free Zone, although the largest foreign institution established in the center remains, at November 2002, Germany's Dresdner Bank Lateinamerika.

The Japanese Bank of Tokyo-Mitsubishi and France's Societe Generale have announced the closure of their operations while keeping a representation office by end-2002 due to global re-organization.

The monetary system

Panama's unique monetary system has largely contributed to her stable economy and healthy growth of the financial sector. The U.S. dollar has been legal tender in Panama from the time that a treaty, without date of expiration, was signed between the U.S. and Panama in 1904 (law 84) and no changes are foreseen. The dollar circulates in bank notes and coins while the official currency—the Balboa (B/.) which is permanently pegged at a value of one dollar—exists only in forms of coins of 10 cents, 25 cents and fifty cents. Documents, bills and check books are written in balboas, dollars or both. Panama's state-owned Banco Nacional de Panama (BNP, Panama's National Bank) plays the double role of commercial bank and fiduciary agent of the Republic. It also distributes US dollars and collects old bills in conjunction with the Federal Reserve Bank of New York. Banco Nacional de Panama is the government's paymaster and holds the reserves and deposits of the Nation.

The bank regulators

Panama's banking system is controlled by the autonomous Banking Superintendency. This independent body regulates the sector and the law gives broad powers to its five-member board of directors, appointed by the executive branch for a maximum of two eight-year terms. Ms. Delia Cardenas, a former minister of planning and economic policy from 1990 to 1994, was named Banking Superintendent in 2000. The superintendent is named for a five-year period, renewable once, that does not coincide with the presidential term. The Superintendency is financed by collecting fees from the center's banks and thus functions independently from the government. It supervises the sector, grants licences, audits banks, imposes sanctions and oversees both voluntary and imposed bank liquidations.

According to decree-Law 9-1998, which follows most of the Basel Committee's recommendations drawn up in the early 1990s, minimum capital requirements for all banks with general licences is $10m and for banks with an international licence (offshore banks) the minimum is $3m of which, $250,000 must be kept in one of several financial mechanisms previously approved by the Superintendency, such as Treasury bills or in Banco Nacional de Panama's deposits. In addition, foreign banks must possess assets of at least $500m, be recognized financial institutions in their country of origin and comply with mandatory reserve ratios. Banks are not allowed to reduce their capital reserves unless authorised by the Superintendency, and are not allowed to distribute dividends or transfer capital to other organizations until their capital requirement is met. In addition, banks may not lend more than 25% of their capital to a single borrower, be it a person or an organization, or more than 30% of their capital to another bank.

They are prohibited from making loans under the following conditions: a non-guaranteed loan for more than 5% of the bank's total capital; a guaranteed loan for more than 10% of the bank's total capital that is without deposit; a guaranteed loan with a deposit amounting to more than 50% of the bank's total capital to people connected to the bank. Loans guaranteed with deposits must make up no less than 25% of a bank's credit portfolio and the regulators may request detailed information concerning a bank's deposits to evaluate their risks. The Superintendency regulates the percentage of banks' assets that must be held in liquid form and the percentage of local deposits that must kept in the country. Currently the required percentage of total local and foreign assets is 30%. Although the Superintendency may change that percentage, the figure may not exceed 35%. By law, 85% of local assets must be kept in Panamanian territory. The law also allows foreign regulators to inspect the local branches of banks under their jurisdiction and use the information they find during investigations to enforce the laws of their country.

With the enactment in June 2001 of Law 43 that regulates e-commerce and provides legal recognition of electronic documents and signatures, the Superintendency requires all financial institutions to submit a request for authorization to offer banking services on-line. As of November 2002, more than 25 foreign and domestic banks offered their customers access to their accounts on-line and some of them allow financial transactions to be conducted on-line.

Since 1998, the Superintendency has published a number of regulations complementing the banking law, on licencing procedures, corporate governance, limitations on investments in equity securities, on electronic banking and on external audit, market risk, bank ratings and interest rates calculations. The Superintendency has pursued Memoranda of Understanding (MOUs) with 16 foreign jurisdictions to facilitate supervision.

Laws 41 and 42, passed by the National Assembly in October 2000, modify Panama's penal code, expanding the definition of money-laundering beyond the sphere of narcotics to cover funds derived from arms and other illicit goods trafficking, financial swindles, official corruption and terrorism. The new legislation provides stiffer penalties, broadens reporting requirements and permits the Financial Analysis Unit (Unidad de Análisis Financiero-UAF) of the executive branch, created in 1996 to track illicit transactions in banking and other sectors of the economy and to share information with its foreign counterparts. Panama has signed memoranda on money —laundering with 11 countries including Belgium, Spain, the US, Brazil and Colombia and some Caribbean countries. The new legislation came in response to Panama's inclusion in June 2000 on a blacklist drawn up by the OECD's Financial Analysis Task-Force (FATF), which alleged non-co-operation by Panamanian authorities in the pursuit of money-launderers. Because of Panama's improved efforts to combat money-laundering, the FATF removed it from the blacklist in June 2001. In a report published in July 2002 the IMF praised the Banking Superintendency's efforts to strengthen supervisory and regulatory frameworks within the banking system. This report and the country's removal from the blacklist drawn up by OECD's Financial Action Task Force is expected to help to boost the banking center and business in Panama in the medium term.

Foundations and trusts

Panama's laws allow for the creation and regulation of private foundations and trusts. The law provides total tax exemptions and makes the creation of a foundation or a trust as simple and fast as establishing a corporation. A total of sixty financial institutions are registered with the Banking Superintendency as trust companies qualified for trust administration and management. Those companies are banks, financial institutions, co-operatives, insurance companies and law firms. The law does not distinguish between family foundations and joint foundations, in which entities or persons that are not members of the same family can participate, neither does it require the members of the foundation's staff to have Panamanian citizenship. The law does not require the payment of the minimum capital needed to establish the foundation before its creation.

The Stock Exchange

The Panama Stock Exchange (Bolsa de Valores, BVP) founded in 1990, is regulated by the National Securities Commission, once a department of the Ministry of Commerce and Industry and now an autonomous entity, under the terms of Decree Law 1 of July 8,1999. It offers trading in bonds, IOUs, and other national and international government and private company issues. Since end-1999 the government has sold Treasury bills on a monthly basis with an average value of $30m per issue. These issues have been generally well received by the market. The stock exchange is primarily national and operates in the same way as exchanges throughout Latin America. Member firms must maintain one or several bank accounts in the country, with balances sufficient to meet the value of purchases made on the exchange. Listing requirements are less restrictive than those of the New York Stock Exchange. Traders and brokerage firms are required to apply for a licence. There is no tax on securities traded on the stock exchange and foreign companies can issue securities on Panama's bourse. A couple of years ago, the El Salvador-based TACA airlines issued a series of five and three-year corporate bonds on the bourse. Institutional investors, such as insurance companies, banks and private pension funds can invest in the stock market. The process of preparing an equity public offer may cost up to $100,000 while brokers generally charge commission fees of less than 1% of the offering.

By June 2002, 29 local firms with total market capitalization of $2.61bn quoted their common stock on the exchange. Total trading volume fell by 23.3% to $1.04bn at the end of-2001 down from $2.79bn in 2000 and from $3.78bn in 1999 because of the slowing domestic economy. However, total trading during the first six months of 2002 increased 41.8% to $596.9m compared to the same period in 2001. The current yield on equities rose to 32.55% at June 2002, though it was somewhat distorted by a $100m buy-out of a local brewery by Colombian investors. The Panamanian bourse trades electronically on both the primary and secondary markets. The bourse's electronic trading is open daily from 10 am to 3 pm.

Insurance companies

Although the insurance sector grew constantly during the 1980s and 1990s it was not immune to the global trend of mergers that had characterized other sectors of the domestic economy. Three large domestic companies, Assa, Compania Internacional de Seguros, and Aseguradora Mundial, control over half the market in terms of premium incomes while other insurers are considerably smaller, including some foreign companies. Insurance companies are allowed to invest in a range of financial assets, including public-sector debt securities, mortgages, mortgage-backed securities and securities issued through Panama's stock exchange. Law 59, of July 29th, 1996 regulates the sector while Law 60 allows the creation of captive companies.

Insurance companies are allowed, by Law 59, to invest up to 75% of their total reserves locally and up to 25% internationally. They are required to meet a mandatory reserve ratio as follows: 20% of net income before taxes, up to and including $2m, and 10% of net income taxes over $2m. When investing funds internationally, insurers may only place these funds in investment-grade securities. The Superintendency of Insurance oversees the sector which can appeal to an Insurance Technical Committee which also promotes the development of the industry. The key industry group is the Panama's Insurance Association.

To establish a captive subsidiary, a minimum paid-up capital of $150,000 is required for non-life risks and a premium-to-surplus ratio of five to one. Applications are submitted to the Superintendent of Insurance and Reinsurance. There are no taxes on premiums, capital gains or profits.

Torch gingers, product of a new flower farm, Finca Jones in Caimito de Capira. *Photo: Focus*

Compensating, in environmental terms, for the clear-cutting by ranchers and the slash-and-burn techniques of peasant farmers throughout the region, is the dramatic growth of re-forestation. Medium and large-scale farmers and investor groups are re-making the forests. These photographs were taken on the 370 acre farm of the Besser brothers in Caimito, near Capira. The photo shows Dr. Israel Besser, an engineer, who grew up on the farm of his Polish father in Chiriquí and now adds precise know-how to his inherited love of the land to make arboriculture his second business. His brother, Dr. Walter Besser, a medical doctor, is a partner in the farm. They have planted 150,000 trees in the five years since they bought the farm, including Mahogany, Purple Heart, Teak, Terminalia Ivorensis and Cedar (Cedro Espino) the spiny trees shown in the inset photo. Between their groves and among the trees, they have cattle, geese and lakes full of fish.
Photo: Focus

The banana industry, "green gold" in its heyday, is in crisis, troubled by high production costs, causing concern in the Bocas del Toro and Chiriquí provinces.
Photo above: Danny Lehman.
At right: Yolande Vicente

Cocoa and pineapple are two other staple crops.
Photos: Yolande Vicente and Jorge Quinzada Loo

Above: Shrimp farms cover vast areas of the Pacific coastal plain from Chame to Aguadulce. *Photo: Jorge Quinzada Loo.*

Left: Chiriquí, home of quality, high mountain coffee.

Below: Orchids thrive in the rain forests– and in captivity, a growing export. *Photos: Yolande Vicente*

The North Corridor, city bypass road which is slated to continue north as an expressway to across the isthmus to the Caribbean city of Colon. *Photo: Jorge Quinzada Loo*

The Panamanian Corporation

**Offshore or onshore...there are many reasons to set up a corporation
in Panama where foreign investors enjoy the same rights as nationals.
The advantages may be for tax, location or just opportunity**

Panamanian commerce is based in one of the world's few truly service-dominated economies. Industries such as banking, insurance, shipping and transport, "offshore" business and import/re-export account for between 75% and 80% of the GNP and the dynamic of the sector requires constant change. The number of companies registered in Panama –the majority of which deal with the aforementioned services– is approximately 350,000, a number exceeded only by those of Hong Kong, which has close to 400,000.

The reason for the popularity of Panama-based corporations are many. Panama welcomes foreigner investors and has given them the same rights as nationals. The country's tax structure is favorable and generous incentives are available, especially to operations devoted to export. Taxes are levied only on net income derived from operations within Panama and there are no exchange controls. There are no restrictions on transfer of profits, dividends, interest, royalties and fees, repatriation of capital or repayment of principal. Finally there is the foundation, Panama corporate law, amended only once since 1927, that is extremely conducive to organizing a company within the country for the purpose of directing operations elsewhere.

In terms of the actual opening and maintaining of a business in general, this equates to a relatively simple unrestricted process.

Business licenses

Law No. 25 of August 26, 1994 most recently modified licensing stipulations and licenses are issued through the Ministry of Commerce and Industry. Exempted from licensing are entities conducting business exclusively in certain agroindustrial and handicraft sectors, as are those companies with a startup capital base of under $10,000. There are two standard types of licenses, which must always be visible in the place of business.

The Class A Commercial License applies to commercial and mortgage banks, financial companies, high-technology companies insurers and reinsurers, international financial brokers and transportation companies, mutual funds and public utilities. The Class B Commercial License is mandatory for bars, drugstores, gas stations, real estate agents, representation agencies, restaurant and other retail-oriented businesses. Class B status is only granted to Panamanians or corporations owned entirely by Panamanians since foreign companies are not permitted to engage in retail trade or certain professional activities. The National Securities Commission or the Superintendency of Insurance and Reinsurance must grant special accreditation for specified financial industries.

Forming corporations

Corporate names are certified by the Official Register of National Industry (Registro Oficial de la Industria Nacional). Names can be in any language, but are required to be suffixed with S.A., Inc., Corp. or Corporation.

There are two types of corporations in Panama: resident and non-resident. Two or more individuals or corporations may start a corporation and articles of incorporation may be executed inside or outside Panama in any language. Corporations may be owned by a single individual or corporation and capital does not have to be held by Panamanians. A foreign company is allowed to have branches or subsiduaries in Panama and numerous entities offer the use of shell companies to those requiring them.

The Board of Directors must be composed of at least three directors. Directors can be individual or corporate, national or non-national. A President, Treasurer and Secretary are required and one person can hold more than one of these positions. Directors and officers need not be shareholders and shareholder meetings need not be held in Panama.

All corporations are required to have a Resident Agent (read : Panamanian lawyer or law firm) and only agents can file incorporation documents. Approval is normally granted within one week. Costs vary, but usually fall within the $900 to $1,300 range.

Corporate taxes

Panamanian income tax is meant to be levied only on income derived from sources "within the territory of the Republic", and the 1964 law specifically states that the following activities do not produce taxable income: (1) invoicing from an office in Panama the sales of goods that do not enter the country; (2) handling offshore transactions from an office in Panama; and, (3) distributing dividends from income derived abroad, including income from (1) and (2).

Taxable income is defined as the balance of gross income less deductible expenses. The resident corporate tax rate on income of up to $500,000 is 30%. For over $500,000, the rate is $150,000 plus 34%. Non-resident corporate income is considered to be offshore, but a yearly fee of $150 is levied. For non-resident banking corporations in Panama, income from activities is also tax-free.

Organizational expenses may be excluded from taxable income in the year incurred or amortized over five years, at the discretion of the taxpayer. The total cost of research and development may also be subtracted.

Labor concerns

Panama has a relatively small labor pool (Government statistics for 1999 listed approximately 1.5 million persons as "employable.") and this tends to limit availability in upper-echelon positions. As a rule, Panamanians respond well to in-house training and the bilingual workforce (especially Spanish-English) is proportionately quite large.

Unionism is not as prevalent as in European countries and the United States and tends to be centered in the construction, government works and private manufacturing sectors. In Panama, union membership includes around 10% of the workforce.

Though modifications are under study, the Panamanian Labor Code still tends to be protective of the worker and somewhat prohibitive for the employer. Under the code, three types of labor contracts are recognized. The Definitive Period of Time Contract allows for employment not to exceed one year. The time period of a Defined Work Labor Contract is determined by the job performed. The Indefinite or Permanent Labor Contract is for a duration which is at yet undetermined by the parties at the time of signing. When special circumstances dictate them, probationary three-month contracts may be signed.

Mandatory employee fringe rights represent an estimated 35-40% of base pay and a Panamanian employee is guaranteed a wide range of benefits by law. Some of special note to employers include:

• An annual paid vacation of 30 days for every 11 months of continuous employment.

• A "Thirteenth Month" compensation that is aggregated at one day's salary for every 11 days worked. The bonus is paid in three installments in April, August and December.

• Termination compensation equivalent to a week's salary for each year worked.

• An unjustified-cause termination payment. This is a lump-sum payment, the value of which is based on labor code indemnification tables. After the amount is paid, the effected employee must be rehired if he or she desires.

• A paid maternity leave of 14 weeks.

The maximum normal workweek is 48 hours for daytime work, 42 hours for night work and 45 hours for mixed day and night work. Executive Decree No. 38 of July 22, 1998 established new minimum wage standards for three geographical regions, cross-referenced by employment sector. The resultant table places the minimum wage rate at between $0.82 and $1.33 per hour.

Foreign labor must obtain a one-year, sometimes-renewable work permit from the Bureau of Immigration. (In certain sectors and for some specialized positions, special temporary permits are granted.) For companies choosing to hire foreign labor, the rule of thumb is that the percentage of foreigners to nationals cannot exceed 10%. Due to the fact that unemployment has averaged between 12% and 14% for the last several years, foreign-labor statutes are strictly enforced in Panama and violations may result in fines and/or revocation of visa status, depending upon the individual case.

In terms of taxation, bonuses to employees in excess of one month's salary or $750, whichever is lowest, are not deductible, nor are profit-sharing payments in excess of 10% of a company's taxable income.

Other considerations

The fiscal year is calculated from January 1 to December 31. Due to the existence of numerous back-to-back holidays, business activity slows down dramatically during the months of November and December.

Business information sources

Those wishing to obtain more information pertaining to establishing a business in Panama may contact:

Chamber of Commerce, Industry and Agriculture of Panama, tel: (507) 227-1233, fax: (507) 225-3653, mailing address: Apartado 74, Panama 1, Rep. of Panama, physical address: Avenidas Cuba and Ecuador, e-mail: infocciap@panacamara.com, website: www.panacamara.com;

Ministry of Commerce and Industry, tel: (507) 227-4222, (507) 227-1222, fax: (507) 227-5604, mailing address: Apartado 9658, Zona 4, Rep. of Panama, physical address: Edificio de La Lotería Nacional de Beneficencia, Calles 31 and 32, Avenidas Cuba y Perú, pisos del 14 al 21, e-mail: uti@mici.gob.pa, website: www.mici.gob.pa; and,

American Chamber of Commerce and Industry of Panama (AMCHAM), tel: (507) 269-3881, fax: (507) 223-3508, mailing address: Apartado 168, Balboa (Ancon), Panama, Rep. of Panama, physical address: Calles Uruguay and 47, e-mail: amcham@sinfo.net, website: www.panamcham.com.

Panama: Golden Gateway to offshore opportunities

**Foreign companies and individuals choose Panama as a base of operations.
The climate is right —in more ways than one**

Panama's economy is largely based on services in the international field. These activities were originally spawned by the Canal which began construction at the start of Panama's existence as a Republic. The vast undertaking needed bankers, brokers, lawyers and agents of all ilks.

Successive governments since the fledgling country raised its flag in 1903, have passed legislation encouraging service business; a growing body of professionals has taken full advantage of the opportunities offered, and today, Panama is a leader in offshore business which includes banking, trusts, ship-registration, corporations, foundations, captive insurance and intellectual property (trademarks, royalties and patents). The main basis of offshore business is the Panamanian corporation, details of which appear in another section of this book, but trusts and foundations are also key elements.

A trust, which can be defined as a fiduciary relationship between a settlor (the person creating the trust) and the trustee, entered into for the benefit of persons or entities, is primarily used for personal protection against litigation or for wealth management for families over generations, or for charitable purposes.

There is also a tax element. It is possible to legitimately reduce or defer taxes. This was a major issue 20 years ago but today this motive has become less common due to more transparency rules, tighter regulation and, generally, lower levels of taxation. The trust route affords the settlor a greater degree of privacy in his business affairs.

Trusts are used mainly by foreigners who have chosen Panama as their offshore base. Although the trust law was first introduced in the 1940s, new concepts were introduced in law No. 1 of 5th January 1984, making it especially attractive for foreigners. Trust services can be offered only by licensed companies of which there are about 58, including some banks.

Panama is one of many offshore centers, a number situated in the Caribbean region, but it has great advantages over its competitors. Having had a continuous business connection with Panama for the last 20 years I have watched the jurisdiction progress through some very difficult times. The one recent, striking development for many people involved in financial services in Panama has been the profound changes which have taken place in many of the island offshore financial services centers where the perceived certainty of their confidentiality has been found to be as permanent as the shifting sands on their shores.

It is indeed an irony that the very thing that many island offshore centers boasted about, being under the protective and prestigious sovereign wing of an OECD (Organisation for Economic Co-operation and Development) country, has proven to be their downfall and highlighted the fundamental difference between being dependent and independent. Panama, in contrast, has its financial services industry built on firm ground, with its sovereignty guaranteeing freedom from the decrees of foreign powers. It is a contrast between coercion and co-operation.

But that said, 2002 has seen significant changes in the attitude toward offshore centers and the manner in which business is conducted in them. The terrorism which struck North America so vividly in September, 2001, has changed the complexion of international financial services. Business privacy has come under the spotlight and the offshore centers themselves have experienced an assault on their bona fides like never before.

Since the day the twin towers of the World Trade Centre in New York crashed to the ground and part of the Pentagon was destroyed, terrorism has dominated political agendas of many leading nations. The United States has been traumatised; the savagery and scale of the mainland terrorist horror, concentrated in one day, had no precedent. The American mainland, protected by two great oceans and unthreatening neighbours, has enjoyed an isolationism from foreign assaults since the British burnt down the White House in 1812. The United States had already spent almost $10 billion and employed 1,000 people in its counter-terrorism campaign before that September, but now the anti-terrorist funding is expected to exceed the entire GDP of Panama and Slovenia combined.

The OECD'S money laundering black list, issued by its satellite body, the Financial Action Task Force, was momentarily eclipsed by a black list of terrorists which was issued by the United States government. The FATF itself, however, far from being overshadowed, has now gained in stature as its role becomes more prominent in the search for terrorist funds, supplementing a team which the United States has assembled and which includes the Central Intelligence Agency, the Federal Bureau of Investigation and the National Security Agency. The United States Treasury Department also plays a pivotal role, employing its Office of Foreign Asset Control, the Customs service and the Financial Crimes Enforcement Network in the hunt for terrorist finances. Terrorism has triggered a chain of events which will affect the way professionals in offshore centres such as Panama conduct business with clients in the future.

Although the Washington and New York attacks were catastrophic, they have served to test the credentials of all offshore centers and have revealed those whose regulatory regimes and response have been found to be wanting. The International Monetary Fund, in a 2001 report, had this to say about one offshore centre:

"The authorities and the banking industry are very aware of the prudential risks associated with money laundering and have in place adequate safeguards to deter improper use of the banking system for illegal purposes. While no system is infallible, the mission team concludes that the legal, regulatory and supervisory systems in place in the banking sector compare favourably with internationally accepted prudential supervision practices... The legal and regulatory requirements are strict and many requirements exceed those in place in industrial countries."

Which jurisdiction is being referred to? Bermuda? The Channel Islands? The remarks, actually, refer to Panama and to its compliance with established international standards for an offshore banking system. The positive tenor throughout the report underlines the fact that the jurisdiction is conscious of the need to have sound financial regulatory and supervisory systems in place. Equally, the jurisdiction has won high praise for its money laundering controls which are also mentioned in the same IMF report:

"The level of supervision dedicated to anti-money laundering is exceptional and under different circumstances disproportionate relative to the risk posed by money laundering".

Against this favourable background Panama has continued to attract offshore business, especially trusts, foundations and offshore companies (known also as IBCs) which form the bedrock (excluding services such as shipping) of its offshore financial services industry.

The country's money laundering legislation goes beyond the narrow confines of drug smuggling and drug trafficking and includes robbery, extortion, trafficking in illegal weapons and terrorism. Panama understands that international crimes and confidentiality are incompatible despite the perennial perception that Panama, along with other offshore centers in the region, consider privacy at all costs paramount in preserving their attractiveness to businessmen and investors alike.

Despite the automatic assumption by many that offshore centers played a leading financial role in the September attacks, what has emerged so far is the appearance of a terrorist operation run on conventional business lines rather than one which had fleet-footed men with sunglasses and briefcases, stashed with cash, visiting the world's offshore centers, putting money on the counter and sand on the carpet. It is, of course, a scenario which sits uncomfortably with OECD bureaucrats who have jumped on the offshore center-bashing bandwagon. Even so, there has been no let-up in the assault by OECD governments on offshore centers, known already for their secretive ways, because perceptions are so well entrenched. In this new climate of concern, therefore, one can no more realistically expect, for example, that the British Virgin Islands' own agenda will supplant Whitehall's any more than that of the US Virgin Islands will supersede Washington's. This is where sovereignty becomes significant, especially if there is a concern that existing confidentiality laws could be either swept aside or compromised by fiat of a controlling foreign power for political or other motives.

Pressure by the OECD has been applied on sovereign states which are also offshore centers (such as the Bahamas) with varying degrees of success. It would, however, be wrong to assume that OECD tactics successfully used, say, in the case of a sovereign island offshore center in the Lesser Antilles would produce the same results in Panama – and it has got nothing to do with the fact that Panama's Canal Zone alone (10 miles wide and 50 miles long) could easily incorporate any regional island offshore center within its boundaries.

The difference is not size but the unique geographical and geopolitical considerations which exist and which can never apply to regional island offshore centers that can only offer, primarily, beaches and banking. The country's canal is a practical illustration of Panama's pivotal geographical position in relation to the flow of world commerce, providing a conduit between the Pacific and Atlantic oceans. Panama, when looking at the geopolitical perspective, is also strategically located, serving, as it were, as an observation post that is ideally positioned between Central and South America.

Panama has good reason to expect its offshore financial services industry to grow significantly in the next few years as growing numbers of people consider doing some business in Panama. The array of financial services which they will find here, all offered in a modern sophisticated environment, will probably be, like the country itself, a real revelation.

Colon Free Zone

A Latin American giant which keeps growing despite regional turmoil

Panama has been a country of commerce almost from the time the New World began to be colonized. Centuries before the Panama Canal was built, merchandise crossed this narrow isthmus between North And South America on mule trains. Gold and silver plundered from the Incas of Peru travelled this way to be loaded onto galleons bound for Spain. The same galleons brought luxuries from Europe, bartered at fairs at the Atlantic ports of Portobelo, Chagres and Nombre de Dios and carried back across by the same mule trains to the "Southern Sea" destined for colonies along the West Coast of South America.

Nowadays, a dozen or so leagues to the west, at the city of Colon, commerce continues at a faster pace, in volumes which those earlier traders would have been unable to conceive. The reason is the Colón Free Zone at the Atlantic mouth of the Panama Canal. Its growth in recent years is eclipsing the Canal itself in terms of the country's progress and reputation. The Free Zone was started 54 years ago on an 87 acre plot adjacent to the city of Colón with a couple of warehouses occupied by a handful of hopeful and ambitious Panamanian merchants. Today, the Zone occupies an area of more than 800 acres. Over 2000 companies operate or are represented there. Containers clog the roads; buyers and representatives of thousands of trademarks flock in and out to generate the staggering $11 billion which the Colón Free Zone turns over now in the course of a year.

The rationale of the Colón Free Zone is easy to grasp. It is a segregated, walled area where companies may import free from import duties or quotas and with a minimum of taxes. The obvious result, from the beginning was that merchants could import in bulk from the Far East, Europe and the U.S.A. and re-export in quantities to suit their Latin American clients. Taking advantage, also, of Panama's position on the major sea route of the Americas, they could deliver the merchandise rapidly and with a knowledge and understanding of customs and import requirements into neighbouring countries with which suppliers in non-Latin countries could not compete.

Expansion has been steady and the original walled area of 94 acres had been filled with warehouses and showrooms by 1978. Hemmed in by the city of Colón around half of its perimeter and with the waters of Manzanillo Bay lapping almost to the foundations of the buildings on the other side, there was nowhere for the Free Zone to go - except into the bay with landfills and across the bay where former Canal Zone land had reverted to Panama under treaties between Panama and the U.S.A.

Accordingly, 131 acres were set aside at Old France Field, so named for an old airstrip which served the Atlantic port before the present France Field runway was built in World War II. This became exclusively a warehouse area in contrast to the original Free Zone, with its mix of warehouses and showrooms, which is now known as the Commercial Area. It is now joined to France Field by a bridge.

The variety of merchandise and brand names available is awesome, hardly surprising when you consider that any day's inventory can be in the region of $1.5 billion. Companies vary greatly in size from mega-stores which carry hundreds of famous brands of luxury goods, down to small variety stores or single agency businesses. A number of large multinationals have also realized the advantages offered.

Not all of the business in the Free Zone involves the merchandise rolling in and out of the gates. If quantities are big enough and transportation suitable, a Free Zone company, although complying with the normal entry and exit paperwork as though the merchandise had passed through the zone, will find it more convenient to have goods shipped direct from source to customer.

Most Colón Free Zone companies have their main offices and showrooms in the Commercial Sector separated from the city of Colón by a high security wall. A visitor's pass can be easily obtained from the administration's reception office just inside the gate.

The area is bisected by streets and avenues —miles of warehouses and showrooms— some with fancy window displays which almost give a visitor the impression of being on a normal shopping street. The impression is erroneous, since the Colón Free Zone is not designed for retail sales, and merchandise cannot be carried out with the purchaser. Some companies will send goods to Tocumen International Airport in-bond to be collected by a visitor on departure.

But the commerce of the Free Zone is in grosses, case-lots and container loads. It is a city dedicated only to commerce, with sidewalks often thronging with people and streets jammed with trucks and trailers. But after 5 p.m. when the workers and the buyers and business people have gone to their homes and hotels, the security guards are the only inhabitants.

Reasons for the phenomenal success of the Cólon Free Zone are numerous. Not least is the use of the U.S. dollar as the currency of the country owing to the special relationship of Panama with the USA since the construction of the Panama Canal. Another reason is that the Zone has access to 5 huge ports all situated within a few miles radius.

The Free Zone is, however, a classic example of interaction between Government and private enterprise. Panama's laws have always been aimed at encouraging business, including the establishment of companies from abroad. The Colón Free Zone is a prime example. The Free Zone laws establish that businesses may operate with the absolute minimum of controls (incredibly, merchandise entering and leaving the Free Zone requires the filling of only one form).

Some tax and other benefits are as follows:
• 0% taxes on income derived from export activities.
• 0% tariffs and quotas on imports and exports.
• Highly competitive costs.
• Immigration benefits for executives and foreigners.

Getting Started

Any person or company can set up operations in the Colón Free Zone by applying to the Administration and supplying commercial and bank references, a Panamanian Government tax clearance (paz y salvo) and the articles of incorporation in the case of a company. No commercial licence is required and no minimum capital investment is stipulated. The only condition is that a minimum of five Panamanians be employed.

Setting up can be achieved in any one of four ways:

1. A premises can be rented from a private owner.

2. A 20-year lease can be obtained on a lot of land and a company can construct its own facilities subject to Administration approval of plans.

3. An existing company can be used as a representative. A number of companies are organised for this service and the advantages they offer provide a convincing argument for this type of operation. The representative company makes transport arrangements, receives goods, does the documentation, packs and re-packs if necessary, re-exports, bills and even collects. The instructing company retains title to the merchandise. Agreements of this sort need approval of the Administration and the condition will be that at least 60% of the goods be re-exported. The advantages of this system are obvious: no capital investment, no overheads, no headaches providing the relationship between owner and representative is a good one.

Devils are a Panamanian speciality.
Photo: Tomás Munita.

Traditional devil masks are donned at festivals and saint days in the interior especially at Corpus Cristi. These photos were shot at a "Festival of the Devils" at Portobelo
Photo by Yolande Vicente.

Congo dancing, an ancient tradition of the Caribbean coast is a frequent spectacle at the ruins of Portobelo
Photos: Yolande Vicente

Ancient artistry is exhibited in this golden huaca, a mythical bird crafted by a pre-Colombian indian. No less skilled but in a different style are these painted ivory nut (tagua) carvings made by the Embera and Wounaan indians of the Darien as domestic charms and for sale in the handicraft stores and to the occasional adventurer who may visit their village.
Photo above: Danny Lehman
Photo left: Bernheim Gallery

Several indigenous tribal groups live in traditional habitats in various parts of the Republic.
Kuna women of the San Blas islands help each other to tie their beaded leg ornaments.
Photo: Danny Lehman.

Above: The San Blas islands, 300 of them, lie in a lagoon protected by barrier reefs.

Left: In the Darien jungle, girls from the Embera and Wounaan tribes of Choco Indians are seen in their body paint and finery, ready for a party.

Below: Fine and artistic basket weaving, and carving in iron-hard cocobolo wood is part of their culture.
Photos: Danny Lehman

President Mireya Moscoso, with some of her ministers, strides out on a muddy road at Los Peladeros in the province of Herrera. To improve the lives of poor people, especially in rural areas, is one of her aims.
Photo: Adolfo Chamorro, State Office of Communication.

4. Merchandise can be handled by the public warehouse system. The businessman stores his merchandise in a public warehouse but in other respects functions like any other business established in the Free Zone. As in the case of employing a representative, the advantages are: no overheads such as salaries, rent, telephone.

Market Factors

The Colón Free Zone functions just like any other marketplace — its success is due in large measure to price and variety. Prices are bound to be competitive because of volume. The basic premise of the Free Zone is that goods arrive in large quantities from factory or supplier in the Orient, Europe, North or Latin America. Variety is constantly improved as the Free Zone grows and ever more companies introduce new lines.

Delivery time is the other vital factor which boosts the commercial movement statistics each year. Weeks and even months can be cut off delivery times for Latin American clients who order from the Colón Free Zone because firstly, the goods are already here on the continent and not subject to manufacturing quotas and freight schedules from half way round the world. Secondly, Free Zone companies, anxious to turn over their inventories as fast as possible, assisted by the almost total lack of red tape and supremely knowledgeable in the paperwork involved in all the countries of the marketplace, despatch the goods in record time.

Thirdly, the transport network from Panama to all parts of the Latin America and the Caribbean is unbeatable. This rapidity of service allows customers to operate on inventory margins which otherwise would be impossible and therefore saves them interest charges.

How the Free Zone Administration Functions

Responsibility for the efficient running and continued development of the Colón Free Zone is in the hands of the Free Zone Administration. The Zone is an autonomous institution of the Panamanian Government and functions under clearly defined laws and precedents. The Administration controls rents, public warehousing, promotion, development and construction. It keeps statistics and administers the flow of imports and exports.

The User's Association

The User's Association of the Colón Free Zone is an active and prestigious body with its own offices, conference and exhibition rooms, whose principal function is to look after the rights and interests of its members and increase the prosperity of the Free Zone. It publishes an annual directory and catalogue, "FOB Zona Libre de Colon". Its website, www.colonfreezone.com, which includes company, product and trademark information, features individual home pages for most of the companies operating in the zone. The Users Association also organizes commercial missions abroad with the aim of introducing its products to foreign companies.

Future of the Cólon Free Zone.

An ambitious project, which unites existing infrastructure and transport entities (maritime installations, airports, railway) into one permanent network to facilitate the movement of cargo from coast to coast across the Isthmus of Panama, will be developed in Colón within the next five years, which entails the expansion of the Colon Free Zone to a further 1200 hectares (approximately 3000 acres). The planning of the project involves coordination of the Civil Aviation Authority (DAC), the Maritime Authority of Panama (AMP), the Interoceanic Regional Authority (ARI), the Colón Free Zone Administration (CFZ) and the Customs Department. From the private sector, port operators of Manazanillo International Terminal, Colon Container Terminal, Panama Ports, Cocosolo Ports Terminal, the Panama Canal Railway Company and the Enrique A. Jiménez Airport to France Field are involved.

The project will integrate the railroad terminal, the three ports, France Field airport and a new road system. This will permit the development and establishment of new companies dedicated to commerce, light industry, service and high tech industries as well as multimodal transportation to complement each other in a secure and integrated area. This will operate within one customs regime, allowing the efficient and economic transfer of goods from one modal to another without paying any fees. As well as reducing the cost of freight and bureaucratic requirements the center will reduce the transport time for cargo making export operations more economic and efficient.

The purpose is to convert the Colón Free Zone into the "Multimodal Logistics Center of the Americas", attracting new investors and buyers and helping to increase international commerce.

Telecommunications Hub of Latin America

Aggressive privatization and Panama's Latin American "Connectivity" are changing the country into a technological pioneer

A few years ago, UNESCO predicted that Panama was destined to become the communications hub of Latin America by the end of the year 2002. Time is proving this to be true as a combination of geographical location, aggressive privatization and a burgeoning, "wired" local market have all contributed to Panama's establishment as a leading location for Latam connectivity and telecommunications services. Within the space of a decade, Panama has changed from a technological backwater to a Latin American technological pioneer.

Cable and Bandwidth

"All of the fiber-optic backbones of the United States, Canada, and Latin America cross Panama. If there's a problem inside the United States, the most obvious place to go outside is Panama." This quote from Nelson Bendeck, a representative of Sun Microsystems company (that is moving into server equipment in Panama) says a lot about Panama's lure for multinational tech companies. Bendeck also aptly summed up what the country has become when he stated, "Why Panama? Because it's one of the most wired places in the world."

Submarine cable is driving bandwidth (the capacity to carry a high volume of internet or telephone traffic at speed) growth at a rapid pace. There are currently five major backbones that touch land in Panama. The $217 million MAYA-1 and ARCOS networks are owned by a 14-member group made up of heavyweights such as AT&T, Cable & Wireless (C & W), France Telecome and TelMex, and connect North and South America and the Caribbean Basin. (In addition, MAYA-1 acts as a restoration conduit for the Pan-American Cable.) The Global Crossing cable links Asia, the Caribbean, Europe and the U.S. The OXYGEN network ties the U.S. with the Caribbean, Brazil, Chile, Colombia, Ecuador, Peru and Europe. Together, these major fiber-optic backbones have ushered out Panama's past reliance on satellite feed while ushering in more modern, faster connectivity options.

Internet and E-commerce

Limited access to the Internet actually came to Panama in the period from 1995-1997 and was provided by trend setters such as Houston's (U.S.) Charter Communications International, Inc. and local entities such as

Sinfonet and Orbinet, which brought the nation out of the email dark ages with basic dial-up access. Today, the Internet has found a welcome home in Panama. Business and home ADSL (enabling you to have internet access and speak on the phone simultaneously) and cable modem connections are currently dominated by C & W and homegrown Cable Onda, though this may change in the coming year (see, "Telephone and Cellular" later in this chapter). Internet access is available in an ever-growing number of Panamanian locations and Internet cafes offer cheap rates and are easy to find. On the information front, the number of Panama governmental agency, national newspaper, tourism and other free sites has grown tremendously in the past four years.

Demand from multinational companies and Panamanian entrepreneurs is causing an increase in online, E-commerce options. Basics such as web hosting and design services and local B2B (business to business) and B2C (business to consumer) portals are already common and have become established entities. More advanced services, such as online banking and purchasing are still in their nascent state and lag far behind their U.S. counterparts, however.

Telephone and Cellular

In 1997, Panama's state-owned telephone monopoly, INTEL, was dissolved. A 49% stake of the company was sold to the British Company, Cable & Wireless for the sum of US$652 million, the highest concession price ever paid for a Latin telephone network at that time. Since the concession was granted, C & W has enjoyed a non-competition grace period and has made significant investment in national infrastructure (especially in outlying areas). Due to C & W's efforts, Panama's phone systems have been completely redesigned and function very reliably, a full-range of basic telephone services are available, rates have dropped and pay phones can easily be found. Starting from a base of 380,000 phone lines, the number expanded to 550,000 by mid-2000 and is now calculated to be 600,000 lines

Telephone service is expected to jump to a new level after January 2, 2003. On this date, C & W will lose their monopoly status and the telephone concession will again be up for bid. As of this writing, 24 companies had announced their intentions to compete with C & W as Panama's telephone provider. Most were interested in offering international calls. Very few intended to offer basic local telephone services.

In 1996, the bidding to construct and operate a cellular phone service network (Band "A") in Panama was won by BellSouth Company (BSC) de Panamá, a partnership formed by BellSouth of the United States, Grupo Boltrán of Guatemala, Multiholding and a group of Panamanian investors including Bancomer. BSC was granted a 20-year license to establish the first cellular web in the country. In its 1997 negotiations, C & W obtained the concession to operate Band "B". During their respective tenures, both companies have invested millions in bringing cellular phone service to Panamanians.

Panama had awaited cellular phones for a long time and cells (both subscription and pre-paid) have quickly become a staple in the Panamanian lifestyle.

According to mobile-phone companies operating in Panama, the spread of mobile phones has also been swift. From 8.6 mobile phones per 100 inhabitants in mid 2000 to 16.5 per 100 in mid 2002, the equivalent to some 500,000 mobile phones. Panama has the highest mobile-telephone penetration rate in Central America, and one of the highest in Latin America. The growth in mobile phones, is attributed to the sale of phones for use with cards.

C&W Movil offers fax and data services that give customers limited access to the Internet over their mobile phones. Although C&W Movil announced the introduction of wireless access protocol (WAP) technology in Panama in February 2000, the company has held off introducing the service until market sentiment becomes more favourable. High-speed broadband access to the Internet is available via the telephone grid (ADSL) from C&W and also by modem cable via local firm, Cable Onda.

BellSouth mobile phone company offers roaming in several countries of Central and South America as well as in the United States. Due to BellSouth's aggressive push into the Latam markets and C & W's attempt to secure its position as a telecommunications force in Panama, the selection and sophistication of cellular-type communications, such as WAN (Wide Access Network) phones are expected to expand quickly in the next few years.

Call Service Centers

Since 2000, "call centers" have made their appearance in Panama mainly due to Law No. 54 of 25th October,

2001, which excludes all call center telephone traffic from taxes applied to other international calls from Panama and provides a generous list of other tax exemptions. In the last two years, companies such as Dell Computers and MasterCard and call center operators such as Cable & Wireless and Sitel have expressed interest in, or have opened their Panamanian operations.

Telecommunications Development and Research

The country's growing prominence in the telecommunications field has not been lost on the nation's technologically-minded progressionists. Panama has proven that it is not only interested in adopting and implementing modern telecommunications technology, but in enhancing it as well. In January of 2000, the autonomous International Technopark of Panama (Tecnoparque Internacional de Panamá, TIP), as a component of the City of Knowledge center (see, the chapter "City of Knowledge"), officially opened its collective doors. The Park represents Panama's first foray into international high-tech research and development.

The TIP edict is to offer prime conditions through which to encourage tech-based industries, scientific research entities and academia to expand both individual and interdependent high-tech (communication) capabilities. TIP members are bound to conduct only tech businesses and projects, to use non-contaminating facilities and to coordinate activities with the National Secretariat of Science and Technology (SENACYT), among other prestigious entities. In order to ensure its mandate, TIP has become a full member in the International Association of Science Parks and is seeking further collaboration with similar organizations worldwide. The idea has caught on and numerous renowned enterprises have joined the TIP team, including the Smithsonian Tropical Research Institute (STRI).

Several local and international companies offer business Internet tecnology solutions, including credit-card-number encryption.

@Altec1 initiated operations in August 2001 as the dirst data centre in Latin America, offering massive web-hosting and co-location. This strategy is based on the network of five fibre-optic submarine cables off Panama, which were interconnected in mid-2001. In the two weeks following the September 11th attacks in the United States @Altec1 received more than 90 calls from US businesses interested in switching their servers or back-ups to Panama. Many of the firms calling had been located in areas that were affected by the terrorist attacks but few followed through. Nevertheless Altec1 doubled its customer base in 2001. Another data centre is in construction in the former Fort Clayton military base's City of Knowledge.

Panama's Canal

The Panama Canal Authority faces a vast challenge—to construct new locks for the superships and keep the waterway competitive

Although Panama's centenary, celebrating 100 years as an independent republic, is in 2003, you could say that the country really came of age three years earlier–when the Panama Canal was handed over to the Panamanians. This was the event which defined the nation's century.

A profound transformation had been underway during the years that preceded the formal transfer and Panama's Canal began its operations as a different organization, renovated, entirely Panamanian and run by an autonomous entity, the Panama Canal Authority (ACP), successor to the former Panama Canal Commission created in 1979 as a binational U.S. -Panama hybrid organization enabled by a treaty between the U.S. and Panama. Radical changes, although imperceptible to Canal users, have taken place at every level of the Panama Canal. The most important was the addition of a new title in Panama's Constitution (May 25, 1995) about the Panama Canal that guarantees independence of its administration, creates the Panama Canal Authority and its board of directors, and the organic law passed in 1997 (Law 19 of June 11, 1997) that organizes the ACP administration. The eleven-member board of directors is appointed by the President for fixed terms of nine years while the Administrator is chosen by the board and named for seven years. The ACP board chairman is also designated by the President, is of cabinet-level rank and holds the title of Minister of Canal Affairs. The Canal should be kept out of domestic politics and free from partisan politics, observing a merit system for employment and bidding process for all business contracts. In addition to the ACP board, an Advisory Board was established and comprises a group of experts in the maritime and business world who will offer their advice and support to the board to ensure the successful operation of the Canal.

The Canal as a corporation

From its inauguration in 1914 under the Panama Canal Company and later under the Panama Canal Commission, the waterway had been managed as a U.S. federal agency under the Department of Defense and, by law, had a break-even budget. For nearly 70 years, the Panama Canal Company was generous and subsidized most of the costs of the former Canal Zone which was in effect a "company town" in addition to the canal's.

The new Panama Canal Authority has a clear mandate to run the waterway as a modern, profitable business.

The waterway Panama received came with a clear financial bill of health and "without liabilities" as written in the treaty, a unique situation in the modern business world. The Panama Canal Authority benefits from permanent cash flow and good financial records. ACP Administrator, Alberto Aleman Zubieta, says it is a solid business operation which needs to eliminate bureaucratic processes established over 85 years, use its resources more efficiently and give greater attention to its customers to make it the best example of business in the region.

Watershed protection key issue for future

Panama defined a protected canal watershed by law to assure the shipping route has plenty of water since prudent water management is needed to avoid draft restrictions such as those implemented during the dramatic El Nino droughts; additional water resources will be needed for any further expansion that would include the building additional locks. However, the plan is already controversial. The issue has attracted the attention of shippers, watershed residents and Canal officials but "water management is definitely the Canal's first goal", says Administrator Alberto Aleman. Any plan that is adopted will not only increase water reserves but provide better deterrent against deforestation and the resulting erosion.

Each vessel transiting the Canal uses 52 million gallons of fresh water to pass through the three locks that allow passage through the Canal. With an average of 36 ships transiting every day, 1.872 billion gallons of water flow out to sea each day. While the water supply is constantly replenished through abundant Panamanian rainfall, in the dry season depletion of water reserves can cause the level of Gatun Lake to fall to levels that affect Canal operations. Any plans to increase traffic or to build a third lane through the Canal to accommodate post-Panamax (Panamax is the designation for vessels of maximum width to pass through the lock chambers) vessels will put an even greater strain on the Canal's water resources and for more than two years the Canal administration has been looking for alternate fresh water sources.

A new law passed in August 1999 by Panama's National Assembly contemplates doubling the water resources for canal operations and future expansion by legally defining the Canal watershed area. The Canal watershed reserve which comprises the artificial Madden and Gatun lakes also provides more than 95% of the drinking water for the cities of Colón, Panama and the district of Arraijan. In addition a water plant under construction by UK-based BiWater will also use water from the lakes to service the capital's expanding suburbs.

The law that defined the watershed established a total area of 1,365,320 acres or 7% of the national territory within that protected space. The watershed will have the potential to supply about six times the active storage and double the land resources available for the canal today. The area comprises land around four rivers that could be dammed or diverted. Studies for the watershed development plan will have to resolve crucial environmental and social problems as they move forward.

The plan will be an opportunity to make the area a model of sustainable development with better standard of living for the families that live there. Environmental groups and non-governmental organizations will likely be asked to participate in drawing up the plan but experts say the plan will be positive for nature conservation, slowing deforestation, a major problem for canal operations during the 1980s when it raised silt levels in Gatun and Madden lakes.

The Canal watershed includes some tracts of land still covered with dense forest, in part because it was within the US-controlled Canal Zone. Other areas have not enjoyed such strict protection despite government controls, excellent on paper but virtually ineffectual in the field.

Some History

The idea of a canal that could shorten the journey between the Atlantic and Pacific oceans goes back to 1524 when King Carlos I of Spain ordered the first topographic studies for the construction of a waterway between the two oceans.

However, it was not until the 19th century when the great powers of the day, France, England and the United States, began to seriously consider the matter. Expeditions were mounted in the province of Darién and in the Atrato region of Colombia which seemed to offer the best possibilities. In 1826, then-U.S. Secretary of State, Henry Clay, suggested to Congress the construction of a path "for navigation purposes" somewhere across the Isthmus.

In 1835, the U.S. Senate urged the president to initiate conversations with the governments of Central

America and Nueva Granada (the northern Andean region) about a treaty that would protect companies interested in building a waterway to eliminate the Cape Horn route.

The construction of a transisthmian railroad in Panama in 1855 demonstrated the necessity to proceed with this monumental feat. In 1878, the French obtained a concession from the Colombian government and created the Compagnie Universelle du Canal Interoceanique, under the direction of Ferdinand de Lesseps, builder of the Suez Canal. De Lesseps wanted a sea-level channel, but the rock formations of the Continental Divide and the tropical diseases, combined with financial problems, transformed the great adventure into a nightmare. Another adverse factor was the scope of the excavations through the continental mountain range. The excavations stopped, but De Lesseps' perseverance got work started again in 1894, only to be abandoned later after an enormous financial scandal in Paris that left the only option in the hands of the North Americans.

In 1903, since the Colombian government had not reached a satisfactory agreement with the U.S. on the Herrán-Hay Canal Treaties, Washington's government backed the aspirations of Panamanian nationalists, and the then Colombian province of Panama declared its independence on November 3 of that year. Several days later, the leaders of the new republic signed a treaty with the United States for the construction of a waterway through the Isthmus. In 1904, the U.S. purchased all the rights and properties of Compagnie Nouvelle du Canal de Panama (the French company which had replaced Compagnie Universelle du Canal Interoceanique) for $40 million and began a task that would last 10 years and cost $387 million. The construction also claimed the lives of some 20,000 workers who perished from yellow fever and malaria.

More than 30,000 workers from the Caribbean islands of Jamaica, Martinique, Barbados and other parts of the world participated in the construction. Many of them remained on the Isthmus and settled around the ports of Cristóbal and Balboa —the maritime facilities at both entrances of the Canal— and continued to work for the Canal Company, the railroad, and within the Canal Zone, under U.S. management.

The "eighth wonder of the world", as many call the Canal, was inaugurated on August 15, 1914, and the steamer, "Ancon" was the first ship to make a complete ocean-to-ocean transit.

Since then, and until 1977, relations between the two countries were often stormy. The 1903 Treaty granted the United States government a strip of land at both sides of the Canal over which the U.S. exercised sovereignty and jurisdiction "in perpetuity". What was known as the Panama Canal Zone was a colonial enclave within Panamanian territory, and became the main source of conflict between the two nations.

The 1903 Hay-Buncau Varilla Treaty underwent a number of modifications, none of which brought major consequences. Due to violent riots on January 9, 1964, Panama broke relations with the U.S. The relationship resumed when both governments agreed to review the treaty. In October, 1968, a military coup brought the National Guard to power in Panama led by General Omar Torrijos, who directed a nationalist movement resulting in two new treaties, signed by both countries on September 7, 1977. The treaties were ratified in Panama through a referendum and by the vote of the United States Senate. The new agreements went into effect on October 1, 1979.

The Torrijos-Carter Treaties.

The signing of the Torrijos-Carter Treaties (one known as the Panama Canal Treaty and the other as the Permanent Neutrality and Operation of the Panama Canal Treaty) began a new relationship between the two countries and established the gradual transfer of the Canal to the Republic of Panama. The perpetuity clause was eliminated as well as the Canal Zone concept. Jurisdiction of the strip of land was handed over to Panama. The U.S. government agreed to return the Canal and its administration to Panama by midday, December 31, 1999. Until then, the Canal would remain under U.S. control with a new body, the Panama Canal Comission responsible for implementing the treaty.

The first Panamanian administrator nominated by the Panamanian government and appointed by the President of the United States in accordance to the 1977 Canal Treaty, was an engineer, Gilberto Guardia Fábrega, who was inaugurated in September of 1990.

Guardia, who presented his resignation in 1996, was preceded by acting Administrator Fernando Manfredo, who took over the post on January 1st, 1990 after serving as Deputy Administrator between October, 1979 and December, 1989. After Guardia's resignation, President Ernesto Pérez Balladares designated a new Administrator, Alberto Alemán Zubieta, who was sworn in on August 18, 1996.

Alemán Zubieta was designated Administrator of the newly-created Panama Canal Authority in 1998 by the entity's Board of Directors. This enabled him to continue in his position after all Canal assets were transferred to Panama on December 31, 1999.

The following were the members of the first Board of Directors of the Panama Canal Authority: Ricardo Martinelli, president (also Panama's Minister of Canal Affairs); Emanuel González Revilla, Fernando Cardoze Fábrega, Eloy Alfaro, Moisés Mizrachi, Samuel Lewis Navarro, Adolfo Ahumada, Roberto Roy, Abel Rodríguez, Luis Anderson and Raúl Montenegro, Jr.

By the time the Canal was transferred, Panama was fully prepared to assume its great responsibility. By the end of December, 1999, nearly all personnel responsible for operating the waterway was Panamanian.

The members of the Board of the Panama Canal Authority are appointed by various authorities for different terms, stated as follows. One member is designated by the President of the Republic, having also the rank of a Minister for Canal Affairs, while another is designated by the Legislative Assembly. The rest are nominated by the President and ratified by the Legislative Assembly. To avoid all designations by a single president, three board members are appointed to three-year terms in the initial assignment, whereas another three serve six-year periods, and the remaining three, nine-year terms. Once their respective initial terms have expired chosen members will serve a nine-year term.

The Board of Directors is also responsible for appointing ACP's Administrator and Deputy Administrator. A number of the Board's duties are similar to those of the former Panama Canal Commission's directives in regard to the establishment of tolls; the establishment of a tonnage system for ships transiting the Canal; the approval of the budget submitted to the vote of the Cabinet and the Legislative Assembly, and the approval of the regulations necessary for the operation and modernization of the Canal.

In addition to this, the organic law of the ACP stipulates that the annual payment of the institution to the national treasury will be no less than the amount Panama received under the Canal's U.S. administration until December 31, 1999. These payments were approximately US$120 million. Another important regulation established by the Constitution and the organic law of the ACP states that Canal employees will be governed by a special employment standard and a merit system similar to that of the former U.S. administration, which guarantees the same conditions and labor benefits enjoyed until 1999.

The Issue of the Third Set of Locks

The Canal's managers and planners face an enormous challenge....the need to expand the waterway to accommodate the larger ships –post Panamax in canal terminology —which are now being built. The prospect is to build a third chamber, wider, longer and deeper alongside the two-chamber existing locks.

"It is not just engineering but a business project" says deputy administrator and project manager Ricaurte Vasquez. Canal authorities will have to look at timing, cost, demand and supply and whether there is enough volume to support the likely US$3BN-5BN cost expansion.

This third set of locks would require additional water supplies. The concept designs will be for locks of 60 meters width by 425 meters length and by 18.3 meters of clearance, compared with the existing 33.5 x 300 x 12.5 meters locks that allow only the passage of container ships up to 4.5000 Teu.

Each vessel transiting the Canal requires approximately 197 million liters of fresh water ultimately flushed into the sea but a post-Panamax ship would need between 2.3 and 7.7 times that quantity. But the engineers are working on water savings systems which could limit the need for extra water to only 1 to 1.5 times.

The Canal Board must assess the results of some 200 investigations and are being assisted by the consortium, Parsons Brinkerhoff International of New York, and Chicago-based Montgomery Watson-Harza. The French-Belgium consortium of Tractebel Development Engineering, Coyne-et-Bellier, Technum N. V. and Companie Nationale du Rhone are developing the conceptual design for one-and three-lift locks on the Pacific side while the U.S.Army Corps of Engineers will do the same on the two-three-lift locks on the Atlantic side.

Four marketing studies-awarded to Louis Berger with the National Ports and Waterways Institute; Nathan & Associates with Richardson Lawrie Associates; and to Fearnley; will address future performance of the liner industry and of some significant segments of the cargo transiting the waterway such as dry bulk which includes grains,

Digging the Gaillard Cut, otherwise known as Corte Culebra (snake cut), through the Continental divide was a monumental task, hampered by constant landslides. When the cut was widened recently, this section of notorious Gold Hill was reinforced with a vast concrete facia.
Photo: Panama Canal Authority.

Pedro Miguel locks on the Pacific side.
Photo: Danny Lehman

Panama has grown into an immensly important cargo hub. In addition to the Canal, the Panama Canal Railway makes a land bridge speeding double stacked containers from the Port of Balboa on the Pacific to the Colon Port complex on the caribbean side, and vice versa.
Photo: Robert Fenton Houser

The railway also affords tourists a memorable trip as the train passes through jungle scenery and alongside the Canal.
Photo right: Danny Lehman
Photo left: Tomas Munita

The gigantic scale of the locks can be appreciated in this photo taken when a chamber was emptied to carry out maintenance.

The photo on the right shows the special locomotives which pull ships through the locks.
Photos: Panama Canal Authority

Above: Birds eye view of part of the Colon Port Complex. Colon Container Terminal is shown in the foreground, with Manzanillo International Terminal behind and Colon Free Zone and France Field warehouse area in the background. *Photo: Tomás Munita.*

Below: The busy docks of Manzanillo International Terminal. *Photo: Jorge Quinzada Loo.*

The Canal and the Bridge of The Americas in the foreground with Panama City spread out behind. The old city, Casco Viejo, can be seen on the right, the modern city spreads around the bay. In the extreme foreground, on the right, can be seen the pilings of what was once the pier of the Thatcher Ferry, at one time the only means for vehicles or pedestrians to cross the Canal for access to the interior.
Photo: Jorge Quinzada Loo.

The impressive foyer of the Melia Panama Canal Hotel in Colon, former school of the Americas, the U.S. Military academy. Inset shows an acrial views of the hotel on its promontory on beautiful Gatun Lake.
Photo: Focus

mineral and coal; liquid bulk for crude oil and chemicals; and the bunkering business. Another study will concentrate on the international economic impact of the construction of a third set of locks and economic value of the canal for international trade.

As an example of Panama's responsible and efficient administration of the Canal, the Panamanian government renounced its right to receive payment from the surplus registered at the end of the first fiscal year. This sum was re-invested in the widening works at Culebra Cut. Culebra Cut is also known as Gaillard Cut in honor of Colonel David DuBose Gaillard, the official in charge of the excavation of the passage during the construction of the Panama Canal. This section was excavated through the rocky mountains of the Continental Divide —a task that claimed many lives. It is the narrowest point of the waterway. The Cut was originally 300 feet wide, but it was later widened to 500 feet in 1969. Culebra Cut now has a minimum width of 630 feet along straight ways, and up to 730 feet around curves. The total investment amounted to approximately US$300 million.

As part of the modernization program, the Authority is gradually expanding its tug boat fleet, and the number of locomotives at the locks.

The equipment currently being acquired to improve transit operations is especially designed to manage the growing number of large ships that transit the Canal daily.

While the Canal undergoes a modernization and improvement process that will increase its transit capacity by 20% (enough to satisfy the waterway's demands until 2012), the Canal Capacity Studies Department is constantly examining the options to increase its capacity even more. One of the options being studied was a recommendation made in 1993 by the Tripartite Alternatives Commission for the Panama Canal (formed by Panama, the United States and Japan), to build a third set of locks for ships up to 150,000 tons. The department is also studying additional sources of water, water saving alternatives and available technologies for the transit of small ships without the need for water.

A study prepared by the Institute of Ports and Waterways of the United States revealed that, providing the third set of locks becomes a reality, the Panama Canal would become a world-class service center by the year 2020. If the Panamanian government makes the decision to build a new set of locks, a number of new dams will be necessary to meet the future water supply needs for the Canal and the metropolitan area of Panama City.

Operations of the Waterway

The tolls

On October 1st, 1994, the Panama Canal Commission modified its tonnage system in order to adopt the universal formula of the International Tonnage Convention, approved in 1969. The chosen formula, known as the Universal Tonnage System Panama Canal (UTS/PC), did not change the toll system applied to Canal customers. In order to calculate the toll rate of a ship in ballast or with cargo, a Panama Canal Ton equals a real income capacity of one hundred cubic feet. In July, 1997, the Canal agency started to charge fees on containers on deck —a decision approved by the Board of Directors. Until then, the Panama Canal did not charge cargo on deck.

A new toll structure was implemented October 1st, 2002 with an increase of 8%, followed by a second phase and increase of 4.5% in July 2003. At the same time, the ACP also decided to change its pricing structure from a one-size-fits-all, in place since the opening of the waterway in 1914, to seven separate categories for container, passenger, general cargo, dry bulk, liquid bulk, reefer and car carrier vessels. In addition, there is a discount structure with a higher rate for the first 10,000 PC/UMS tones, another rate for the following 10,000 PC/UMS with the lowest rate for the remaining tonnage. Based on the new tolls pricing structure, if larger ships use the Canal, then the average toll increase is actually lower.

The toll increase was approved by the board of directors and ratified by the Cabinet after the Panama Canal Authority consulted its customers during a public hearing in Panama, in July 2002. The tolls were last raised in 1996. That was a two-phase increase of 8.2% in 1997 and 7.5% in 1998.

The present toll rate is $2.80 per ton for laden and $2.22 for ballast, for the first 10,000 tons PC/UMS, and $2.78 per ton for laden and $2.21 for ballast for the following 10,000 tons PC/UMS. For the remaining tons, the rate is $2.75 for laden and $2.18 for ballast.

On July 1, 2003, the second phase will raise the rate to $2.96 per ton laden and $2.35 for ballast for the first

10,000 tons PC/UMS. It will decrease to $2.90 for laden and $2.30 for ballast for the following 10,000 tons PC/UMS and the remaining tons will be charged $2.85 laden and $2.26 in ballast.

The new tariff system aims at attracting more traffic for the canal. It is what "our customers want" said Panama Canal Authority administrator Alberto Aleman Zubieta. It reflects "a change of philosophy" and the first step towards charging clients for the value they receive from the Canal.

The Authority, which had frozen toll charges since 1998, also announced a new fee to use locomotives during ship transits in canal locks on top of special fees already charged to use tug boats and line handlers. The charge will help recoup the ACP's $300M investment in new locomotives and tracks. The ACP had also imposed a new security fee from June 1, 2002 on all vessels transiting the canal to cover significant investments to expand vessel monitoring and tracking and protect its operations. A flat fee of $400 is charged for vessels over 3,000 Panama Canal Universal Measurement System (PC/UMS) and $50 for vessels below this tonnage.

The users

Some four percent of world trade passes through the 80-km Panama Canal, moving cargo from the Far East to the coasts of the United Sates and to Europe and vice versa, saving some 4,800 kilometers compared with rounding Cape Horn. The waterway has also recently become an increasingly important passage for exports of goods and commodities from South America to the U.S., Europe and the Far East.

In its ongoing efforts to satisfy the demands of the maritime industry, the Panama Canal Authority's new corporate mission is market-driven and customer-oriented. That is the reason why several members of the international shipping community sit on the Panama Canal advisory board where their experience, recommendations and permanent advice are of extreme value to the Panama Canal Authority officials. The recent reorganisation of the department of corporate planning and marketing brought about the creation of a new strategic services division and the consolidation of a marketing division to get a better understanding of the market and customers' needs. The new marketing division now includes the office of customer relations, pricing and tolls, dry bulks, liquid bulks, liner services, other specialized services and new business development.

The main users of the Panama Canal in 1999 were: the United States, with a total of 135.3 million metric tons (59.7% of the total); Japan, with 40.6 million tons (18%); mainland China (18.5 million tons, 8.2%); Canada (16.5 million, 7.3); Chile (15.5 million, 6.8%); South Korea (14.9 million, 6.6%); Peru (11 million, 4.8%); Taiwan (11 million, 4.8%); Venezuela (10.4 million, 4.6%); Mexico (10.2 million, 4.5%); Ecuador (9.5 million, 4.2%); Panama (6.9 million, 3%); Colombia (6.7 million, 2.9%)' Belgium (5.2 million, 2.3%), and Australia (4.6 million, 2%).

Some of the Canal's main customers are shipping lines that have been transiting the canal for decades. Many companies may have changed names after mergers or global purchases but several of them can recall the first vessel of their companies transiting the waterway in its early years. In fiscal year 2002, the Canal's main customers are the following : Mitsui. O.S.K, Maersk, Nippon Yusen Kaisha (NYK Line), Kawasaki Kisen (K Line), CSAV (Compania Suramericana de Vapores), COSCO, Hyundai Merchant Marine, Evergreen, Pan Ocean Shipping, Hanjin Shipping Co.

An interesting historic note: A total of 1,058 ships transited the Canal during its first year of operations, and total fees amounted to 4.4 million dollars (1914-1915). During the Canal's last year under U.S. administration (1999), 13,003 large-draught vessels transited the waterway, paying a total of U.S.$565.5 millions.

Physical features

The Panama Canal measures 50 miles in length, extending from the deep waters of the Atlantic, to deep waters of the Pacific. It was excavated through one of the narrowest and least mountainous regions of the Isthmus of Panama, which links North and South America. The point where the Canal meets the Continental Divide originally measured 328 feet above sea level. The waterway runs northeast to southwest, The flying distance between both entrances is 43.2 miles.

The average ship takes between 8-10 hours to transit the Canal. During this short journey, passengers have the opportunity to observe one of the marvels of the world in operation. Its main features are: a terminal port on the Pacific (Balboa) and four maritime facilities on the Atlantic (Cristóbal, Manzanillo, Colón Container Terminal and Colón Port Terminal); three sets of locks (Gatún, Pedro Miguel and Miraflores); Gatún Lake and Gaillard Cut.

A ship transiting the Canal from the Atlantic to the Pacific enters the channel at the Bay of Limón, after passing through the breakwaters of Cristóbal. This sea-level stretch measures approximately 6.2 miles in length and passes through an area of mangrove. Vessels ascend or descend up to 86 feet through the three chambers of Gatún Locks. Each chamber measures 1000 feet long by 110 feet wide. The length of Gatún Locks, starting at the access walls, is almost 1.25 miles.

Gatún Lake and Dam

Ships navigate some 27 miles on Gatún Lake, which extends from Gatún Locks to the northern end of Gaillard Cut. During the construction era, it was the largest man-made lake on the planet, and its still among the world's greatest. It covers an area of 42,500 hectares (425 square kilometers) and was created by damming the waters of the Chagres River, located beside Gatún Locks. The two sections of the dam and the spillway have a total length of approximately 7,800 feet. The damn measures almost 2,624 feet wide at the base, and gradually becomes narrower toward the top, where its 100 feet wide. It is 105 feet above sea level and 19.7 feet over Gatún Lake's level.

In March 2002, the Presidents of Panama and Brazil jointly launched the seven year US$190M deepening of the Panama Canal navigational channel. The project, first major improvement since the transfer of the waterway to Panama, will be done "in house" including the design phase and will provide an additional one meter of water storage in Gatun Lake. It will require considerable drilling, blasting and excavation of material. With the Canal expansion feasibility studies to conclude in 2003, several dredging projects are being evaluated to determine their feasibility.

Gaillard Cut

Gaillard Cut has a special appeal to the passengers of the more than 300 cruise ships that transit the Panama Canal each year, due to its history, its extraordinary geology and the fact that it bisects the Continental Divide. It was known as Culebra (snake) Cut during the construction days of the Canal because of its sinuous extension, but it was later named Gaillard Cut to honor Colonel David DuBose Gaillard, the chief engineer in charge of its construction. The Canal's main excavation work took place there, as well as the devastating land slides that occurred during the construction, and shortly after the waterway's official opening.

A southbound vessel (toward the Pacific) enters the Cut where the Chagres River meets the Canal, in Gamboa. More than any other section of the waterway, Gaillard Cut gives passengers the sense of being in a gigantic ditch. Shortly before the ship enters the Pedro Miguel Locks, it passes beside Gold Hill, located on the eastern bank of the Canal. The hill towers 539 feet above sea level, but its height has been substantially reduced due to the widening works on the Canal. Contractor's Hill, on the opposite bank, originally measured a little over 410 feet, but was reduced to 370 feet in 1954 in order to stabilize it. The hill will be further leveled with the current widening works.

The original width of the Canal was 300 feet.. During the 1930's and 1940's, the straightway located immediately to the north of Gold Hill was widened to 500 feet to improve navigation for large ships in the straight. Between 1957 and 1971, the Cut was widened to 500 feet.

After the Cut, ships enter Pedro Miguel Locks, on the southern end of Culebra Cut, where they descend —26 feet in a single step— to the level of Miraflores Lake, which separates both sets of locks. The ship descends two more steps (54 feet) to reach sea level at Miraflores Locks, which measure approximately 5,248 feet (1.600 meters) in length. The Miraflores Locks are the tallest of the entire system due to the great tide variations of the Pacific.

Completed a year ahead of schedule in November 2001, the Culebra Cut Widening Program increased the Panama Canal's operating capacity by 20 percent, it also enables the simultaneous transit of two Panamax-type vessels and a more flexible traffic scheduling of vessels in the waterway. In a simple ceremony attended by former Canal administrators, Fernando Manfredo and Gilberto Guardia, Administrator Alberto Alemán Zubieta conceded to Gilberto Guardia the honor of operating the dredge Christensen for the final shovelful, at the precise historical site which had constituted the greatest challenge for the construction workers of the waterway.

On July 4th, the Panama Canal Authority (ACP) had wrapped up the drilling and blasting portion of the Cut's widening program. On August 16, the last shovelful of the land-based wet excavation project was accomplished by excavator LIEBHERR. A total of 23.2 million cubic meters of dry material and 12 million cubic meters of wet material were removed.

The completion of the project widens the narrowest passage of the Panama Canal from 152 meters to 192 meters along straight stretches and up to 222 meters on curves. Originally scheduled to be concluded in 2012, the Culebra Cut project was sped up by more than 10 years, in order to meet increasing traffic demands. Widening Culebra Cut was part of the Canal's $1-billion modernization and improvement program. Under $300 million were invested in this project, originally estimated to cost more than $600 million. During the Canal's construction, the Culebra Cut was the portion which required the greatest volume of excavation and it has been the site where the biggest landslides have occurred throughout its history. This part of the navigational channel is approximately 12.5 kilometers long, and here mostly rock and slate were excavated during the waterway's construction.

General Information
Legal Maximum Dimension (for regular transits)
Beam: 106 feet; Length: 965 feet (depending on the type of ship); Maximum draft: 39.5 feet

Main products (percentage of total tonnage)
In Fiscal year 2002, the main products (in millions of Long tons) transported through the Panama Canal were: oil (7,508 m), oil products (18,538m), grains (37,703m) coal (5,720m), containerized cargo (39,520m), vehicles (2,384m), refrigerated products (8,441m), nitrates, phosphates and potash (10,232m), lumber and products (5,411m), mineral and miscellaneous (9,139m),chemicals and chemical products (9,288m) and others (33,947m).

Distances from the Canal (nautical miles)
Guayaquil: 824; Hong Kong: 9,195; New Orleans: 1,444; New York: 2,018; Rotterdam: 4,842; San Francisco: 3,245; Yokohama: 7,682

Panama City's Old Quarter

New life has come to the Casco Viejo. Restoration continues apace and the narrow, streets with their balconied facades, where all the best people lived at the beginning of the century, are fashionable once more

The small district of Panama City known officially as San Felipe and referred to as Casco Antiguo or Casco Viejo, is rich in history and is now regarded as a national treasure. It was originally built around 1673, by the Spanish garrison, the Catholic Church and the settlers, after privateer Henry Morgan sacked the original site of Panama City (Panama Viejo). Next, the area housed the French officials during their attempt to construct the Panama Canal; what was left behind was a unique, culturally diverse neighborhood with buildings featuring a charming mix of Spanish colonial and French provincial architectures.

Since the 1920s however, Casco Viejo has gradually become to all intents and purposes, a semi-elegant slum. The inner city syndrome gripped the area. Maintenance and development stagnated and it was basically forgotten, except by those tourists wishing to see some of the historical landmarks that are interspersed throughout.

Over the years, attempts were made by various organizations and groups to stimulate the refurbishment of San Felipe. The hopes were to imitate the successful rejuvenations of Cartegena in Colombia, San Juan in Puerto Rico and Cuba's Old Havana. Despite these attempts, up until the mid 1990s Casco Viejo remained slumped in its continuing deterioration —the vicious circle of poor tenants not paying the rent and landlords losing interest in maintenance.

The advent of the Ernesto Pérez Balladares administration in 1994 proved to be the necessary catalyst for the long-hoped for metamorphosis. With the passage of Law 9 of August 27, 1997, special restoration incentives were delineated. Coincidentally, UNESCO chose Casco Viejo as one of its 46 historic areas in the same year. Local and international investors liked the offer, and slowly but surely new life has become evident among the narrow, balconied streets.

The incentives apply to San Felipe, along with parts of neighboring Santa Ana, Salsipuedes and Terraplén. Under the law, buildings are classified as historical structures and the approval granted for restoration depends on the architectural characteristics of each individual building. (Before the law, no such distinction existed).

The law seeks to accelerate the restoration process by providing incentives such as: preferential mortgage rates for investment into restoration projects (financing available); no tax on rental revenue generated in Casco Viejo; no property tax for the first 30 years; no Transfer of Title tax; and no importation tax.

An investor usually must conduct an investigation in order to locate the owner or heirs of the owner in order to purchase a property. To do this, the identification numbers of the property must be obtained from the Ministry of Housing. This information must then be taken to the Public Ministry to see if any ownership and contact information exists, which is not always the case, since many landowners have moved away or have died without leaving proper wills. Once the requisite channels have been identified, the sale negotiations can be initiated.

The next major hurdle is tenant relocation. In theory, the district government offices are supposed to lend assistance in the transition process. But, in order not to upset their constituents, officials tend to be rather lax in this department. So, the bottom line is that it is usually up to the new landlord to contact those families living on the premises and arrange for them to move.

This is not a simple process. A large percentage of previous landowners have relegated their Casco Antiguo assets to write-off status. As a result, they have ceased to administrate the buildings, including rent collection. This has created a large number of what are literally squatter families who have been in the same residence for a number of years. Although there is no actual legal basis for such persons to remain, Panama civil statute recognizes squatters' rights to a point, so eviction can be a long and convoluted process.

To avoid messy complications, those developing in Casco Antiguo employ a buyout strategy, which supplies a one-time payment for vacating the premises. In general, experienced developers supply only the money. This can represent a considerable expense. For example, say the agreed figure is $1,000 per family. This sounds like a bargain until one realizes that a single building can easily house up to 50 families or more. They do not arrange for future residences, except in extreme situations. To save time and frustration, it is a good idea to have a real estate agency specializing in the area or an experienced legal firm conduct the entire owner-location, tenant-eviction process.

Stringent guidelines for restoration have been set by the Directorate of Heritage of the National Institute of Culture (INAC), which, in turn, reports to the a new commission appointed by President Mireya Moscoso. Blueprints must be drawn by a licensed architectural entity and submitted to INAC, which judges the architectural merit and period compatibility. Once approved, the plans move on to the municipality, which studies infrastructure, such as electricity and plumbing. The approval process usually takes less than three months. Although when the actual time for drawing up plans is added, the final approval average reaches approximately six months. Final construction prices average around $500,000. When all the incidental costs are tallied, the total for a restoration rises to the $700,000 mark.

Parking can be a problem due to the narrow streets of the San Felipe district. If a building is located near one of the quaint plazas that pepper the area, parking can be obtained there for free. If this option is not viable, there is another strategy that presents an option to the parking conundrum. Edifices built before 1940 must be restored, but those constructed after can be demolished. Some developers have taken advantage of this stipulation by buying a newer edifice near the building targeted for restoration, demolishing it and building a structure that contains parking facilities. (As of yet, no actual parking lots have appeared.)

The move to obtain Casco Viejo investments is escalating. Restored buildings can be seen on nearly every block and specialized Casco Viejo real estate web sites can be found on the Net. (We recommend that you visit Mayhew Cook's www.cascoviejo.com). A majority of the buildings have been purchased (if not yet renovated), but opportunities still exist. Buyers can expect to pay from $150 to $400 + per square meter. Once the building is restored, the values escalate from $1,000 to $1,600 per square meter so money making opportunities still exist.

As one walks the streets of today's Casco Antiguo, it becomes obvious that things are changing. Beautifully restored mansions owned by Mayor Juan Carlos Navarro and entertainer Ruben Blades delight the eye. From inside gutted buildings, their facades intact, ring the sounds of hammer and saw. Cobbled red-brick surfaces on the streets are being repaired. The new Panama Canal museum and trendy sidewalk restaurants have opened their doors. This time the long-awaited revamp of Casco Viejo is indeed a reality, and there are no signs that the trend will lose its momentum. Every sign augers well for the preservation of one of Panama's most interesting and enduring sociohistorical legacies.

This article was written from material supplied by Compañía Inmobilaria.

A stroll through the Old Quarter

Remembering the lost elegance of the early years of the Republic

Memories of the society which inhabited Panama City's Old Quarter when the Republic was young seem still to haunt the narrow streets where, perhaps, spirits of the past are anxious to regain the lost elegance of the early days of the last century. There, in the district of San Felipe or Casco Viejo, lived the illustrious founders of the nation and their families, men such as: Don José Agustin Arango, Dr. Manuel Amador Guerrero, the first president of Panama, Don Constantino Arosemena, Don Nicanor de Obarrio, Don Ricardo Arias, Don Federico Boyd, Don Tomás Arias y Don Manuel Espinosa Batista. Nobody needed an "address" in the Casco Viejo of yesterday. Everybody knew where everybody lived.

Some of the old and well-loved houses of these families are still habitable but sadly affected by the passage of the years. The families formed a close–knit group which met frequently, giving each other a respectful and friendly greeting when they promenaded in the evenings in Independence Plaza, or Cathedral Plaza as it is better known nowadays, or at the famous concerts of the Republican Band which enlivened the square on Sundays and during the week at Santa Ana Plaza.

On these occasions, it was the custom for the gentlemen to perambulate round the square in one direction and the ladies, in their Sunday best, in the other, permitting discreet coquetry and courtship.

Many of these families, both wealthy and of limited resources, later moved to the new suburbs such as La Exposicion, Bella Vista and Calidonia which grew up in the third decade of the past century.

It should be explained that this short essay does not pretend to be a historical review, but an agreeable stroll through the small world of the Panamanian community which resided within the "walls" of the old city and also 'outside' to the Santa Ana Park.

Some of the houses have already been restored, such as that formely occupied by the Jimenez —De la Guardia family. Its owner, Don Enrique A. Jimenez was president in 1945. His residence was purchased and restored a few years ago by Juan Carlos Navarro, Panama City's current mayor. The three-storey mansion overlooks French Plaza and the imposing monument honoring the constructors of the French Canal. The monument is dominated by a tall obelisk surrounded by an arcade of carved marble plaques on which is carved, in the words of Dr. Octavio Méndez Pereira, the story of the valiant achievement of the French.

Flanking the monument is the stone façade of Las Bovedas – prisons in the colonial era and up to the beginning of the last century. The buildings surrounding French Plaza have all played a part in Panama's history. The French Embassy is there and another complex of buildings houses the National Institute of Culture.

First Street, where there are a number of well-restored houses, brings us to the ruins of the former Union Club which, since the beginning of the last century, has been the principal social center of the old families. The old club was also, for decades, the official headquarters of Carnival in the capital. The first Carnival Queen was Manuelita Vallarino who later became Mrs. Frank Morrice.

Bernhart and Fonteyn

On the seafront a little beyond the old Union Club is a beautifully-restored building, one floor of which is owned by Ruben Blades, the famous Panamanian screen and music personality. Close by is the former residence of Luisa Aguilar whose superb nativity scenes were so much admired by her neighbors... and the *refresqueria* Purruñotis whose ice cream was famous. On the way to the Plaza Bolivar the stroller will pause to admire the National Theatre where the immortal Sarah Bernhardt took to the stage in her early years; and where, in 1974 the equally-immortal Dame Margot Fonteyn, wife of Dr. Roberto Arias Guardia, gave unforgettable perfomances . The ceiling of the auditorium, and the foyer of this historical jewel is decorated with exquisite work by Roberto Lewis, the famous Panamanian painter.

Plaza Bolivar, with its monument to the great liberator Simon Bolivar, is flanked on one side by the church of St. Francis of Asisi, restored by the Jesuits, and on the other by the elegant façade of the old Hotel Colombia. Just past the church, on the street leading back to the sea, is the Salon Bolivariano, the old meeting hall of the Convent of St. Francis of Asisi where Simon Bolivar held the *Congreso Anfictonico* in 1826 to propose unity for the region.

In the same building , the monks gave schooling to children of the families of San Felipe.

Further down the street one arrives at the residence of the Arias —Espinosa family. This mansion was buit in 1929 and has been featured in various movies. Further round the bay is another school, a boarding school where the sisters Teresa, Maria y Josefa Ucros are still fondly remembered.

Palace of the Herons

Close by, is the presidential palace, known as El Palacio de las Garzas, the Palace of The Herons for the tame family of elegant birds which live around the fountain in the Moorish patio at the main entrance. The palace was built in 1673 and re-constructed in 1921 by liberal politican and three-times president Dr. Belisario Porras.

In the Yellow Room, hang oil paintings of all the Panamanians who have occupied the highest office of the Republic: Manuel Amador Guerrero, Manuel Espinosa Batista, José Agustin Arango, Tomás Arias, Federico Boyd, José de Obaldía, Carlos A. Mendoza, Pablo Arosemena, Rodolfo Chiari, Ramón Valdés, Ciro Luis Urriola, Pedro A. Díaz, Ernesto T. Lefevre, Tomás Gabriel Duque, Florencio Harmodio Arosemena, Harmodio Arias Madrid, Ricardo J. Alfaro, Domingo Díaz Arosemena, Juan Demóstenes Arosemena, Ezequiel Fernández Jaén, Augusto Samuel Boyd, Arnulfo Arias Madrid, José Pezet, Ernesto Jaén Guardia, Ricardo Adolfo De La Guardia, Enrique A. Jiménez, Daniel Chanis, Roberto F. Chiari, Alcibíades Arosemena, José A. Remón Cantera, José Ramón

Guizado, Ricardo Manuel Arias Espinosa, Ernesto de la Guardia, Sergio González Ruiz, José Dominador Bazán, Bernardino González Ruiz, Marco Aurelio Robles, Max Del Valle, José María Pinilla, Bolívar Urrutia, Demetrio Basilio Lakas, Arturo Sucre, Gerardo González, Aristides Royo, Ricardo De La Espriella, Jorge Illueca, Nicolás Ardito Barletta, Eric Arturo del Valle, Manuel Solís Palma, Francisco Rodríguez, Guillermo Endara Galimany, Guillermo Ford, Ernesto Pérez Balladares, Tomás Altamirano and the current president, Mireya Moscoso.

The offices of the president are at present in the building erected over the original residence constructed in 1716 by the couple, Don Joseph Arillaga y Doña María de Flores. Close to the palace is the famous Casa Gongora which was constructed in 1760.

The Cathedral, gleaming with mother of pearl

If your route through the Old Quarter follows the old tramway, you pass the neo-classic building occupied by the Ministry of Government and Justice and following Avenida Central you arrive at Cathedral Plaza. The twin towers of the Cathedral, gleaming with mother of pearl, face the Hotel Central which, for three decades of the last century was the best hotel in town. International personalities in the words of politics, commerce and art stayed there; among them the immortal stars of silent films John Barrymore and Dolores Costello who spent their honey moon there.

By tram, horse-drawn coaches and motor cars with canvas hoods, the visitors enjoyed sightseeing tours, perhaps to admire the spectacular Municipal Palace with its marble sculpture by Italian artist Enrico Braga or the building which now houses the Panama Canal Museum.

The tramline continued along Central Avenue to the Fifth of May Plaza and the "outskirts" which today are La Exposicion and Bella Vista. On the other side of Cathedral Plaza are commercial establishments such as IL Maduro Jr., Libreria Preciado, Felix B. Maduro, Eisenmann and Eleta (Bazar Americano) and in this area were the offices of Brandon Brothers whose operations in Panama were handled by Ernesto (Neco) De La Guardia, and Bazar Frances operated by the Heurtematte family.

Santa Ana Plaza

Further along Central Avenue was the Vander Hans pharmacy in front of the clinic of the famous physician of the Panama Hospital, Dr. Herrick. Then came the Lyons hardware store and the Panama Radio Corporation where one could buy the latest models of the "Victor" gramaphones.

On to the Santa Ana Plaza, one could admire the La Merced church, the residence of the Arias —Feraud family, today "Municipal House", and in the 1930s, as old-timers will recollect, the *refresquerias* Rendezvous, Viu and Mihalitsianos, this last still operating today as also is the Preciado Pharmacy and the stores La Mascota, La Joyeria, Ponce Rojas, Salomon Antonio and Lupi which specializes in the famous "Panama Hats".

We also remember, in this area, the Amador Theatre, the El Dorado Theatre, and fronting the Santa Ana Plaza, the Variedades Theatre; where silent movies, later talkies and always variety shows, were presented. A few yards away was the Colon Hotel which is still open today.

If you were to leave Las Bovedas by "B" Avenue you would experience just as much vibrant history; noble houses such as that of the Calderon family with its private chapel have disappeared but others await restoration. They are mute witnesses of past splendor; the ruins of the Flat Arch, and of the Santo Domingo church with its beautiful golden altar which was saved from the old city which was sacked by the pirate Henry Morgan. In this area, too, were the original headquarters of the newspapers founded by Don Alejandro A, Duque G; *the Star & Herald* en 1848 and *La Estrella* de Panama in 1853.

Wandering here, you will also discover Herrera Plaza dedicated to that illustrious Panamanian son, General

Tomas Herrera. Attractive wrought-iron balconies lend dignity to the houses and from here can be glimpsed part of the "Boyaca" building surrounded by the city wall of the colonial city.

And returning by this route again to the historic Santa Ana Plaza where the domino enthusiasts have their private "casino", the curious stroller may pause awhile to savor a *"tinto"* coffee in the traditional Coca Cola Café on the corner where the latest happenings in sport, international affairs and politics have always been and still are the main item on the menu.

By Madelag (Manuelita A. de Tribaldos).

Note: Information about the families which lived in the Casco Viejo and its environs can be obtained at the offices of the San Felipe Foundation at the building of the old Convent of San Felipe de Neri at the junction of Fourth Street and Bolivar, Plaza and at the offices of the Old Quarter at Las Bovedas.

Aviation outlook excellent

COPA, Panama's national airline, sets records and continues growth

The Aviation business is alive and well in the Republic of Panama. The country is a hub and gateway for travel in Latin America stimulated by the acquisition by Continental Airline of the majority of shares in the private national airline COPA.

The progress and prospects of general and domestic aviation are also excellent due to new developments and state strategies.

Planes of 12 international carriers make scheduled stops at Panama City's Tocumen airport. Panama has other international airports with customs and immigration facilities which accommodate overseas flights. At the last count there were over 60 airports and landing strips in regular use on the isthmus, and internal airlines give comprehensive coverage. All of this activity, including the fact that a high volume of traffic between the U.S.A. and Latin American destinations overflies Panama's airspace, has led to the development of relatively sophisticated air navigation and control facilities.

Tocumen International Airport is one of Latin America's most modern and well-equipped. Completed in 1978, it is 21 km from the centre of the city. The new airport was built adjacent to the original Tocumen Airport, the runway and terminal facilities of which have been converted to a cargo centre and base for the National Air Service so that the old and the new airports form one single complex. The airport is only 15 minutes from the center of Panama City on the South Corridor expressway.

The full list of international carriers using Tocumen Airport (or with offices in Panama) and their main destinations, is as follows:

AEROFLOT (Russia)
AEROLINEAS ARGENTINAS (Argentina)
AEROMEXICO (Mexico)
AIRES (Colombia): Baranquilla, Cartagena, Bucaramanga
AIR FRANCE (France)
ALITALIA (Italy)
AMERICA WEST (US)
AMERICAN AIRLINES (US): Miami
AVIANCA (Colombia): Bogotá, Cali

CONTINENTAL AIRLINES (US): Guayaquil, Houston, Newark, Quito

COPA AIRLINES (Panama): Barranquilla, Bogotá, Buenos Aires, Cali, Cancún, Caracas, Cartagena, Guatemala, Guayaquil, Kingston, Havana, Lima, Los Angeles, Managua, Medellín, México, Miami, Orlando, Port-au-Prince, Quito, San José, San Juan, San Salvador, Santiago de Chile, Santo Domingo, Sao Paulo

CUBANA (Cuba): Havana

DELTA AIRLINES (US): Atlanta

IBERIA (Spain): Miami

JAPAN AIRLINES (Japan)

KLM (Netherlands)

KOREAN AIR (South Korea)

LACSA (Costa Rica): San José

LLOYD AERO BOLIVIANO (Bolivia): Cancún, Santa Cruz, México

LUFTHANSA (Alemania)

MEXICANA (México): México, D.F.

TACA (El Salvador): San José, San Salvador

UNITED AIRLINES (US)

US AIRWAYS (US)

WEST CARIBBEAN (Colombia): Medellín, San Andrés, San José

Panama City's other international airport is Marcos A. Gelabert Airport, at Albrook, which is the main airport for general aviation. Between domestic carriers, charter airlines, helicopter companies and private aviation, it is a busy airport.

Among the airlines which operate from Marcos A. Gelabert at Albrook are: Aeroperlas (Bocas del Toro, Contadora, Changuinola, Chitré, David, France Field); Mapiex S.A. (Bocas del Toro, Changuinola and David); Aero Taxi (San Blas), Arrendamientos Aéreos (charter), Aviatur (Contadora, Darién, San Blas, San Miguel and charter flights), Helipan (charter), Helix Craft (charter).

Other international airports are the Enrique Malek Airport in David, the Manuel Niño Airport at Changuinola, Puerto Armuelles Airport and Bocas del Toro Airport.

All of these airports have been re-built or improved in recent years. David's airport has been completely re-built in anticipation of increased international traffic especially since it is now the best alternative airport for flights in and out of San José, Costa Rica which formerly used Managua as an alternative.

There can be no other country of comparable size with as many airports and airstrips as Panama, from ex-World War II airfields to strips built by indigenous tribes for access to their remote reservations.

Tocumen International Airport is equipped with ILS (Instrument Landing System), VOR (Visual Omni Range directional radio) DME (Distance Measuring Equipment) and NDB (Non-Directional Radio Beacon).

Panama's aviation control centre is at Balboa, where both CERAP and Panama Radio are housed in one building. CERAP (Centro de Radar y Aproximación) is also known as Panama Center or Panama Approach Control and is equipped with a radar with a primary coverage of a 60 mile radius from the antennae which are located on Isla Perico on the Causeway at the Pacific entrance to the Canal. Coverage for aircraft equipped with transponders is 200 miles, which is adequate to cover the entire isthmus. The station is equipped to offer surveillance approaches to either Marcos Gelabert or Tocumen Airports.

Panama's Air Control Center at Balboa also performs an important international function in being the only Latin America base for AFTN (Aeronautical Fixed Telecommunication Network), an international network for the exchange of information. A bank of computers at Balboa talks to Kansas, U.S.A., the control center, and passes messages relating to weather and overflight permissions, as well as flight plans to countries in the Latin American and Caribbean area from Mexico to Brazilia. This service is controlled by ICAO (International Civil Aviation Organization).

The pollera with its intricate headdress is worn with pride.
Photo: Jorge Quinzada Loo

Left: A float which captured the essence of country culture entitled "On my grandmother's patio" parades on a cart pulled by two oxen at the Festival of the Mejorana, Guararé.
Photo: Jorge Quinzada Loo

The Mejorana Festival, one of the most outstanding of the many traditional events of the interior, is enjoyed to the full by young and old.
Photo: Jorge Quinzada Loo

Senobia Cerrud, aged 80, who lives in the remote village of Paritilla near Pocri in the province of Los Santos is a compulsive collector. Any oddment to her is a valuable artifact – and deserves a place in her museum which she calls "El Museo de Antiguedades de Todas Las Especies", which, approximately translated, means – The Museum of Antiquities of All Things. She will be glad to show you round.
Photo: Gustavo Araújo.

Reverence for Christ and the saints and belief in miracles leads thousands of Catholic pilgrims each year to the Santa Librada Church at Las Tablas at the province of Los Santos.
Photo: Jorge Quinzada Loo

Reverence and wonder are shown on the faces of this mother and daughter in ceremonial robes which they wear to the Santa Librada mass.

A candle-light procession through the streets of the town.
Photos: Jorge Quinzada Loo

Children of the Darien, whose family dwellings are on stilts to protect from floods and jungle beasties help with daily chores like unloading the boat after a trip to gather provisions. The little girl above has her own boat and is an expert driver.
Photos: Tomas Munita

Above: Father and son. Photo. *Jorge Quinzada Loo*

Below left: An old cow hand. *Photo: Danny Lehman*

Below right: A young girl of the Embera tribe of Darien Indians, clothed in body painting of exquisite and intricate design, helps to prepare for a feast.
Photo: Danny Lehman

Perhaps one day this little boy of the Wounaan tribe in the jungles of the Darien will be a hunter, too.
Photo: Tito Herrera

The fight to protect our green heritage

The perennial problem —development versus ecological protection— is being tackled in Panama

Biology specialists in Panama enjoy monitoring the species that inhabit the country's tropical geography. A recent animal inventory of the tiny island of Barro Colorado —a forested ecological haven located in the middle of Gatún Lake—demonstrated an interesting aspect of Panama's diversity: there are over 100 species of roaches on the Isthmus, none of which appears in the country's list of endangered species.

The beauty and the ecological richness of Panama's forests and coasts are known around the world. Local governments, with the aid of non-profit organizations such as the National Association for Nature Conservancy (ANCON), and the Smithsonian Tropical Research Institute (STRI) promote sustainable development programs in a wide range of areas, from agriculture to tourism.

However, there is still a lot to be done. The percentage of Panama's territory covered by tropical forests has dropped from 70% to approximately 40% in the last 50 years. The rest remains threatened by inadequate farming practices, deforestation, the construction of roads and by the growth of unplanned human settlements. Only a small part of Panama's territory is adequate for agriculture. Approximately 78% of the country's land is part of the Cordillera Central mountain range —the backbone of the Isthmus—which makes it an easy target for erosion.

The greater part of Panama's agricultural activities are performed by small farmers who cut down forests for cattle raising purposes (which obviously erodes the land). There is little control over the colonization of remote, forested areas. Deforestation is also affecting the country's bio-diversity and approximately 80 plant species are now listed as endangered.

Panamanian cities also have their share of ecological problems. The contamination levels of the Bay of Panama are so high that only a few species are known to live in its waters. According the 2000 Census, the population of Panama City and surrounding areas (the districts of Panama and San Miguelito) surpassed the one-million mark.

Every day, approximately 575,000 cubic tons of raw sewage are poured into the Bay —an extremely critical situation, since Panama City has not been able to solve its solid waste problem and re-cycling activities in the metropolitan area are limited.

During his tenure as mayor of Panama City, Juan Carlos Navarro, former executive director of ANCON, reaffirmed his commitment to solving the capital's environmental problems, starting by improving garbage collection and reforestation programs to later continue with the Bay's sanitation plans coordinated by the national government.

The Panama Canal watershed, the forested area that provides the large amounts of fresh water needed for the daily activities of the famous waterway (52 million gallons are needed for each ship transit) is also threatened by the colonization of forests and low-scale industrial pollution.

However, the first steps have been taken to correct the problem. In June of 1988, Panama passed a law targeted at strengthening the country's ecological policy. A new governmental agency, the National Environment Authority (ANAM) was created with greater powers than its forerunner (the Renewable Natural Resources Institute -INRENARE). Since its creation, ANAM has started a re-structuring process with the aid of the Inter-American Development Bank (IDB) which has resulted in the development of a more coherent environment protection strategy for Panama.

Established in 1985, ANCON has expanded its activities with the creation of the International Center for Environmental Training, which trains individuals in order to foster the conservation of the Panama Canal watershed, and also strengthen other non-governmental organizations.

ANCON's priorities are also concentrated in two potential risk areas: Bocas del Toro (due to the growth of the tourism industry) and the jungles of Darien, Panama's least-developed province. The IDB currently supports a US$70-million program targeted at paving the leg of the Pan-American Highway that extends to the town of Yaviza, Darién —a segment which is virtually impassable during the country's rainy season.

There are a number of important issues related to the environment which are expected to yield results in the next few years. First to be seen is the way in which Panama will manage the forested areas surrounding the Panama Canal, which was gradually transferred from U.S. to Isthmian control during the last two decades of last century. This area includes the Panama Canal watershed, which is no longer under the control of the Panama Canal Commission (a former U.S. federal government agency), but under the Panama Canal Authority (ACP —an autonomous entity of the Republic of Panama).

The successful management of the area will be a great challenge for the newly-created entity. One particular idea currently studied by the ACP —and carefully analyzed by environmental groups—is an ambitious plan to create more fresh-water sources for the Panama Canal through three great reserves. If approved, the project will take 10 years to complete and will entail relocating approximately 8,000 people that inhabit the area. It is thought the above-mentioned area is not very forested, although the corresponding environmental impact studies are currently taking place.

A large part of the forests of the former Panama Canal Zone has been in Panamanian hands since 1979 and is currently protected under the country's national park system. One of Panama's greatest challenges is to stop the colonization of the forests. The rest of the former Zone was divided into human development areas for a number of purposes, both in the Pacific and Caribbean coasts.

Panama is currently conversing with United States' authorities in regards to the issue of the former fire ranges used by the U.S. military in the Isthmus, which are contaminated with explosive artifacts. Panama has stated that the North Americans have not done enough to clean these areas while, on the other hand, U.S. officials insist that contaminated forested lands need not be cleaned, as they could be declared protected areas that would guarantee the supply of fresh water for the Canal.

ANCON believes environmental issues are gaining popularity among Panamanians. The organization has given special attention to the school-age children that visit the country's national parks, as well as to actions taken by local communities. In early 2000, the residents of an upper-class Panama City neighborhood protested against the cutting of a full-grown tree that supposedly prevented the construction of a new building. The incident, which received full coverage by the local media, motivated those involved to relocate the tree to a nearby park.

According to ANCON, poverty constitutes the greatest threat to the environment. Over 30% of Panama's population lives under the poverty level. If this reality continues, the greatest ecological problems will not be solved, according to the organization's officials.

Barro Colorado Island – a scientific mecca

The Smithsonian is a permanent part of the Panama scene

The Smithsonian Institution has had a fruitful partnership with Panama for most of the century. When Gatun lake was filled, a group of Smithsonian scientists established a laboratory on Barro Colorado Island. Nearly eighty years later, Barro Colorado is no longer an unknown island. Today it is the piece of tropical forest with the longest history of scientific investigation in the world. It was the take-off point, the seed that would give rise to the Smithsonian Tropical Research Institute (STRI), the extension, in Panama, of the prestigious Smithsonian Institution of the U.S.A.

The Smithsonian Institution was created in 1846 with funds endowed by James Smithson, an English scientist. It is an independent entity whose objective as set forth in James Smithson's own will and testament is "to increase and diffuse knowledge among men." The Smithsonian, although it is best known as the largest complex of museums in the world in Washington, D.C., is also dedicated to public education and the study of art, science and history. The Smithsonian Tropical Research Institute, created in 1966, is the only branch of the Smithsonian Institution located outside U.S. territory.

Why have sites like Barro Colorado become scientific Meccas? Why is the Republic of Panama one of the most intensively studied tropical countries on the planet? The answers lie in the ecological importance of the Isthmus, itself. To better understand its present importance, let's consider a bit of history—or geology, to be more exact…

Some 3.5 million years ago, the formation of this Isthmus of dry land that connected South and North America (present day Panama and Costa Rica) was complete. From then on, the Isthmus has been a biological bridge for the migration of plants and land animals and a barrier for marine organisms. Before the Isthmus formed, the opposite was true; a series of unconnected volcanic islands allowed open communication between the oceans. Terrestrial animals and plants in North and South America were separated; not the marine organisms of the Atlantic and Pacific.

When the Isthmus formed, events began that would impact the ecology of the entire planet. The barrier between the two oceans redirected the flow of the Atlantic into the Pacific and gave rise to the Gulf Stream. The change in the direction of warm tropical waters from eastward to northward altered global climate patterns. Massive migrations of animals began. Northern mammals proved to be more successful colonists in most cases; their southward migration resulted in the extinction of certain species and in the dispersion of others. The northern fauna remained relatively unaltered.

Few of us are aware that these migrations continue today. Less than four decades ago the Capibara (Hydrochaeris hydrochaeris) arrived in Panama from South America. It has yet to extend its range into Costa Rica.

And probably the Coyote (Canis lactrans), the wild dog species, moving South from North America now forms part of the fauna of Panama's Darién Province. Coyotes have been sighted in Campana National Park in central Panama.

But Panama should not be considered only as a biological crossroads but also as a geographical barrier between two oceans and as a bridge for migrating plant and animals. There is more to the story. Mountain ranges bisect Panama from East to West, creating different climatic conditions on the Pacific and Caribbean slopes. The variety of animal and plant life is so great in Panama because of the diversity of habitats. This is a small tropical country with an immense (and still not completely catalogued) diversity of organisms.

More than 150 rivers spill into the Atlantic; nearly 350 flow into the Pacific. And it is here that we find the narrowest point between the two oceans: 49 km between the Gulf of Carti on the Caribbean and the high tide of the Pacific. More than 4,500 km2 of Panama's shoreline is protected by mangroves, an area similar to the mangrove swamps of Colombia and greater in extent than the mangrove forests of any other Central American country.

It is commonplace to hear that there are more bird species in Panama than in all of the territory north of Mexico. We know more about the flora of Panama than we do about any other tropical country of similar size. On Barro Colorado Island (15 km2) more vascular plants are represented than in all of Europe.

Some of the research projects at STRI are also directed to answer some more pressing questions—potential environmental problems that face society in the coming century. The tropics, with their rainforests and coral reefs, shelter the majority of the diverse organisms of the planet. What gave rise to such diversity? How stable are these systems considering the changes provoked by agriculture, industrialization and human population growth? How does the biosphere interact with the geosphere?

In Panama, the Smithsonian Tropical Research Institute maintains a comprehensive array of facilities. The best-known is the 5,400 hectareas of forest designated as Barro Colorado Nature Monument, which includes Barro Colorado Island.

Marine laboratories are maintained on both coasts of Panama and a modern research vessel that provide access to two very different oceans, divided by the Isthmus of Panama only a few million years ago: a magnificent " natural experiment" in evolution.

Construction cranes are located in the dry tropical forest near Panama City and also at the former Fort Sherman site, in a humid tropical forest on the Caribbean slope. These two cranes have proven to be excellent scientific tools for access to the tropical forest canopy and have resulted in pioneer studies of insect diversity, plant physiology, and plant interface with the atmosphere in a part of the forest that is still poorly understood.

The Smithsonian's Earl S. Tupper Center in Panama City is the best and most complete of its type in Latin America, and one of the best in the world. Located in the Ancon area, the center honors Earl Silas Tupper, pioneer of the plastic industry and prestigious inventor, researcher, philanthropist, and businessman. The Tupper Center is a campus-like facility that includes a research center with laboratories and offices for scientists, an administration building, a tropical sciences library, a conference facility with a 176-seat auditorium, exhibit hall and meeting room, a small cafeteria, and a bookstore.

The Institute also maintains dormitories and labs in Gamboa, with access to 54,340 acres of Soberania National Park and another field station in Fortuna, a montane tropical forest in the province of Chiriqui.

The facilities and the knowledge accumulated at Smithsonian in Panama, in conjunction with the knowledge base generated by researchers at universities, government institutes and independent institutions in Panama, annually attracts hundreds of researchers from all over the world. STRI has more than 200 permanent employees in Panama.

Ecotourism, stands out as a real possibility for sustainable use of the national flora and fauna. Tourism based on the natural and cultural heritage of Panama, will be fed by the knowledge that results from research that has been done here. This is "value added" for the tourism industry.

A series of actions has been taken to insure the continuity of scientific work of the Smithsonian in Panama, and that will contribute to expanding the position of Panama as a source of tropical biology information. Since 1985, the Panamanian government has granted STRI International Mission status; STRI has signed accords with the most prestigious universities and research centers in the country and has made an agreement with the government to guarantee uninterrupted use of all of its installations through the beginning of the new millenium.

From material submitted by Georgina de Alba, Administrative Director of Education and Scholarships, Smithsonian Iropical Research Institute .

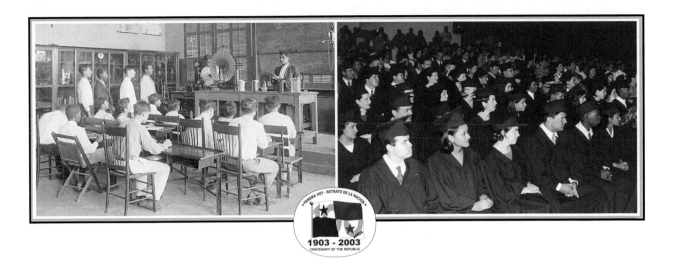

Expansion continues in private education

New universities, a broader range of courses to prepare for the age of the technocrats

Basic education in Panama is obligatory and free according to Panama's Constitution, but it is a struggle for the Ministry of Education to find the money for all the new state schools that are needed. Nevertheless, education is a national priority and although there are difficulties at the primary and secondary levels, higher education is forging ahead.

The Government budget for the education sector amounted to $544.7 million in the year 2001. The cost of rebuilding, repair and equipment for schools was $37.5 million. It is made up from a special education tax and contributions from abroad: Banco Internacional de Reconstruccion y Fomento (BIRF) the Banco de Desarrollo (BID), Spain and the European Union.

Another government involvement in education is through the Instituto para La Formacion y Aprovechamiento de los Recursos Humanos (IFARHU) which was created to solicit and distribute scholarships to students and professional Panamanians from foundations, public entities, and private Panamanian and foreign companies. IFARHU also offers student loans. During the last four years IFARHU has awarded almost 20,000 scholarships per year to Panamanian students.

The illiteracy rate in Panama dropped from 10.7% in 1990 to 7.8% in 2000 and was concentrated mainly in the poor rural areas and particularly in indigenous groups. The general student population climbed to 797,014 in 2001.

Pre-School Education

The total matriculation for pre-school education was 60,471 children under four or five years of age who attended 1,441 schools with 2,962 teachers.

Primary education.

Primary schools receive children between six and twelve years of age. In 2001 total enrollment in primary schools rose to 400,408. These students attended 3,043 schools of which 2,805 were public and 238 private schools. The total number of teachers in these schools was 16,187. The student teacher ratio was 25 to one.

Secondary schools

Secondary schools, whose educational programs are divided into two three-year stages called first and second "cycles", admit students from 12 to 18 years of age.

Total high school enrollment in 2001 was 234,153 students. There was a total of 429 secondary schools in the country, of which 246 were public and 183 private. At this level, during the same period, there were 14,404 teachers. The average student teacher ratio was 18 to one in the public schools and 10 to one in the private schools.

The area of post-secondary education made important strides in the year 2001 with the diversification of technical and specialized learning centers and in public and private universities. One of the most important developments was the creation of seven centers, including the Instituto Superior de Ciencias y Tecnologia Aeronauticas and the new Panamericana University (UPAM)

Special Education

Special education is the responsibility of the Panamanian Institute of Special Rehabilitation (IPHE), in coordination with the Ministry of Education. This institution handles children with physical or mental disabilities and prepares them to integrate into their society.

Included in this area are the National School for the Deaf, the Special Education School, the National School for the Blind, the Autistic Program, the School for Precocious Children, the Special Vocation School, the Cerebral Palsy Program, the Andres Toro Adult Rehabilitation Program, and the Agricultural Center (CJAC). In 2002, a total of 8,556 students matriculated in these special centers.

Higher Education

Four state universities and 14 private universities serve the needs of advanced eduction in the Republic of Panama. University matriculation in 2001 rose to 117,806 students.

The University of Panama, founded in 1935 is the main university of the country as well as the official university of the Republic. The University of Panama is located in an extensive campus in the residential sector of El Cangrejo in the center of Panama City.

Entrance requirements include presentation of a high school graduation certificate and passing several exams (psychological, academic capacity, and general knowledge exams). Students who fail to obtain the minimum 70 percent for a pass are not rejected, but instead enter a training course which automatically accepts them. Matriculation in 2001 was 68,013.

The University of Panama offers both undergraduate and post-graduate degrees. At the postgraduate level eight degrees are offered. At the undergraduate level, 61 courses are offered for the diploma designated " licenciatura" and 17 technical courses are offered. These courses are in the areas of Business Management and Accounting, Public Administration, Architecture, Fine Arts, Agriculture and Fishery Sciences, Education Sciences, Natural Sciences, General Sciences, Social Communication, Law and Political Sciences, Economy, Nursing, Pharmacy, Humanities, Medicine, Veterinary Medicine and Odontology.

The University offers specialization in International Trade, Public Affairs, Advanced Teaching. The masters programs are: Mathematics, Educational Development Systems, Medical Entomology, Agricultural Entomology and General Entomology, Nursing, and Public Health Care.

The University has eight Regional Centers in the provinces of Azuero, Coclé, Colon, Chiriquí, Los Santos, Veraguas, San Miguelito and Western Panama and branches in Bocas del Toro, Barú, Azuero, Coclé and Darién.

The Technological University of Panama, "La Tecnológica", as it is called, is the second state university and has its central campus in the capital, with seven regional centers, in the Provinces of Bocas del Toro, Chiriquí, Veraguas, Coclé, Herrera, Los Santos, Colón and La Chorrera. In the year 2001 matriculation was 16,102.

It has six faculties: Civil Engineering, Electrical Engineering, Industrial Engineering, Mechanical Engineering, Computer Systems Engineering and Science and Technology.

La Universidad Autonoma de Chiriqui (UNACHI) is the third state university and is located in the province of Chiriqui. It offers degrees in nine faculties as well as post graduate courses, masters and doctorates in higher education. Matriculation in 2001 was 9,722.

La Universidad Especializada de las Americas (UDELAS), situated in Albrook, is the fourth state University.

In 2001 matriculation was 2,039 students. It offers very specific careers in the areas of social sciences, medicine and special education.

State universities had a total teaching staff of 6,516.

Private Universities

The Santa María La Antigua University (USMA) is Roman Catholic, private and non-profit. It began in 1965 in the compound of the Archbishop's Palace in the Cathedral sector of Panama City. The USMA Campus is now on Ricardo J. Alfaro Avenue, and has modern facilities. It accepts approximately 5,000 students who study 24 degree courses in the areas of Administrative Science, Technology, Natural Sciences, Law and Political Sciences, Humanities, Religious Sciences and Social Sciences. It also offers 32 postgraduate and masters academic programs and three intermediate degree courses. It is the only university in Panama which has an obligatory General Studies program. It has regional centers in the provinces of Colon, Chiriqui and Los Santos. There are more than 580 teachers and an administrative staff of 300. The university has well-equipped laboratories, a library and book shop and other student services.

Florida State University, another private university, with its principal headquarters in Tallahassee, Florida started up in Panama through an agreement with the U.S. Government to offer higher education to members of the U.S. armed forces stationed here but it has always had Panamanian students and professors. Now it continues to operate from its new installations on the campus of the former Panama Canal College in Balboa.

The Inter-American Correspondence Course University of Panama (UNIEDPA), was created officially in 1986. In has branches in Chiriqui, Hererra, Veraguas, Darién, Colón Penonomé, Chorrera and Ocú.

Nova University, is the second largest private educational institution in Florida. It was established in 1964 and has graduated more than 25,000 students in fields such as business, banking, law, data processing, education, psychology and health. Nova began its programs in Panama in 1977 and was the first private American university to be authorized by the Ministry of Education.

La Universidad Del Istmo is sponsored by the Michelsen family and by the foundation Politécnico Grancolombiano, which operates in Santa Fé de Bogotá, Colombia. It has a central headquarters in the capital city and a regional center in David, Chiriquí. It offers degrees in marketing, human resources and financing.

Universidad Latinoamericana De Ciencia y Tecnología (ULACIT) is a private, non-profit institution which opened its doors in Panama in 1991. Its main headquarters is in Costa Rica It offers various degrees, postgraduate studies, masters and doctorates.

Other important universities are the Universidad Interamericana which offers bachelor degrees in Arts and Engineering and masters degrees in Business Management in its new and modern building in the district of Cangrejo in Panama City. The Universidad Latina de Panama which offers bachelors, masters and post-graduate degrees in Business and Education Administration. There are also faculties for Education Science Politics and Law, Business Administration, Technology, Tourism, Communication, and Medicine and Health Science. It has branches in Chiriqui, Veraguas and Herrera.

The Columbus University on Calle 50, Panama City, offers degrees and post-graduate studies and has branches in David, Veraguas and Herrera.

The Correspondence Course University; Universidad Abierto y a Distancia de Panama offers qualifications up to masters degrees.

The University of Louisville in Bella Vista offers only masters degrees.

The Latin America University of Foreign Trade (La Universidad Latinoamericana de Comercio Exterior) in El Cangrejo offers technical studies as does the Universidad Panamericana. A university specializing in communication techniques is Universidad de Technicas de la Comunicacion with courses in graphic design, TV production and related fields. Other recently created private universities are the Universidad de la Paz in Diablo and the Cartago University of Costa Rica.

A committee of rectors of private universities in Panama has been formed to act as a watchdog on standards.

Although in former years, education in Panama was for the privileged, the years have passed, and doors are open now to schools, colleges, universities and technical schools. Within this new range of opportunities the private universities are in the forefront.

Technical education

Besides the universities, higher education is offered in educational centers such as the International Banking Institute (IBI), the Institute of Management (ISAE), the Center for Higher Management Studies (CESA - APEDE), the Hotel and Tourism College, the Nautical School of Panama, and the National Agriculture Institue (INA).

National Culture Institute

The National Institute of Culture (INAC) was created in 1974 together with cultural centers, and schools of art, sculpture, music and dance. INAC also took over responsibility for museums, national exhibition halls and national showpieces, as well as being made the guardian of Panama's historical heritage.

Great emphasis is placed on art, education and folklore. In addition to holding seminars of folkloric art, tours have been made in recent years to support the work of the following schools of fine art: National School of Plastic Art, National School of Dance, National School of Music, National School of Theater, The Estelina Tejeira School of Penonomé, Chiriquí School of Fine Arts, Chitré School of Fine Arts, Colón School of Fine Arts and the Veraguas Extension of the National School of Plastic Art.

Retirees are moving to Panama

**Panama gets top ranking as a place where expatriates
can find a good lifestyle in the tropics — and the price is right**

Another Panamanian secret has been revealed during the past few years—it is a great place to retire to. In 2001, International Living, the renowned magazine and recognized expert for promoting U.S. expatriate lifestyles, stated that Panama is the best place to live outside of the United States. The American Association of Retired People's (AARP) Modern Maturity Magazine, has ranked Panama's town of Boquete as fourth in its listing of the "Fifteen best cities in the world for U.S. retirees."

Panama's popularity as a retirement destination is easy to define. This country's mixture of a high quality of life, easy life-style, retirement incentives and modern amenities allow persons to change their location and lives, with very little problem.

To begin with, Panama is an incredibly beautiful country. It has a diversity of flora and fauna that is found in no other place, due to the Isthmus' position as the crossroads of North and South America. Potential residential opportunities range over city, mountain, beach and island communities so that a special place can be found to suit anyone's taste. Once you decide where to settle, you have the security of knowing that, as a foreigner, you can own property easily and are granted exactly the same rights and protections as a Panamanian property owner.

Due to the pull-out of the American military and other factors, prices for Panamanian real estate have remained basically unchanged from the early 1990s (except for "hot" areas like Boquete in Chiriqui and the islands of the Bocas del Toro archipelago). As of this writing some representative prices in the better known areas include: a three-bedroom, apartment in Panama City, $60,000; a two-bedroom condo in a new high rise, $175,000; a four-plex building in the old Albrook military base, $155,000; a three-bedroom house with lot in Boquete, $100,000; and, a home on the beach in Colon, $40,000.

There are a number of real estate land developments ideal for retirees. Foremost among these is Altos de Cerro Azul and Altos del Maria, both within reasonable distance from Panama City but situated in cooler, mountainous areas and with their own residential infraestructure and services such as clinics and supermarkets close by.

Once you purchase your home, you can also bring your personal and house belongings with you tax-free and a new car (for private use) every two years, plus you pay no property taxes on your residence. If all this is not beneficial enough, English, is spoken widely enough so chances are you can converse with at least some of your new neighbors.

Panama is one of the safest countries in the world and has the highest rating for tourist safety from the prestigious Pinkerton Intelligence Agency. Panama is a constitutional democracy with no dictator and no standing army. Due to the presence of the Panama Canal, Panama also enjoys international protection and monitoring.

In terms of health standards Panama is among the top countries in Latin America. Life expectancy is around 75 years. A large percentage of Panamanian doctors are bilingual and have been trained in Europe and the United States. Private medical facilities are among the best in Central America (many are affiliated with major hospitals in the U.S.). In addition, health standards in most parts of the country are quite good as a result of massive sanitation programs initiated during the construction of the Panama Canal. Water is also potable in most of the country and in the cities you can drink straight from the tap.

Making the most of their money is, of course, a prime concern for retirees. The U.S. dollar has always been the republic's currency. Panama is known for its banking center, which boasts branch banks from nearly all of the international players. On another note, the cost of living is reasonable and is much less than in the States and Europe. Inflation rates are some of the lowest known, normally hovering between 1% and 2%. Plus, pensioners, or "jubilados" to use the Spanish term receive generous price discounts such as 50% on movies and cultural events, 30% on transportation, 25% on utilities, 15% on personals loans and 1% on personal mortgages.

Those settling in Panama can expect the tab for day-to-day living to be significantly less than in "first-world" countries. Nice apartments and homes can be rented for $1,000 or less per month. Grocery prices are 25%-30% lower. A meal at a good restaurant can be enjoyed for $15-$40. First-run movie tickets are $3.75. Concert tickets range from $20-$100. Maid service is around $180 per month. Gardeners cost under $10 a day. A bottle of Scotch whisky can be found for $6.

Purchasing just what you need is not usually a problem. Due to its mixture of cultures and positioning as an international trade hub, Panama offers a wide range of top-quality goods and, therefore, shopping options.

Keeping in touch with friends, family and the rest of the world is no problem. High-band Internet connectivity, cellular phone networks and ADSL in-home phone capability are readily accessible. Full service satellite and cable TV are common.

Regarding accessibility, many major airlines call at Panama's Tocumen International Airport, including American and Delta. Panama's international airline COPA flies to 29 cities in 19 countries and now has direct flights from Houston, Los Angeles, Miami (2 1/2 hours), Newark and Orlando. There are also direct flights from the major Central and South American centers. Anyone wishing to travel from the Eastern Hemisphere will probably be routed through the U.S.

Finally, obtaining a retiree visa is a very simple and inexpensive process. All you need is a "clean" police report from the area in which you lived before Panama, a certificate of health from a Panamanian doctor and proof of personal income of $500 per month, with $100 monthly for any dependents.

Given all the benefits listed above, it is no wonder that for those looking to retire, Panama has become the Latin American location of choice.

If you desire more information about retiring in Panama, numerous legal firms offer a full line of advisory and relocation services. Retirement-related reading includes: "Getting to Know Panama", "The Visitor" and "Focus on Panama", published by Focus Publications (Int), S.A. email: focusint@sinfo.net "Living in Panama" from the American Chamber of Commerce and Industry of Panama (amcham@panamcham.com, http://www.panamcham.com, under "Publications") and the Panama Country Kit from International Living's Panama branch (panama@internationalliving.com, http://www.agora-inc.com/reports/pvom/wilvbb31/). Another good source of information is Panama Info (http://panamainfo.com).

Americans may want to contact the American Society of Panama (info@amsoc.org, http://www.amso.org). There are a number of organizations for foreigners and of interest to foreigners including active groups of Alcoholics Anonymous (panamakevin.com)

Panama Relocation Services was created to offer full-assistance in the process of moving and relocating in Panama or from Panama to another country. Services include airport pick-up, orientation to Panama, search for and installation in new residence, help in finding schools and doctors and everything a person or family could need in starting a new life. (www.panamarelocation.com)

The Azuero peninsula extends far into the Pacific Ocean where the big waves roll in unhindered until they crash on the majestic shores. Surfers travel from many parts of the world to sample the waves on Venao Beach in Los Santos, photographed above. Another famous Panama beach for surfing is Mariato Beach in Veraguas province. Both are far from conventional tourist amenities. For other water sports, take your choice.
Photos: Panama Government Tourist Bureau.

Adrenalin rush or calmer pursuits... the choice is yours. On the left is the birdwatching mecca, the Canopy Tower (www.canopytower.com), close to Panama City in the Gamboa area.

Above: Pony trekking, mountain biking or braving the rapids. Panama has it all.
Photos: Panama Government Tourist Bureau.

The Government Tourist Bureau's recent promotions describe Panama as "The path less travelled" with thanks to the poet Robert Frost whose line they adapted. The phrase is nowhere more apt than on Panama's islands.

Above: is shown the Pacific island of San Jose, outermost of the Perlas group where a small cabin resort, Hacienda del Mar (www.haciendadel mar.net) recently opened.

Below: is the Caribbean resort of Punta Caracol in Bocas del Toro (www.puntacaracol.com). Small, charming resorts have proliferated in Bocas del Toro in recent years.

You need a sharp eye and great stealth to catch sight of the shy animals of the jungle. If you do not see them, they see you. A spider monkey and a crocodile are two of the watchers. *Photo above :Ancon. Below: Yolande Vicente*

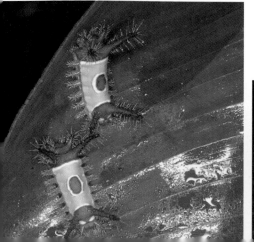

The rainforests of Panama's National Parks are home to mysterious and colorful species: tree frogs of all the colors of the rainbow, fruits you will never find in you supermarket and thousands of varieties of insects, many of which have yet to be classified by the scientists. *Photo of the rainforest: Panama Canal Authority.*
Photos of the species: Jorge Quinzada Loo.

The beautiful but violent world of the seashore. A Pelican grabs a snack and a Portugese Man o' War, the large and deadly jellyfish which navigates by its purple sail, hovers over a reef trailing poisonous tentacles in search of prey.
Photo: Jorge Quinzada Loo

The giant turtle comes to the beach at night to lay her eggs. That is the extent of her motherhood. Back she goes on the next tide leaving her eggs to hatch. When they do, the baby turtles must face the gauntlet of the predators as they stumble toward the sanctuary of the sea.
Photos: Jorge Quinzada Loo.

White sand, black sand reflecting myriad colors, flowering trees, blue skies. Summertime on Panama's Pacific beaches, hundreds of miles of them. *Photo: Lina Isaza*

Panamanian girls are especially beautiful at Carnival, a happy tradition in Panama with parades, music and extravagant costumes. *Photo: Ruben Flores*

PROFILES

of companies and institutions in Panama.

The following section of profiles is offered to give readers some idea of the scope of the business world in Panama. It reflects the diversity of the country's economy and also emphasizes the services backing the country's strong institutions such as the Canal and the maritime industry, the Financial Center and the Colon Free Zone.

INDEX OF PROFILES

MORGAN & MORGAN
ATTORNEYS AT LAW

A case in point for the service industry

Legal firms are at the forefront of Panama's service industry. One of the leading firms, which can be used to demonstrate the importance of the service sector in Panama is Morgan & Morgan, with over 40 attorneys and more than 300 supporting staff members, and offices in the major financial centers of the world.

ORIGINS

The origins of Morgan & Morgan date back to 1923, the year in which Dr. Eduardo Morgan Sr. (1902-1988) began his law practice in David, Chiriqui, Republic of Panama. In 1945 Dr. Morgan, seeking new challenges, moved to Panama City and with his expertise and reputation quickly occupied one of the highest positions in the legal community. In the early sixties his sons Eduardo Morgan Jr. and Juan David Morgan joined their father to give the firm its present name.

As its professional activities grew, Morgan & Morgan incorporated new partners and associates and in 1970 began to expand internationally. Today, some of the partners and associates of Morgan & Morgan work in subsidiary offices of the firm in London, Zurich, Geneva, Madrid, the British Virgin Islands, and most recently Beijing. Also, for shipping, corporate and trusts services, Morgan & Morgan has affiliated offices in Hong Kong, Singapore, Piraeus, Lugano, The Bahamas, Belize, and New York.

LEGAL PRACTICE

The extensive general practice of Morgan & Morgan in Panama covers all areas of the law. Teams of attorneys concentrate in specific areas such as litigation, commercial law, tax planning, estate planning, government contracts, labor law, intellectual property, immigration law, mining law, and others. The firm is also considered the leader in the commercialization of Panama's open ship registry which has now grown to be the largest in the world. Our attorneys in the Maritime Department specialize in litigation of all types of claims before the Maritime Court of Panama and the Panama Canal Commission, as well as in ship sales and ship financing, and in the registration of vessels and mortgages.

OFFSHORE CORPORATIONS AND SHIPPING

Besides its general practice in Panama, the firm places high value on the international training and experience which its associates and partners have attained, especially with regard to formation and administration of corporations and other holding companies both "offshore" and "onshore" and in various tax haven jurisdictions such as Panama, British Virgin Islands (Tortola), The Bahamas, Hong Kong, Belize, Luxembourg, Gibraltar, and Liechtenstein, depending on the needs of the client.

Morgan & Morgan has been very successful in developing an international offshore and shipping practice. Since 1970, it has been establishing a network of offices in important financial and shipping centers around the world. These offices, managed by internationally trained attorneys and professionals, provide selected clients with offshore and fiduciary services that not only include setting up legal instruments such as offshore corporations, trusts, and private foundations, but also engaging in fiduciary and other types of related services such as company and trust management, opening and management of bank accounts, back-office service, tax planning, and others.

ESTATE PLANNING

In 1984, the Panamanian legislature enacted a modern and flexible law for the creation of trusts. Morgan & Morgan has the capacity to prepare any type of trust agreement including shares trusts, administrative trusts, investment trusts, trusts for the protection of minors or incompetents and any other permitted under the laws of the Republic of Panama.

Moreover, in June of 1995, the National Assembly of Panama enacted Law No. 25, whereby the Private Foundations were created and regulated. In response to the availability of this new instrument Morgan & Morgan organized a department specializing in structuring and managing private foundations. With the availability of this instrument, Panama became the first country in the American continent to adopt such legislation, ensuring its leadership as a provider of services to meet the needs of its clients.

Other specific areas within the firm are banking, administrative services, trademarks and patents, and general proceedings.

In Panama City, Morgan & Morgan has its offices in the Swiss Tower Building, 16th floor, Cl. 53E, Urb. Marbella. P.O. Box 0832-00232 World Trade Center, Panama, Republic of Panama. Phone: 265-7777. Fax: 265-7700.
E-mail: info@morimor.com. Webpage: www.morimor.com/lawfirm

Boyd & Sucre

Offering a broad range of legal expertise

One of the most prestigious law firms in the region, Boyd & Sucre was born as a result of the merging of Boyd & Associates, Sucre & Associates, and R.J. Alemán and Associates, which together account for close to a century of legal expertise.

The main objectives of the firm are two-fold: to provide legal business advice to international companies, and to colaborate with local companies and clients, offering them a broad range of legal services.

All members of the firm are professionals educated in renowned universities of Panama, Europe and the United States. The majority of these well trained attorneys perform their practice in both English and Spanish.

The changes on the international scene in the past 60 years, especially those related to the globalization era, have resulted in diversification of legal services in all parts of the corporate world and public and private administration. Among Boyd & Sucre's areas of expertise are:

1) Litigation
Boyd & Sucre's experience in litigation matters is vast. The firm litigators provide counsel and representation in lawsuits, class actions, administrative and adversarial proceedings, involving areas of the law such as: civil law, labor law, maritime law, arbitration, and dispute resolutions.

2) Comercial Law
Boyd & Sucre's expertise in commercial law includes areas such as: business law and contracts, corporate law, corporate governance, and International trade and trade regulations.

3) Antitrust, Antidumping and Unfair Competition:
The firm attorneys have participated in cases involving Safeguard measures, Antidumping and Antitrust. The firm expertise in antitrust matters, derives from participating in investigations regarding price discrimination and fixing, cartels and other unlawful practices restricting fair competition.

4) Mergers and Acquisitions
Boyd & Sucre's experts provide counseling and representation to owners, directors, officers and managers about structural, tax, corporate, labor and antitrust implications derived from mergers and acquisition transactions.

5) Securities and Commodities
Boyd & Sucre expertise on issues related to investment and securities regulation, allows them to provide advice on matters such as: incorporation of a corporation; its registration before the local Securities and Exchange Commission and the issuance of stocks, bonds and offerings.

6) Computer and Technology Law and Intellectual and Industrial Property:
Boyd & Sucre's experience on legal issues about computer and technology protection, provide their attorneys with the expertise to advice clients about electronic contracts and signatures, regulation, business to business transactions, and the implications of this technological developments on intellectual and industrial property matters.

7) Banking and Financial Institutions and Insurance
Boyd & Sucre's attorneys vast expertise allows them to serve their clients needs on financial transactions in areas such as: banking, financial institutions, leasing and insurance as well as to offer legal advice about new regulation and policies with respect to financial institutions.

8) Foreign Investment, Privatization and Cross Border Transactions
Boyd and Sucre's attorneys have attained the necessary expertise and skill in: negotiating with the local government the acquisition of enterprises publicly managed; facilitating business with local companies and foreign investment in domestic or private project infrastructures, and providing assistance for their foreign clients in all the aspects related with inmigration law with a view toward investment and cross border transactions as well as responses to any inquiry about panamanian labor law .

9) Government Contracts and Administrative Procedures:
Boyd & Sucre's attorneys are experienced in negotiating contracts with the government, preparing documentation for public bids, obtaining permits to operate in the Colon free Zone, acquiring Comercial and Industrial Licences as well as Radio and Telecomunications Licenses, and any other related administrative transactions.

10) Maritime and Admiralty law:
The firm offers to its clients legal assistance in all aspects of vessel's registration under panamanian flag, navigation patents, radio and fishing licenses, and any other necessary permits to follow up such aspects; the drafting and inscription of title deeds and ship mortgages in the public Registry; the negotiation and drafting of vessel's contracts such as are: charter and credit, and maritime agreements.

Other areas of expertise are: Trademarks, Copyrights and Patents; Estate Planning Trust, Private Foundations, Inmigration Law, Labor Law, Family Law, Real Estates Transactions, and Concessions, Natural Resources and Enviromental Law.

ABS   Boyd & Sucre

Boyd & Sucre, Attorneys at Law, Apartado Postal 6335, Panamá 5, República de Panamá, Teléfono: (507) 263-7400, Fax: (507) 263-8737, E-mail: abs@abs-law.com Website: www.abs-law.com

FABREGA, BARSALLO, MOLINO & MULINO

Focussing on business – delivering the goods

Fabrega, Barsallo, Molino & Mulino (FBM&M) is one of Panama City's main law firms, with a tradition of excellent service in local and international affairs, efficient and quality service, and a reputation for maintaining close ties with its clients.

Its partners and associates are backed by a competent staff whose qualifications permit them to respond to the demands of any situation in which a client needs to be represented.

In Panama, the offices of FBM&M are located in the heart of the finance and banking center. The firm has a vast number of correspondents in the main cities of the world, making international transactions swift and efficient, especially with the assistance of their communications network which converts to "real time" the differences in the time zones of the countries where their clients are situated or wish to be represented.

The firm offers a wide range of services to many companies and individuals, especially in the Asian Pacific region, the United States and Europe. Clients include Panamanian and international banks, manufacturers, international traders, ship owners and shipping agents and also businessmen with substantial commercial interests, also acting as liaisons to represent clients with transactions in Latin America and the Caribbean.

The advice provided by the firm to international clients is especially valuable in taking advantage of the benefits granted by Panamanian legislation in the fields of investment, corporations, trusts, private foundations and captive insurance, among others. It also offers a 24 hour service for ship registry under the Panamanian flag and for structuring different kinds of financing, assisting banks and law firms in different parts of the world in the preparation of necessary documents.

On the local scene, FBM&M has become a key player in many interesting transactions and is recognised for its experience with the stock exchange law and in the area of mergers and acquisitions, having participated as legal counsel to the most important transactions in Panama in recent years.

All of this expertise is supplemented by its experience in litigation, which assures clients that their interests will be protected in case of dispute.

In Panama, the main offices of Fabrega, Barsallo, Molino & Mulino are at the Omega Building, Ave. Samuel Lewis and Calle 53, P.O. Box: 4493, Panama 5 Republic of Panama

ABOGADOS

FBM&M

Teléfono: +507 263-5333.
Fax: +507 263-6983; 264-0181.
E-Mail: fabamm@fabamm.com
Site: http://www.fabamm.com

ORILLAC, CARLES & GUARDIA
Attorneys at Law

Roberto I. Guardia Rabell, Alexis Carles Barraza, Javier Orillac Icaza.

After working for a variety of law firms and private and government institutions, lawyers Alexis Carles Barraza, Roberto Guardia Rabell and Javier Orillac Icaza decided to open their own law firm with the purpose of offering the community a wide scope of services, with an efficient and personalized approach.

The office of lawyers Orillac, Carles & Guardia, even though it has grown as a company, is still a small firm, which permits them, among other advantages, to offer a prompt service and to treat each of the cases in a personalized manner.

A professional team to assist you

The bureau of Orillac, Carles & Guardia has expert personnel in the various fields of law, and offers legal advice to a great number of clients, among which are private individuals, Panamanian and foreign, companies, and associations, in the different areas of law that are grouped in their departments: Corporations, Commercial Law, Civil Law, Taxation, Patents, Maritime, and Trademark Registry. The firm's ethics are based on guaranteeing each client confidentiality and seriousness in the administration of all their dealings, and the assurance that the law firm partners will handle all matters personally.

Priority: Client Satisfaction

Each case at Orillac, Carles & Guardia is considered of utmost importance, whether small or large. This has been one of the main characteristics that have contributed to the stability and continuous growth of the firm.

Current efforts are centered in consolidating within the local market, as well as broadening the international market through the diversification of services and offering a wide range of options to the clients. At the same time they keep working on the continuous develpment of the company through personnel training in various areas, with the sole purpose of being able to offer clients the best quality in service.

In this firm the client may be sure that he will be dealing directly with Orillac, Carles or Guardia, that is, always with one of the partners .

Orillac, Carles & Guardia is located in the ADR Technology Tower Building, HP, Samuel Lewis Avenue and 58th Street, 7th floor, Suite #7-A. Telephones (507) 223 9957/ 8763, 263-3917/ 18, Fax 263-3924.
E-mail: orcag@orcag.com
Website: www.orcag.com
P.O. Box 83-0588, Zone 3, Panama, Republic of Panama

SUCRE ARIAS & REYES

ABOGADOS • LAWYERS

FUNDADO EN 1969

Taking care of your business

SUCRE ARIAS & REYES is a Panamanian International Law Firm characterized by its premier legal service, dynamism and long standing tradition.

With the aim of continuing the private practice first begun by Mr. Carlos Sucre C. in 1928, the Panamanian law firm SUCRE & SUCRE was founded in 1969, by the father and son partnership of Carlos Sucre C. and Carlos Sucre. Following the admittance of new partners, the firm is currently known as SUCRE ARIAS & REYES.

On June 2001, SUCRE ARIAS & REYES merged with the firm MARQUEZ & PRECIADO. This merger of the firms has strengthened and broadened the scope of the legal and professional services offered by SUCRE ARIAS & REYES to clients. To this end, our lawyers are highly qualified and recognized for their expertise and legal skills in a wide range of areas of legal practice, as well as for their extensive experience in business

advisory services. The Firm's legal team is currently made up of twenty two lawyers, eight of which are partners and over one hundred staff members.

The firm's main office is located in Panama City. The firm also has affiliated branch offices in British Virgin Islands, Bahamas and Aguilla.

Our firm's main policy and principal goal is to provide premier legal service that meets all client needs. In this sense, we pride ourselves in providing a personalized and professional service to each of our clients. In order to achieve this, the firm has formed a group of specialized Lawyers that center their professional expertise on individual fields of practice. The firm offers professional services in the following areas:
• Asset Protection
• Banking, Finance and Securities
• Commercial International Trade & Competition
• Corporate Structure and Planning
• Energy, Environmental and Natural

Resources
• Foreign Investments
• Insurance Matters
• Intellectual Property
• International Business
• Labor and Administrative Procedures
• Litigation
• Maritime
• Privatization and Government Contracts
• Taxation Matters
• Telecommunications and Technology
• Tourism and Industry

SUCRE ARIAS & REYES offices in Panama City are located at Sucre Building, 48th East street, Bella Vista, P.O. Box 6277, Panama 5, Republic of Panama.

Telephone: (507) 264-1355
Fax: (507) 264-1168.
E-mail: sucre@sucre.net,
Website: www.sucre.net

The main office building of Sucre Arias & Reyes, a reflection of the city's current style combines colonial architecture with contemporary design.

TRUST SERVICES, S.A.
Centralizing International Wealth Management

Trust Services, S.A. is Panama's specialist in offshore corporations and trust formation, providing services to professional firms and private individuals since 1981. Panama is a bridge between two oceans and Trust Services, S.A. is a bridge between two objectives: the successful planning and then implementation of a sound, secure offshore strategy. The firm is a licensed independent trust company which reached its 20th anniversary milestone in 2001, and although many changes have taken place in the offshore financial services industry during that time, the one constant for clients of Trust Services has been the standard of service. The firm has adopted the Code of Professional Conduct of the Society of Trust and Estate Practitioners in the United Kingdom, of which the Managing Director is a member.

A visit to the website www.trustservices.net will be rewarding, especially for the international and regional newsletters, "Offshore Pilot Quarterly" and "Letter from Panama" by the firm's managing director, who is a former member of the Latin America and Caribbean Banking Commission as well as a former offshore financial services regulator for the British government.

The specialist expertise of Trust Services, S.A. is unrivalled in Panama particularly in the case of common law trusts. A dedicated, trained and bilingual staff (with most senior staff having worked for the firm since the 1980s) offers clients efficiency and continuity. The firm's partners have been business associates for over 20 years and the firm's auditors for almost an equal number of years have been Deloitte and Touche.

Centralizing international wealth management under the control of specialists means that financial institutions such as Trust Services, S.A., for exam-

ple, are able to offer co-ordination of bank and investment accounts, administration, bookkeeping and liaison with other professional providers. And if Panamanian tax advice is needed, this can also be provided in-house.

Clientele is international and in many cases the partners serve as advisers (particularly in the case of trusts) offering solutions and designing structures that are architecturally sound for implementation by overseas parties. British-managed, providing similar fiduciary services to those offered in the British offshore centres, makes Trust Services, S.A. unique in Panama. It has been simplifying the complex for over two decades and offers a package, not just a product. It can, in turn, structure a corporation with bank and brokerage accounts, debit and credit cards which can be managed by a trust or foundation to complete the process of estate planning.

Continuity is guaranteed with additional protection afforded under the banking laws of Panama. The three directors and long-serving, skilled staff are qualified to deal with fiduciary, corporate, accounting and banking requirements within the confines of secure offices.

The following checklist should be followed when seeking financial services:

1 Look for licensed professionals.

2 Consider obtaining references and find out how long the service provider has been operating.

3 Take into account the calibre of management, particularly their qualifications and experience.

4 Don't base your choice of service provider on the lowest fees.

Vasco Núñez de Balboa, discoverer of the Pacific Ocean– symbol of progress and trust.

Things that are cheap can often prove to be costly in other ways.

5 Try to meet the senior personnel of the service provider before conducting business: don't just visit their website, visit them.

6 Don't ignore the need to take tax and legal advice.

What is the next step? A meeting with Trust Services, S.A. would be a good place to start and, hopefully, finish.

Balboa Plaza Building, Office 522
Balboa Avenue.
P. O. Box 0832-1630, World Trade Center, Panamá, Repúblic of Panama.
Tel.: (507):269-2438.
Fax (507) 269-9138
marketing@trustserv.com

BANCO NACIONAL DE PANAMÁ

100 years growing with the nation

Banco Nacional de Panamá, the country's first banking institution, started operations one year after the birth of the Republic. It was created on October 12, 1904 by Decree Law No. 74 of that year, with the name Banco Hipotecario y Prendario (Mortgage and Securities Bank). The institution was established as an autonomous and independent legal entity.

In its beginnings, the bank fostered the development of the cattle and agriculture industries, later becoming an entity devoted to mortgage and securities loans. This helped the country recover from the negative effects of the War of the Thousand Days, which took place in the year 1900.

In 1911, after a series of internal changes, the institution was given its current name: Banco Nacional de Panamá.

Banco Nacional de Panamá is not a central bank. However, due to legal dispositions, it carries out a number of tasks normally attributed to central banks such as being fiscal agent for government, a clearing house for commercial banks, and holding international reserves.

Banco Nacional is the Republic's financial entity *par excellence* and, in addition to the specific objectives stated in its organic law, the bank is responsible for exercising banking duties within the public sector, just as defined by Panamanian law.

As a governmental institution, Banco Nacional plays an important role in the country's economy by granting credit to private-sector producers. In special circumstances, the bank offers loans to the public sector for the purposes of developing the nation's economic and social infrastructure.

Since its creation, Banco Nacional has grown steadily, not only physically (with 58 branches, it is the largest banking chain in Panama), but through continuously preparing, upgrading and modernizing its products, services and human resources as well. The bank strives to maintain the positive corporate image

it has exhibited for almost a century.

Banco Nacional's participation in all sectors of the national economy has continued in the form of loans to the private sector totaling US$378.7 million up to December 31, 2001, which represents an increase of US$46.8 million compared to the year 2000's figures. This helps foster the development of agricultural, commercial and industrial projects, in addition to strengthening the self-supporting projects of small and medium-sized firms.

As Banco Nacional's centennial draws near, the institution prepares to join the rest of the nation in celebrating the Republic's 100th anniversary –a time of great historic significance for all Panamanians. In this context, the institution reaffirms its commitment to support the nation's social, economic and cultural components, always honoring its motto: "Banco Nacional de Panamá, It's ours".

CITIBANK⊕®

Citibank: Investing in Panama since 1904

Citibank first opened in Panama on August 17, 1904 under the name of International Banking Corporation. Eleven years later, the National City Bank of New York purchased IBC' and changed the name of the bank, which was later relocated to La Merced building, in the "Casco Viejo", Panama City's old quarter.

Since then, Citibank has been an important part of Panama's history, consistently offering the best solutions to the financial needs of the Panamanian community. The bank offers a complete range of products, from basic, traditional services such as credit cards with special benefits and personal loans, to investments and all types of complex solutions needed for corporate operations. All of this is done with the support of Citigroup, one of the world's most important financial institutions, operating in over 100 countries.

Innovation and leadership are two terms that describe Citibank, the first bank to offer ATMs and electronic banking. These services have transformed the way traditional banking affairs are conducted, offering new alternatives for completing transactions and monitoring accounts in a rapid, efficient and secure manner. These services are complemented by the bank's Customer Services Center, which operates 24 hours a day, seven days a week and the excellent attention of its staff.

It is important to mention that part of the philosophy of Citibank, N.A., is to contribute to the wellbeing of the communities it serves. Therefore, Citibank has devoted the last 98 years in Panama to improving the quality of life and contributing to the development of Panama. An example of this is seen in the bank's contributions to Operación Sonrisa (Operation Smile), Junior Achievement, COSPAE, the Simón Bolívar School, and the Rotary Club's children's soccer team, among other projects. These contributions have been supported by the bank's employees, who actively participate as volunteers.

Throughout the years, Citibank has demonstrated its commitment to supporting the guilds and associations in which its employees participate. In addition to this, the bank has been among the founding institutions of the Chamber of Commerce and Industry of Panama, the Banking Association and the American Chamber of Commerce. The bank's officers have served in a number of highly responsible positions in these organizations.

Citibank has served Panama for almost 100 years, shaping the history of a nation that has trusted "a North American bank with a Panamanian heart." The bank will continue to make history for decades to come.

A solid financial group of specialized companies

Founded in 1972, the Banco Continental de Panamá has 30 years of experience in the national banking arena and ranks as the third private bank in Panama. It is a bank that has grown and evolved through the years and today boasts a first class team of more than 650 employees guided by firm principles and dedicated to offering its clients advice, individual treatment, confidentiality and quality in all the products and services on offer.

The aim is to develop and cultivate lasting relationships, anticipating clients' needs both on a national and international level.

In October 2002 the bank had assets in excess of US$1.9 billion , a credit portfolio of US$1.2 billion, a net worth of more than US$ 180 million and deposits of US$1.4 billion, all of which makes the bank a solid financial group.

For greater convenience, the bank offers clients national coverage which includes a network of 16 branches and automatic tellers throughout the country.

Banco Continental consists of a group of specialized companies each tailored to cater to the financial needs of its clients.

Banco Alemán Platina: with 27 years of experience in export financing, Banco Alemán Platina merged with Banco Continental in October 2002 as part of the bank's strategy to enter new industries, offer new products and services and widen its business base in the markets of Central America, Mexico and Colombia where Banco Alemán Platina has representative offices. Banco Alemán Platina will operate as a subsidiary of Banco Continental and will develop traditional banking activities, both at the corporate and personal banking levels.

Norfolk & Hampton Bank: Created under the laws of Grand Cayman, this bank offers clients international banking services such as deposits, trusts and current accounts payable through the United States.

Bantal Brokers: The main activity of this firm is securities brokerage, which entails trading Panamanian and international securities. Such securities can be stocks, bonds, short-term tools, options,

Banco Continental Building on 50th Street, Panama City.

BANKS

notes and mutual funds, among others. In addition to this, Bantal Brokers represents the main mutual fund families, which can be acquired through the company's offices. This firm offers consulting services to companies and private individuals regarding financial and stock trading matters.

Leasing Empresarial: offers financial leasing for equipment both in and outside Panama. With the establishment of financial leasing programs under flexible terms, Leasing Empresarial offers a financing system that adjusts to the needs of its clients.

Naka: is one of the most important

credit entities on the national scene, offering personal loans especially for retirees, teachers, nurses, and other public-sector employees in Panama. Naka has 14 branch offices throughout the country.

Product: Banco Continental offers a wide range of traditional and innovative products designed to cover the specific needs of individual and corporate clients. Services include savings accounts, current accounts, time deposits, mortgage loans, car and personal loans, credit and debit cards. The bank also offers financial structuring and Trust Services, local and international investment accounts, repurchase agree-

ments and products created for all types of business such as Cash Management, lines of credit, overdraft facilities, medium and long term loans, leasing, structuring, distribution and investment advisory services for commercial issues and public and private bonds.

Services: among the services offered to clients are:

Internet Banking (BCnet and E-b@p) which allows client access to banking accounts and services via internet, as well as allowing transfers between accounts in a simple and secure manner.

Banking by Telephone where clients can request loan quotations, credit cards and third party payments.

E view, online access system which allows clients to see their international investment accounts.

Banco Continental de Panama is located on 50th street and Aquilino de la Guardia Avenue.
Telephone: (507) 215-7000
Fax: (507) 215-7134.
P.O. Box: 135, Panama 9A,
Panama City.

To learn more about Banco Continental de Panama please visit www.bcontinental.com

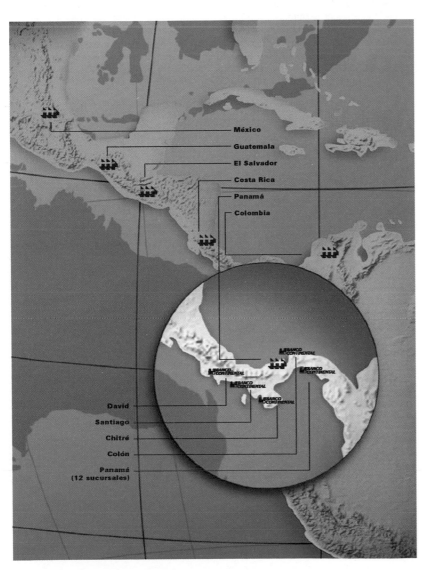

Branch Network of Banco Continental and Banco Aleman Platina.

Investing in High Technology
Atomic Capital: New Firm Breaking Records!

The explosive growth of high technology in the late 1990's provided the springboard for the launch of a new offshore hedge fund that has achieved surprising results and caught the attention of investors in Panama.

The firm is Atomic Capital S.A. and was founded on December 4, 1998 in the Republic of Panama. Its funds are actively managed by Humberto Lopez Jr., a Magna Cum Laude graduate of the University of Miami. Mr. Lopez is a young entrepreneur whose trading philosophy has been derived from a collection of experiences at the University of Miami Business School, SEGUMAR, S.A., and his intensive research on the investment strategies of the most successful financiers and entrepreneurs of our time: Warren Buffett, George Soros, Peter Lynch, Benjamin Graham, John Templeton, Bernard Baruch, Sam Walton, Bill Gates, Michael Dell, John Doerr, Henry Kravis, Masayoshi Son, and Li Ka-Shing.

Mr. Lopez began trading high-tech stocks for his own portfolio before founding Atomic Capital and became a regular winner of investment competitions organized by MarketPlayer.com. During his tenure, the fund has achieved double-digit returns since inception by going long during the Internet boom in 1999 and mostly shorting the market since March of 2000. He is also the author of several works on negotiation, security analysis, and solar energy.

The following are two questions frequently asked by potential investors:

Is it safe to invest in a U.S. technology sector that is increasingly volatile?

Yes, if you are a long-term investor in companies that have proven to be consistent over-achievers. Furthermore, though the best companies seem to be perennially overvalued there are numerous opportunities during the year where

due to temporary market or sector disruptions one is able to purchase stellar companies at prices that are inexpensive relative to their growth rates. Notwithstanding, a highly volatile investment environment requires the ability to protect ones capital and profit from occasional market downturns; the company has successfully achieved this through strategic short sales.

What is the firm's investment style?

The fund looks for companies at the forefront of their field that are developing new products and new markets with the potential to significantly increase profits. In addition, the positions are actively traded in order to capture gains both on the way up, as the market discovers it and on the way down, when the market sentiment changes. Investment categories include:

High-Tech: All sectors, from software to semiconductors and Internet to wireless communications.

Renewable Energy: Leading edge companies in the fields of photovoltaics, fuel cells and energy storage.

Biotechnology: Biopharmaceutical companies with the mission to discover, develop, manufacture and market new gene-and protein-based drugs.

Exchange Traded Funds (ETFs): A basket of stocks that provide quick exposure to different sectors or market indices such as the NASDAQ-100 or the S&P 500.

ATOMIC CAPITAL S.A.

For performance details, please contact:
Atomic Capital S.A.
Suite No. 386 APDO 0832-2745 World Trade Center, Republic of Panama,
Phone: (507) 315-1463 • Fax: (507) 315-0843 e-mail: atomic@sinfo.net

PanAmerica Capital Group, Inc.

PanAmerica Capital Group, Inc., a Panamanian-based full service securities brokerage and investment house, provides its clientele with a diversity of international investment and wealth-enhancement vehicles. As a Central American correspondent of the Pershing Division of DLJ Securities Corp., a wholly owned subsidiary of Credit Suisse/First Boston, PanAmerica provides its clientele with asset safety and security within a private and confidential framework.

PanAmerica is a licensed Casa de Valores or "Investment House" within the jurisdiction of Panama and as such represents a host of other internationally respected financial institutions such as: Alliance Capital Management, AIM International Funds, Bank of America Advisors, Janus International, MFS Meridian, Morgan Stanley/Dean Witter, Oppeheimer, Putnam, Scudder and Selligman to name a few.

Through Pershing, PanAmerica can execute and process securities transactions of all sizes in more than 27 major markets across the globe. Pershing has in excess of US$400 billion on account with more than 6 million accounts and processes 12-15 per cent of the daily volume on the NYSE.

Within this framework PanAmerica Capital Group focuses on providing specialized advisory, trading and asset custody services to high net-worth individuals and institutions. All customer accounts are individually titled and held in custody by Pershing, although client information resides within the jurisdiction of Panama.

PanAmerica follows the NASD guidelines of service and quality standards to ensure the highest level of customer satisfaction. With a full staff of multi-lingual investment advisors, they offer complete account services allowing you to efficiently manage and access your account and its assets 24 hours a day/seven days a week, anywhere in the world.

Clients of PanAmerica have encoded online access to their accounts through Pershing's NetExchange Client™ and can perform transactions on a real-time basis from any computer anywhere in the world.

PanAmerica Capital Group also provides its clientele with ProCash™, a complete asset management account that consolidates a client's money market accounts, CDs, stock and bond accounts, margin accounts, MasterCard™ debit card services, checking accounts, and worldwide ATM access all under the umbrella of one brokerage account.

Benefits:
• Encoded online access and real-time trade execution

• ProCash Plus™, the complete financial organizer
• Credit extensions and margin at U.S. interest rates.
• Corporate and personal checking accounts
• International tax-exempt money market funds
• Corporate and personal MasterCard™ debit card services with ATM access at over 80,000 locations worldwide
• CDs insured by FDIC
• The highest level of SIPC & excess account protection available

Spectrum of Financial Services:
• Money market accounts
• FDIC insured time deposits
• US Government bonds
• U.S. agency bonds (Fannie Mae's)
• U.S. investment and speculative grade corporate bonds
• Emerging market sovereign and corporate bonds
• Brady bonds
• Offshore mutual funds
• Offshore hedge funds
• Managed portfolios
• Trading advisory
• Common and preferred stock
• Options & derivatives
• Private equity participation

PanAmerica Capital Group, Inc.
World Trade Center, 12th floor
P.O. Box: 832-2522
Panamá Rep. of Panama
Tel: (507) 213-8874, Fax: (507) 213-8875
info@panamerica-group.com

Correspondent: Pershing division of DLJ Securities Corp., a wholly owned subsidiary of Credit Suisse/First Boston – Member: SIPC

Bankers: HSBC Bank PLC
                Bank of America

Auditors: Deloitte & Touche

Advisors: Greenberg Traurig, LLP
                Quijano & Associates

Member: Panamanian Assoc. of Securities Brokers.
                American Chamber of Commerce.
                Panamanian Chamber of Commerce.
                Panamanian Association of Business Executives.

Steamship Agent at the Panama Canal
C. FERNIE & CO., S.A.

The Steamship Agent C. Fernie & Co., S.A. was established in the Atlantic port of Cristobal in 1920 by Cyril Fernie, a native of Liverpool, England.

When Mr. Fernie first established the agency, among the ships he represented were vessels enroute from Norwegian ports and the United Kingdom through the Panama Canal to the North Pacific coasts of the United States and Canada.

During the Second World War, Fernie & Co. handled most of their old Norwegian, Danish, British, and U.S. customers whose vessels had been placed on government service. Many of these ships were tankers carrying oil from Aruba to the U.S. Navy in the Pacific. Since the war, Fernie's business has gradually increased. It now has fully manned offices to cover the main ports in the Republic of Panama. The head office is located in Cristóbal, with an additional office at Balboa. In addition to standard agency work, the

Fernie business also represents most of the world's major Protection and Indemnity Clubs.

Another example of Fernie's vigorous competition and close involvement with all maritime affairs in the Republic is that in the late 1980's Fernie & Co., S.A. worked very closely with Smit International Harbour Towage, of Rotterdam, and on behalf of that company, obtained the harbor towage concession in the ports of Cristobal and Balboa under the name Servicios Fernie, S.A.

Fernie's most recent project is to attract cruise ships to call at the Atlantic side. The company pioneered a project to utilize, with the co-operation of the Panama Canal Authority, the Gatún Yacht Club on Gatún Lake as a cruise ship "port of call". Ships transiting Gatún Locks may arrange to anchor in Gatún Lake, where launches shuttle passengers a short distance to the lakeside club. Tourists are welcomed to step

ashore for a close-up look of the Canal and its surrounding areas. Fun filled activities and relaxation opportunities are offered right on the banks of the Canal: folkloric dancing, sampling of local dishes, and the chance to shop for hand-made local handicrafts. Before returning onboard, passengers can also enjoy unique touring experiences such as the Chagres River Eco Cruise, the Fort and Forest Tour, or the Bird Watching Tour.

For the first half of the year 2000, Fernie scheduled more than twenty-five cruise ship visits to Gatún Yacht Club and the Panama Canal.

All of the company's offices are on a 24-hour a day basis and have full telephone, telex, and VHF communications. P.O.Box 212, Balboa, Panama, tel: 433-2494, fax: 441-7504, e-mail: fernops@cfernie.com, webpage: www.cfernie.com

ASSOCIATED STEAMSHIP AGENTS, S.A.
(PAYNE & WARDLAW AND W. ANDREWS & CO.)

Associated Steamship Agents, S.A. is a locally owned company which can trace its origins on the Isthmus of Panama back to 1889 when Captain William Andrews opened a Steamship Agency, W. Andrews & Co., in the City of Colon.

With the opening of the Panama Canal, Captain Clifford Payne who was formerly a Captain with the Pacific Steam Navigation Company and Mr. Robert Wardlaw, who worked for the Panama Railroad, opened an Agency in Balboa in 1914, known as Payne & Wardlaw.

Both Captain Andrews and Captain Payne worked closely toge-ther and when Captain Andrews returned to England in the early 1920's he left his business in Captain Payne's charge and on his death in 1926 bequeathed it to his good friend, Captain Payne.

The two companies retained their separate identities until 1975, when they merged to become Associated Steamship Agents, but for historical reasons continue to use the two original company names in their present day letterhead.

The company maintains offices in both Balboa and Cristobal, where their operations departments work 24 hours a day, 7 days a week, responding to the needs of their principals from around the world who use the Canal and ports in the Republic of Panama.

In addition to representing many ship owners and operators, Associated Steamship Agents are also the agents for Lloyd's of London at the Canal and undertake hull and machinery surveys on behalf of underwriters from Europe, the United States and the Far East.

ASSOCIATED STEAMSHIP AGENTS, S.A.
Williamson Place #798X, La Boca, Balboa, Republic of Panama
P.O. Box 2007, Balboa, Republic of Panama
Tel (507) 211-9400. Fax: (507) 211-9450
E-mail: asa@shipsagent.com   www.shipsagent.com

Left to right: Alexei Oduber, Administrative Manager; Charles M. Langman, President; Gian Carlo Calvosa, Operations; Edmund A. Blennerhassett, Chairman; Fernando Chang, Operations Manager Atlantic; John Bamber, Director; Alessandro Risi, Operations Manager Pacific; Enrique Lindo, Finance Manager.

Colón Container Terminal forges ahead

Expansion to phase 2 will upgrade facilities

With an excellent gowth record behind it, Colon Container Terminal was poised, at the end of 2002, to begin its second phase of development to place it in an even better position to attract new shipping business to Panama's Caribbean gateway.

Located in Coco Solo North, on the Atlantic side of the Panama Canal, Colon Container Terminal covers 25 hectares and incorporates 612 meters of quay with 14 meters of depth of water and five Mitsubishi panamax gantry cranes capable of serving simultaneously two panamax vessels.

Volume through the port rose significantly in the third and fourth quarters of 2001 and although global recession and the September 11 terrorist attacks disturbed the market, CCT closed the year with a gain in volume of 50,000 teu compared to the previous year. The trend

continued into the first quarter of 2002 when thoughput grew by 31% compared to the same period of the previous year.

"We are optimistic because the global economy is slowly recovering", says CCT president Eric Wang. Evergreen, CCT's main customer and one of its eight clients including Unigreen, added a new service to the West Coast of South America in May 2002. The four-vessel weekly service will call at Colombia, Ecuador, Peru, Chile and back to the Colon terminal. And East Asia exports to the Caribbean are picking up which will boost CCT's activity, as the port is the natural transshipment hub for all steamship companies in the region for containers and dry bulk.

Colon Container Terminal is ready to move forward and proceed with Phase II of its concession. The expansion plans will increase present capacity

of 500,000teu to 750,000teu, in the next couple of years. "We expect more container volume in this year and next", forecasts Mr. Wang.

The Phase II project includes the construction of an additional 360 meter berth and a 12-hectare yard area. It is hoped that work can be completed by end of 2004. The expansion will upgrade the service including terminal and shipping operations with the addition of two or three post-panamax cranes.

In November 2001, Colon Container Terminal received the ISO 9002. The classification did not come in a fortune cookie but was the result of a long time quality service. It also recognized excellent port operations and personnel. CCT is the only terminal in Panama to have it. CCT is open to all shipping companies that want to use it.

PORTS

Manzanillo International Terminal-Panama, S.A.

Most productive port in Latin America

Manzanillo International Terminal-Panama, S.A. is strategically located on the Atlantic side of Panama in the Colon Free Zone, the largest free trade zone in the Western Hemisphere. Within a few kilometers of the Canal entrance, MIT offers reliable port services to the shipping lines transiting the Panama Canal or serving the Caribbean region. An investment of over 300 million dollars, sophisticated computer systems managing all aspects of vessel and terminal operations, a well-trained labor force with more than 700 employees, and impressive facilities and equipment have helped make MIT the largest and most productive container transshipment hub in Latin America.

MIT-Panama is a joint venture between SSA Panama Inc. and the Motta and Heilbron families.

FACILITIES AND SERVICES:

To provide the highest quality service and only five minutes away from trans-isthmian highway linking Colon and Panama cities, MIT offers outstanding facilities, including the following:

- 1,239 contiguous meters of container berth (2.5m MSL)
- 200 meters of Ro-Ro/ Breakbulk berth (2.5 m MSL)
- 25 meters of Ro-Ro ramp (1.75m MSL)
- Dedicated breakwater opening, separate from the Panama Canal entrance
- 14 meters of draft in the access channel
- 13 meters of draft alongside the berths (capacity for 15 meters)
- 600 meters of turning basin
- Two Super Post Panamax rail-mounted gantry cranes (50LT)
- Six Post Panamax rail-mounted gantry cranes (50LT)
- Two Panamax rail-mounted gantry cranes (40LT)
- Container Equipment Maintenance (CEM) services and 500 connections for refrigerated containers
- Highest level security in compliance with standards of the U.S. Customs Service
- On-site office accommodation for steamship lines
- Near-dock rail facilities
- Lighting and security for operations 24 hours a day

WORK FORCE: The labor force at MIT-Panama is a great source of pride. To date, MIT has provided more than 700 direct jobs. Furthermore, from each direct job the port provides, five indirect jobs are created, generating a considerable injection to the economy of the country.

PRODUCTIVITY: In 1995, MIT-Panama was rated as one of the top 10 most efficient ports in the world by Containerization International, and for 1999 and 2000, was awarded the prize of "The Port of the Year for Outstanding Performance" by Caribbean Shipping Association. Averaging over 40 moves per hour per, MIT-Panama is certainly the most productive container port in Latin America.

VOLUMES: Of the cargo that MIT-Panama handles, roughly 70% is transshipment, 25% is Colon Free Zone cargo, and 5% of the cargo is for Panamanian consumption (cargo that enters the Panamanian fiscal territory). In 2000, the terminal handled 1,015,000 TEUS (twenty foot equivalent unit), becoming the first port in Latin America that handled over a 1 million TEUS.

HIGH RISK ZONE: MIT-Panama is certified by the Ministry of Agricultural Development (MIDA) as a Quarantine High Risk Area. This certification allows MIT-Panama to handle agricultural and animal cargoes.

WAREHOUSING SERVICES:

MIT-CFS offers several services for consolidated and breakbulk cargo, with a warehousing facility of more than 15,000 cubic meters.

ADDITIONAL SERVICES

Direct access gate to Colon Free Zone.
Container Equipment Maintenance (CEM).
Office space for customers and all government agencies.
Private pilots, tugs, and bunkers available through agents.

Tels.: (507) 430-9800 (507) 430-9900. Fax: (507) 430-9809
P.O. Box 320039, Colon Free Zone, Republic of Panama.
E-mail: info@mitpan.com
Webpage: http://www.mitpan.com

Alianza Viva

The strongest and most visionary grouping in communications

Alianza Viva a Panamanian company, leader in IP communications . Its robust local network offers private circuit voice, video and data services from Panama to Colon by using its own failure-proof infrastructure. Without a doubt, it is the most important competitor. Alianza Viva has made major global agreements with different providers, utilizing international fiber optic networks, thus offering security, quality and speed in telecommunication services.

Alianza Viva will enter the telephone market in 2003 to offer local, national and international long distance services to the public. Using high technology and latest-generation equipment the company will satisfy the needs of communications in Panama with excellent voice quality which will benefit the customer.

The consortium known today as Alianza Viva has strengthened its position with the launching of a holding company, which, without a doubt is the country's strongest and most visionary grouping in the communications field.

Alianza Viva was formed by the following companies: Net Direct, S.A., a provider of wireless and fiber optics, last-mile links; MetroCall, S.A., a company offering fiber optics and satellite international links and Net2Net considered the leading and fastest-growing company in Panama in regards to Internet-based communication solutions, boasting a solid infrastructure, both in Panama and abroad. They have recently created a fiber optics highway in the Colón Free Zone. In addition to this, the consortium

Attention to clients 24 hours a day, seven days a week.

The most complete network of international connections in America.

www.alianzaviva.com

features a Hosting Center capable of hosting a large number of servers, using the highest technological standards available.

Alianza Viva has two links with a 155-Mbps bandwidth. With this bandwidth capacity, the consortium is able to satisfy the current communication demands of the Republic of Panama. Alianza Viva also boasts a highly-trained workforce that offers exceptional service 24 hours a day, seven days a week.

The services that Alianza Viva offers are:

Network Access

Viva Wireless Premium Access provides companies with Internet access through wireless or optical fiber from your LAN (local area network) to Alianza Viva's network. They offer robust and reliable connections using ATM or Frame Relay protocols and advanced IP technologies.

Web Hosting

The solution for reliable, secure and affordable shared hosting of websites.

Guaranteed 24-hour online availability. For this service Alianza Viva has created an exclusive Web Hosting environment which includes high quality hardware, reliability and high-speed Internet connectivity.

Co-Location services

The company offers connections with the flexible bandwidth that meets the client's needs. These range from 128Kb to 155Mb, and from 1/4 rack to rack equipment. The clients can choose among several levels of guaranteed bandwith to ensure optimum performance.

Private Networks

If you require privacy between your offices or branch stores, Alianza Viva's network offers secure links while maintaining good data, video and voice communication. It is possible to handle a wide range of broad bandwidth to obtain the maximum speed and necessary privacy.

International Links

Alianza Viva offers solutions to clients' international communication needs, with highly reliable and secure optical or satellite links. With the most complete network of international connections in America, using their own and their associates' resources, they carry the client's information to anywhere in the continent and beyond.

Tel.: 206-3000, Fax: 269-9177
info@alianzaviva.com

Staff of Alianza Viva at the company's headquarters at Bal Harbour Plaza, Paitilla

High quality hardware and robust, reliable connections.

BELLSOUTH

BellSouth Panama: Pioneers

BellSouth, pioneer in Panama's cellular industry, began operations in 1996, installing the first 100% digital network of the Americas (including U.S.A.) with the latest digital technology available TDMA; (Time Division Multiple Access), placing Panama at the forefront of cellular communications.

In 1998, BellSouth launched the first prepaid cellular service in the country, offering an option to the Panamanian consumers and providing them with a viable alternative for their personal communications.

Once again, BellSouth confirmed its leadership in the wireless telecommunications sector by installing on December 2002 the only Third Generation (3G) Network in Panama and the first 3G Network in Latin America with national coverage by offering CDMA 20001X (Code Division Multiple Access) service.

With the opening of the telecommunications market in January 2003, BellSouth enhances its service offering with the introduction of international long distance, national long distance, public telephony and fixed phones services in addition to its cellular and internet offering.

Availability and service

BellSouth is committed to offer a top quality service catering to the needs and requirements of its customers by offering the best coverage in the Interamerican Highway from Paso Canoas through Chepo, including Panama City, the Panama Canal area, the Transisthmian Highway to Colon City, as well as the areas of Volcan/Cerro Punta, Boquete, Bocas del Toro and the Azuero Peninsula. Customer needs are met through ten modern Customer Centers in a network that includes offices in the cities of Panama, Colon, David, Chorrera, Santiago and Chitre.

Throughout its six years of opera-

tions in Panama, BellSouth has established itself as the leading wireless service provider in the country by offering new products and services that have enriched the life of the Panamanian community. The main offices of

BellSouth in Panama City are located at Centro Magna, Calle 51 Este y Manuel Maria Icaza. Main telephone 265-0955. Fax number 265-0333. Webpage www.bellsouth.com.pa

Sales executives assisting customers in Service Centers.

Cintel and Western Union –symbols of trust

Without complications, in cash, in minutes.

Cintel Corporation serves as an agent of Western Union Financial Services in Panama and is the leader in the market of personal money remittances on the Isthmus.

Founded by Mr. Jaime Lacayo in 1991, it has organized and developed a net of more than 65 offices throughout the country to service the money transfer market from and to Panama, connecting with more than 200 countries in the world.

In February of 2002, Cintel inaugurated a new office in Plaza Concordia, situated in the heart of the banking area of Panama City. The major function of this office is to fulfill the orders of transfers and payments through Western Union. This office also offers a modern and fast service of internet to the public, as well as national and international telephone services.

Another service is that of Western Union Quick Pay, which enables the customer to make payments in the United States, such as: credit cards, university expenses, medical bills, emergency situations or even your Saks Fifth Avenue Card.

Cintel Corporation is a family business that maintains as a priority excellence in service 24 hours a day, 365 days of the year, because all clients expect their transfer to reach its destination; executed without complications, in cash and......in minutes. For the customer, Cintel and Western Union are symbols of trust.

Website: www.wupanama.com

New office in Plaza Concordia.

HOSPITAL NACIONAL

Medical Center with the highest level of technology located in the heart of Panama City

Serving the community since 1973

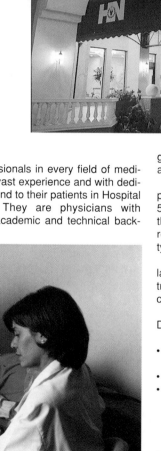

Hospital Nacional has been distinguished for many years by its continuing efforts to offer efficient medical services, supported by the most current technology and assuring the highest level of warm and caring attention towards the patients.

Professionals in every field of medicine, with vast experience and with dedication, attend to their patients in Hospital Nacional. They are physicians with excellent academic and technical back-grounds, who received their education and training in Panama and abroad.

Through the hospitalization and out-patient medical services, an average of 500 patients are attended to each day in the hospital. Many are surprized by the resort-like facilities, spaciousness, beauty and comfort.

Hospital Nacional boasts a clinical laboratory with the strictest quality controls. The Blood Bank is the best in the country.

The Radiology and Imaging Department is equipped with:

* A Tesla 1.5 MRI (Magnetic Resonance Imaging)
* Helicoidal CT/Scan.
* Room of Hemodinamia with an excellent angiograph for the treatment of cardiac catheterisms, positioning of stent and embolizations.
* Cardiac Electrophysiology.
* Digital Fluoroscopy
* Special Three dimension Ultrasound.
* Advanced general Ultrasound.
* Nuclear Medicine.

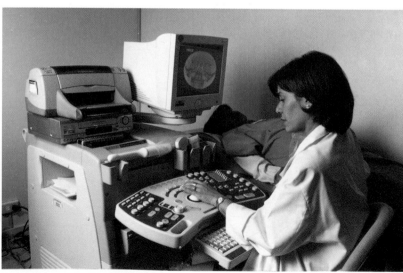

3D Ultrasound.

HEALTH

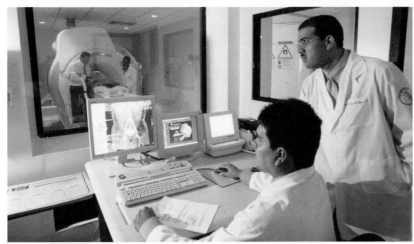

Magnetic resonance imaging, 1.5 Tesla. Cholangiography, angiography and perfusion - difusion diagnostic imaging with extraordinary image.

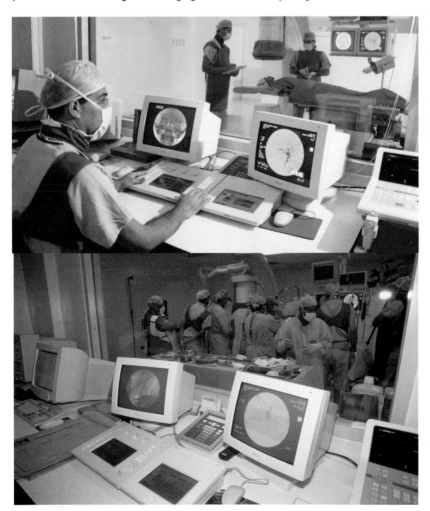

Also located in the hospital are the National Institute of Cardiology, Neumology Services, Physical Therapy and Rehabilitation, Hyperbaric Medicine, the National Center of Genetics, a mammography clinic, Center of Diagnosis and Fetal Therapy, and the Laboratory of Neurophysiology, among others.

The doctors can perform all types of surgery, including complex procedures like open heart surgery, organ transplants and intrauterine transfusions.

The Emergency Room operates 24 hours a day and all the personnel have received the proper certifications (ATLS: Advanced Trauma Life Support and ACLS: Advanced Cardiac Life Support).

Hospital Nacional has also developed diverse committees such as:

- Nosocomiales Infections Committee;
- Code Blue;
- Teaching Committee/ Continuing Education;
- Credentials Committee;
- Disaster Response Committee;

Hospital Nacional has an agreement with Care Group, an integrated healthcare network which includes several Harvard Medical School affiliated institutions, for support and assistance with continuing medical education (CME).

Hemodinamic laboratory - cardiac catherisms, angioplasties, stent placements.

HN

HOSPITAL NACIONAL

centro médico integral

Ave. Cuba, Calles 38 y 39, Ciudad de Panamá Tel.: (507) 207-8100/ (507) 207-8102 Fax: (507) 207-8337 Apdo. 6-2200, El Dorado, Panamá e-mail: mercadeo@hospitalnacional.com Website: www.hospitalnacional.com

CENTRO MEDICO PAITILLA

Centro Médico Paitilla
A prestigious private hospital

Founded in 1975, Centro Médico Paitilla is an essential element in the development of Panama's health sector. It is a private hospital that provides tertiary attention. It has a prestigious group of around 300 professionals of the most diversed medical specialties and a working force of around 400 employees. It was created to offer the community medical and hospital services of excellence.

The center stands out for its technological leadership and modern facilities. The most prominent among these is the intensive care unit for adults and newborns, and the Paitilla Oncology Center, inaugurated in 2000. The hospital has 170 beds and is supplied with the latest diagnosis, treatment, surgery and emergency equipment, including the hyperbaric chamber, magnetic resonance, laparoscopy, helicoidal computerized tomograghy, digital angiofluoroscopy for cardiac catheterization and coronary angioplasty with stent placements, etc.

The quality of Centro Médico Paitilla is guaranteed by its affiliation to well-known international health institutions, such as "The Methodist Hospital" in Houston, Texas; "The Cleveland Clinic Foundation" in Cleveland, Ohio, and the "Fundación Jiménez Díaz", in Madrid, Spain.

It was honored in 2001 with the "Royal Crown to Excellence" award, granted by the Marketing Worldwide Organization, whose headquarters are in Mexico City, for its excellence in the quality of medical and hospital services.

The philosophy of the hospital has remained immutable since its origins, and it is described by the following phrase, which inspired and motivated the founders of Centro Médico Paitilla and still inspires those who work for the enterprise: "In this Center, offered to the Panamanian community, are crystallized the dreams and efforts of few, for the recovery and preservation of the health of many."

The hospital is located at Balboa Ave. and 53th Street, one of the most important avenues in Panama City. P.O. Box 7503 Zone 5, Panama, Republic of Panama. Phone Number 265-8800. Fax: 265-8861.
E-mail: cmp@pty.com.

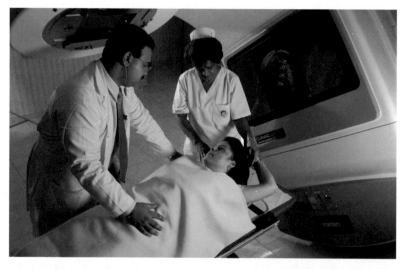

Experience makes the difference

81 years

Serving its customers

C. G. De Haseth & Cía., S.A.
Botica El Javillo, S.A.
Droguería el Javillo, S.A.

Grupo De Haseth was founded by Christiaan G. de Haseth E. at about the beginning of the new Panama Republic. It is now made up of many companies, among them de Haseth & Cia S.A., Drogueria El Javillo, S.A. and Botica El Javillo. Today they can boast 81 years of experience in the market of representation and distribution of pharmaceutical products of famous laboratories. Presently they represent 40 laboratories & consortiums such as:

Alcon, Arsal, Atral Cipan, Apotex, Ancla, Algodón Superior, Cia. Farmaceutica Americana, Biochemie, Elli Lilly, Glaxosmithkline (Pharma y OTC), Grunenthal, Halgam, Interfarma, Janssen-Cilag, Johnson & Johnson, Kimberly Clark, Kincoral, Lafsa, Lacofa, Laboratorio Javillo, Merck Pharma, Merck Químicos, Merck Diagnóstica, Palm, Prieto, Pura Vitta, Pfizer, Rigar, Roche, Rotta, Rowe, Sanofi, Synthelabo, Schering Plough, Senosiain, SSL Américas, Wyeth, Unipharm y Yercu

The company has a motivated workforce, innovative products, an enterprising sales force, an effective marketing strategy and dynamic administration. This well-balanced combination of factors has put the group in the position it holds today.

The sales force of the group for the private market is made up of a sales manager, the supervisor and 24 representatives including salespersons and promotors at a national level, as well as two salespersons for chemical products and one salesperson for the diagnostic line. The salesforce in the rest of the country (Central & Chiriqui) reside in their areas of work, enabling them to attend to business matters immediately. The salesforce has a radio communication system with national coverage which facilitates order-placing and deliveries with the group's fleet of 16 delivery vehicles.

In the Institutional market the group has a specialized department with a sales manager and specialized personnel with vast experience in institutionalized sales procedures, having contacts at all levels of the different health institutions in the republic. Business is handled at the highest level of the company, maintaining the confidentiality of the represented laboratories.

There is also a distribution system of specialized products for private clinics at a national level, maintaining products at the correct temperature and observing the technical procedures required in these delicate transactions.

Grupo De Haseth in its commitment

to offer better service to its customers every day, including an excellent relationship with its representatives, maintains the philosophy of total quality.

As an avant-garde company it has created new activities in the market such as the Pharmacy Fair, the seventh version of in January of 2003 along with the centenary celebrations. This fair, year after year, has grown to be the leading event at a national level in the pharmaceutical market where customers can acquire products of excellent quality at bargain prices to supply their inventories at the beginning of the year.

Towards the future.

The growing Panamanian market and constant evolution of pharmaceutical laboratories worldwide make this a dynamic field with ample scope for development. That is why Grupo De Haseth aims to be the leading company in the pharmaceutical distribution field, using its teamwork to make sure that all the products of the represented laboratories reach the customers in a timely manner. The company looks towards the future growth of the market, being a leader in technological advances and constantly improving procedures and customer service.

"The oldest distributor with the most innovative ideas".

De Haseth Plaza   Vía Cincuentenario final, tel. 224-7000/9644   www.grupodehaseth.com; e-mail: dehaseth@psi.net.pa

REAL ESTATE

Altos del María
Living in the mountains–close to the city

An interesting trend in real estate in recent years has been the growth of "country living" developments outside Panama City. Leading this movement is Altos del Maria, a mountain project developed by the Real Estate Division of Grupo Melo, founded in 1980 with the object of developing land and selling lots in the cool-weather mountainous areas of the Republic of Panama.

These developments are proving very popular with retirees from abroad who are looking for a good climate, splendid views and "first world" amenities not too far from the city. There is also a demand from Panamanians living in the city who seek a country home for week-ends and holidays.

The first important and highly successful project of the Real Estate Division was Los Altos de Cerro Azul, located only 45 minutes from Panama City and within the limits of the Chagres National Park. Here Grupo Melo created a unique country housing development complex, compatible with the principles of environmental protection. To date over 1,800 lots have been sold of which more than 600 included homes.

In 1994 another mountain resort community, Aires del Gaital, was established in El Valle of Anton, an area famous for its eco-tourist attractions and cool climate. One hundred and nineteen lots were sold in a relatively short time.

The success of these developments led to the ambitions project of Altos del Maria in beautiful mountains of the Cordillera in the region of Sorá. This was begun In 1995, after a number of location and environment impact studies had been made. Altos del Maria, is approximately one hour and thirty minutes drive from Panama City along a modern, four lane highway to the town of Bejuco and from there a short drive into the mountains.

Located between 1,400 and 3,300 feet above sea level and with a climate of approximately 63°F, the landscape surrounding Altos del Maria is characterized by rivers, ponds, waterfalls and mountains with breath-taking, panoramic views of both the Pacific and Atlantic oceans from its highest points.

The company has developed a diversity of lots ranging from 1,000 to 3,000 square meters, without altering the natural topography of the mountains. The parcels can be flat, sloped, high or low according to taste.

There are four separate developments: El Valle del Encanto, with 101 lots at the foot of majestic Cerro Picacho, went for sale in October 1998 and sold out in its first year.

Valle del Laurel, with 135 lots, surrounded by impressive rivers and waterfalls, was the second sector.

El Valle de la Toscana, with 211 lots, offers panoramic views of the Pacific Ocean.

Altos del Piamonte, 3,300 feet above sea level, finished in January 2001, is the most important project. Lots range between 1,700 and 3000 square feet with magnificent mountain landscape. A total of 25 km(15 miles) of asphalt roads have been constructed throughout the project. Three aqueducts, under the management of the company, provide drinking water. All of the segments have electricity, street lighting and telephone service. There is also 24 hour security and entrance check points.

Supermarkets restaurants gas stations and beaches all lie within easy reach of Altos del Maria, along the Panamerican Highway, only 12 miles from Sorá.

ALTOS del MARÍA

For more information: Telephones (507) 260-0290, 260-2662. Fax: (507) 260-1557 PostOffice Box: 8-125, Zona 8, Panamá Rep. of Panamá
www.altosdelmaria.com

CONGLOMERATE

EL MACHETAZO
A legend in its own time
one man's philosophy created this business empire

New El Machetazo superstore at the "24 de Diciembre" district near Tocumen to the east of the city.

This is the story of an immigrant family which has built a commercial empire in Panama. It is the story of one man's business philosophy, a blend of altruism and acumen, which made his family's enterprise into a legend in its own time.

It is the story of El Machetazo, a name coined from "machete", the ubiquitous cutlass of the Latin American countryside, and roughly translated as "the big cut".

Machetazo, a celebrated name in Panama, sums up the philosophy of the late Sr. Juan Ramon Poll, who with his wife Vilma and their three daughters Carmen, Vilma and Lilian fled the tyranny of the communist regime in their native Cuba in 1966.

In Santiago de Cuba, Sr. Poll had established two El Machetazo stores and on the same block a shop caled "Casa Goly", after the nickname "Goly" which he had acquired. These establishments sold clothing and fabrics at "Big Cut" prices by passing on to the customer the benefit of lower costs earned by buying in large quantities, a practice which has been carried through to the present day.

But free enterprise was killed when Fidel Castro came to power and Sr. Poll the entrepenuer chose Panama as the new arena in which to wield his symbolic machete.

A small store on Avenida Central, Panama City's famous shopping street was the beginning of the family's Isthmian empire. Word of the bargains at El Machetazo soon spread and further stimulated by catchy slogans from the creative brain of Sr. Poll (there are few Panamanians who do not remember: *"El hombre crea, el mono imita y con El Machetazo no hay quien compita"*) a second store was opened in nearby Calidonia.

There was no stopping El Machetazo. New stores opened in the suburb of San Miguelito and then further afield in Chitre, and Santiago.

In the year 2000 El Machetazo opened a store in Arraijan. A year later, the company's expansion strategy led to the construction of the El Machetazo Tocumen, with more than 14,000 square meters. Also as part of its new strategy the seasonal store Navidad El Machetazo was opened in Chanis, as well as another store in Penonome and yet another is due to open in Chiriqui.

The Machetazo stores offer more than 30 departments such as:

- Haberdashery
- Florist
- Home
- Lamps
- Religious articles
- Furniture
- Music
- Electrodomestic
- Gardening
- Pets
- Hardware
- Auto Parts
- Construction
- Good Luck (incense potions etc.)
- Books
- Sports goods
- Dry goods

- Ladies Clothing
- Mens and boys clothing
- Girls and babies clothing
- Handbags and accessories
- Costume Jewelry
- Boutique, imported
- Clothing
- Jewelry
- Cosmetics
- Clothing fabrics
- Party items
- Toys
- Gifts and Cards
- School items & Books
- Office Supplies
- Footwear

You can find everything at El Machetazo.

Today, the family business, the Machetazo Group of Companies, encompasses many diverse enterprises. The most recent are:

CASA GOLY

A mega hardware store with Ace Hardware products among other brands, located in the Commercial Shopping Center of Punta del Este in Tocumen.

POLLMART

A specialized store offering party supplies, toys, children's department, housewares and others, with branch stores in Los Pueblos 2000 and Avenida Ricardo J. Alfaro.

FABRICA GOVIL INTERNACIONAL, S.A.

This company started in 1973 with six operatives and eight sewing machines making shirts for school children. New styles, quality fabric and buttons soon led to high demand and expan-

sion into other lines such as pants, gym shorts and shirts, and lab coats. Later were added jeans, dressware, uniforms underclothing, bed covers and many other lines until, today, Govil's production covers over 60% of the national market with 100 operatives and the most modern automated equipment available.

INDUSTRIA EL TORERO

The Machetazo group bought this company, located in the district of Arena in Chitre in 1987 and began production of brand name shoes, expanding later into satchels, briefcases haversacks and belts. Seventy operatives and three management personnel run the factory.

EMPACADORA DE GRANOS POLAR, S.A.

This is a recent addition to the group which began in 2000,

The latest store to open at Los Pueblos.

The Govil clothing factory.

Govil's production of many types of clothing covers over 60 % of the market.

CONGLOMERATE

Children's paradise at Poll Mart.

a packing operation for grains, vegetables and other types of foodstuff.

POLAR FRIGORIFICOS, S.A.
Dedicated since 1984 to the import and distribution of fresh frozen greens, vegetables and fruits, meat products and dry goods.

PUNTA DEL ESTE RESIDENTIAL AREA
With the aim of providing housing at community—affordable prices, this associate company established a pleasant residential area close to Tocumen International Airport.

GANADERIA EL TECAL
This is the group's biggest farm—2,300 hectareas in Chepo. Five hundred of these hectares are reforested with a variety of timber and fruit trees. Cattle and iguanas are also grown on the farm which also boasts a nursery for raising endangered species.

GANADERA PACORA S.A.
This farm of 500 hectareas is dedicated to cattle, producing heifers of between 350 to 700 lbs exclusively to provide meat for the supermarkets of El Machetazo stores.

FINCA BREMER, S.A.
In Pedregal, this farm produces poultry and pork for the supermarkets of El Machetazo stores.

MASISA
In Chitre buys and sells vegetables, foodstuffs, dry goods and supermarket items.

FESISA
Also in Chitre, is dedicated to buying and selling hardware, plumbing and building supplies.

HOTEL HAWAII
In Chitre, this hotel offers 33 comfortable rooms.

COMMUNICATION MEDIA
Radio Ritmo and Radio Lasser offer news, comment and music.

The Machetazo Group has a workforce which now numbers over 4000, all dedicated to the business and following the ethic brought to Panama by Sr. Poll. About 70% of of the employees are permanent and enjoy benefits which make it a privilege to work for the group. Staff benefits include life insurance, medical attention, scholarships for children, bonuses for Christmas, births, long service, marriage and carnival time. Benefits also cover transport and even food and expenses after a death in the family.

Juan Ramon died in1999 at the age of 77. His widow Vilma carries on as president of the group. In a company memorandum for the anniversary of the group, Vilma commented that in spite of the difficulties of carrying on without him, the path he cut out was so clear and the foundation so well laid that the family "knew the direction we must take". She added: "following his philosophy and way of working we are sure we can continue the work he started so many years ago".

CONSTRUCTION

Building the FUTURE...Today

Cemex has operations in 30 countries, including nations such as Spain, Phillipines, Venezuela, Mexico, Colombia, Costa Rica & Panama.

CEMEX is a global leader in the production and distribution of cement, with operations strategically situated in the most dynamic markets throughout the four continents. Cemex combines a profound knowledge of the local markets with its worldwide net of operations and information technology systems in order to provide exceptional products and services to its customers, whether the project be a one-man construction job or that of industrial contractors.

Cemex has operations in more than 30 countries and commercial relationships in more than 60 nations, including: Indonesia, Philippines, Thailand, Mexico, Spain, Venezuela, Colombia, Puerto Rico, USA, Egypt, Costa Rica, Nicaragua and Panama.

THE SUCCESS OF CEMEX

If the success of Cemex were to have a secret, it would be its proven ability to reap the benefits of integration and efficiency, through which a process of continued improvements constantly seeks cost effective solutions and to maximize productivity through the inexhaustible analysis and revision of both old and new operations.

CEMEX IN PANAMA

Cemex is the principle provider of cement in Panama. The company operates a dry processing plant in Calzada Larga, in the sub-district of Chilibre; as well as a distribution network of six ready mix concrete plants.

HISTORICAL DEVELOPMENT

1978: Cemento Bayano initiates its operations with a plant built by the FLS Denmark Company, which was commissioned by the Panama Government as a "Turn Key" project.

1994: Cemex acquires a majority interest in Cemento Bayano (until then a state-run company) by means of a public bid organized by PROPRIVAT.

1995: Through the acquisition by Cemex the company initiated the production and distribution of ready mix concrete by installing of two producing plants, one in Panama City and the other in Colon.

1996: Cemento Bayano's operations are reorganized and optimized by investing strategically and opening a cement distributor in Panama City.

1997: The production line of Portland Grey Cement Type I of Cemento Bayano's plant is certified under the international norm of ISO 9002. Later, all the other products of Bayano's plant: Flexicem, Type II and Type GU, are included.

1998: Another cement distributorship is opened in Chiriquí.

1999: An exclusive contract is signed to provide all concrete utilized in the maintenance of the Panama Canal locks.

2000: On January 1, 2000, Cemento Bayano starts operating under the commercial denomination: Cemex Panama. Six new concrete plants begin operations in various parts of the Republic of Panama.

2000: Cemento Bayano receives honorable mention in the Cemex Safety Award 2000 ceremonies for reaching a record of 248 accident-free workdays in the plant.

2001: Operations begin at the new concrete plant in David, Chiriquí. Cemento Bayano exports Clinker, for the first time. The plant passes the fifth audit of continued quality, thereby obtaining the validation of the Certificate of Quality, ISO 9002, for another year.

2001: Cemex signs contracts with Skanska Corporation to supply the Cement required for the construction of the Esti Dam.

2002: Cemex Concrete receives the Cemex Safety Award 2001, and the Cemento Bayano Plant once again achieves an honorable mention in the ceremonies.

2002: Cemex Concrete obtains the ISO 9001 certification 2000 version, which placed the company as the premier cement company at a national level; and, certification under the 2000 version, as the premier company at an international level.

2002: Cemex Concrete negotiates a contract to supply the cement needed for the construction of the Multicentro Commercial project on the site of the old San Agustín College.

Cemex positions itself as the leader in Panama's market and is recognized to be the best provider in the construction industry, thereby contributing to the development of the country.

Whether it be an individual constructor building his own house or industrial contractors, they all rely on the local brands of Cemento Bayano, Flexicem and Cemex Concrete and their range of value-added services.

Cemex Panama fulfills its commitment: build the future of Panama now...

Cemex Bayano, S.A., Credicorp Bank Bldg., Floor 28, 50 Street, Tel.: 278-8700, Fax: 278-8765, Customer Service 800-CEMEX, www.cemex.com

From individual contractors to industrial contractors, they all prefer Cemento Bayano, the local brand of Cemex Panama.

ELECTROINDUSTRIAL DE PANAMA, S.A.
A new star shines in the corporate world of Panamá

Launching a multi-million dollar company during a recession takes courage, foresight and luck. A couple of years after the launching of Electroindustrial S.A. in July 2000 the president Dr. Augusto Robinson and a group of prominent businessmen on its directorate can congratulate themselves on having established the biggest electrical supply and service company in Panama during a difficult period

They not only were able to anticipate the market potential of this business but seized an opportunity presented by the closure of the Triangulo group of companies whose assets, including those of one of its subsidiaries El Electrico, S.A. were sequestered by the banks. Dr. Robinson and his directors negotiated to

buy over $3 million worth of supplies from the banks and took over two warehouses and showrooms with over 5,000 square meters of space on the busy Transisthmian Highway at the junction of Via Brasil.

Electroindustrial was born and has prospered although it began as a company specializing in industrial low voltage and automatic systems. The holding company also incorporated Inversiones Murcia, S.A. which since 1994 has been offering services and supplies in the medium and high voltage fields, thereby offering clients totally integrated solutions to electrical problems.

Their own workshop provides a complete range of services and assem-

bles capacitor banks, motor control centers, panel boards and starters. Electroindustrial is the only company in Panama which offers all these alternatives, with personnel qualified to design and build the systems. The company also has links with overseas companies such as Grupo Ethus, Electricas de Medellin, Mejía Villegas, Turbo Care and Santos CMI to assist major projects.

The company was able to negotiate contracts to distribute 95% of the trade marks contained in the inventory purchased from the banks. These include Schneider, Telemecanique, Square D, Siemens, Alcap, Distrielec, Sylvania, Durman Esquivel, AB Chance, 3M and International Paper.

CONSTRUCTION

This is in addition to trade services and products which Inversiones Murcia represents or distributes. These are:

- AB Chance— *tools, equipment and hardware for electric and telephone lines and sub-stations.*
- Alfa Laval— *heat regulators, centrifugal pumps*
- American Air Filter— *industrial filters*
- Ametek— *analysis and processing instruments Panalarm*
- Anderson— *hardware for electric lines*
- Atlas Copco— *compressors*
- Beckwith Electrics— *protection controls*
- Bowthrope— *lightning arresters and protection equipment*
- Cablofil— *cable management*
- Caddy— *fasteners*
- Caldweld— *welded electrical connections*
- Climatronics— *weather equipment*
- Critec— *surge protection equipment*
- Corning Cable— *fiber optics cables*
- Dataradio — *GPS, communications*
- Emcocables—*aluminum clad cable and guy wires*
- Erico— *lighting protection systems*
- Eritech— *ground and line connectors and electric telephone substations*
- Essex— *cables for telephone lines*
- Exide— *batteries and chargers for industrial bateries*
- Federal pacific— *dry type transformers and switchgear products*
- Ferrogalván— *electrical hardware and fittings*
- Forjasul— *electrical hardware and*

Partial view of the warehouse.

fittings
- Florida Welding— *special steel*
- Fuji Electric— *starters*
- GEA Spiro— *special tubes*
- Grafco– *asphalt sealing applicators*
- Haug Fritz— *compressors*
- Security tools and equipment of diverse brands
- Hitachi Maxco— *industrial chain*
- Inner-Tite— seals and security sealing rings.
- International Paper— *wooden poles*
- JOY—*compressors*
- Leviton– *wiring devices*
- MOOG— *valves, servo-valves*
- Mouvex— *pumps*
- Megger— *measuring equipment*
- Nulec— *reclosers*
- Passoni & Villa— *lightning conductors and protection equipment*
- Peerless— *pumps*
- Pielstick— *motors, spare parts and services*
- Power Line Hardware— *hardware and insulators for electrical and*

telephone lines
- Powell Esco— *medium voltage switches*
- Ritz— *potential and current transformers*
- Rymel— *conventional, power and padmounted transformers*
- Sadelec— *transmission towers*
- Senior Industries— *equipment, tools and hardware for electrical and telephone lines*
- Siemens— *medium and high-power equipment and spare parts*
- Southern States— *switches and circuit switches*
- Southwire— *electrical line cables*
- Stielectrónica— *photoelectric controls, switches and cutouts*
- Stevens— *water and weather measuring equipment*
- Thermal Ceramics— *cement and refractory bricks*
- Up Right— *scaffolds, personnel and cargo elevators*
- Voit— *hydroelectric control*

The slogan of Electroindustrial S.A. is "Follow our current --we know what we are talking about", which is backed up by the policy of Dr. Morgan and his board to give the best service through qualified personnel and a complete inventory.

In order to guarantee a strong financial structure, the directors created a holding company, Pistar Holding S.A. whose logo symbolizes, as Dr. Robinson said in his inaugural address "the ying and yang of the traditional and wise oriental culture which simbolizes crisis/opportunity....and the "Pistol Star" the bright object in the firmament to match the shine of our companies...and the color green for hope and a better tomorrow".

Workshop where assembly and testing is performed on some of the equipment.

Electroindustrial DE PANAMA, S,A

Pistar Holding

The Pedregal branch, Avenida Jose Maria Torrijos.

PAZKO®

A trajectory marked by excellence!

More than 40 years ago, in 1961 to be precise, Mr. Marshall Ross joined forces with other Panamanian investors to found Metales Industriales, S.A., the first company of the group, which was created to satisfy the heavy local demand for mosquito screens.

Towards the end of that decade, the product range was expanded into the fields of construction, with the manufacture, among other things, of galvanized laminates for roofing and plastic products such as PVC pipe. At the same time that this important expansion was taking place, the trademark Pazko was launched to assist in the distribution of the company's products.

During the following years the company successfully reached a sustained annual growth of 20%. This growth helped prepare the way for a change in

the concept of the company during the late 80s. Emphasis was placed on commercialization and global distribution of Pazko products, and products made by other companies. The purpose of this change was to directly serve the end-user with the utmost possible efficiency. But, it does not end there. As a company interested in the development of the country, with the help of top technology and creativity, Pazko kept expanding its range of products for the construction industry especially with pipe systems, light construction and metal structures with efficient, versatile and accessible solutions.

By 1996 Pazko was ready for two great events, brought about by constant work and dedication. The first change was Pazko's consolidation as the leading company of its kind in the

Panamanian market. In second place but just as important, it began the globalization process by establishing a strategic alliance with Amanco the leading company in Latin America, with more than 30 companies in 13 countries of the region.

Today Pazko keeps improving. Proof of this is that in the first months of 2002 the new administration of Amanco Panama and Pazko went through great changes and internal adjustments in which the principles and vision of the future of the companies were redefined. After extensive planning the company now practices a new client-oriented philosophy to satisfy the needs of the customer and offers service of excellent quality while incorporating the dynamic creativity of the company.

CONSTRUCTION

Corporate headquarters, Via Tocumen.

The branch of Pazko in David, Chiriqui Province.

The process of re-structuring the company led to notable improvements especially in the range of products offered, which include the following:

- **PVC Pipe Systems**
  PVC pipes, fittings, drain pipes, hot water CPVC pipe, Polipropilene, PVC gutters, valves, hydrants, steel rings and manhole covers and geosynthetic textil.

- **Roofing Systems**
  Pazko corrugated sheet zinc, coated and galvanized sheeting, policarbonate transparent sheets, Plycem roof panels, channels and flashings, screws, roofing, fittings and purlings.

- **Metal**
  Corrugated steel girders, WF steel beams, angles, square steel pipe, electrowelded netting, Masterdeck system and welding rods.

- **Ceiling System**
  Light ceiling steel structures, Plycem and Gypsum board, screws and fittings, insulating, fiberglass rolls and insulating Polipropilene rolls (Low-E)

- **Dry Wall Systems**
  Plycem boards (skirting, cornices), Gypsum board, studs, tracks, screws and accesories.

- **Other Products**
  Galvanized and coated chain-link fencing, wire gauze insect screening, treated and untreated lumber.

- **Services**
  Irrigation systems, drinking water treatment plants, and waste water treatment plants.

One phrase sums up what PAZKO means to Panama: When PAZKO is there, progress follows.

For the convenience of its customers, Pazko has three stores: Vía Tocumen, telephone 220-8285; José María Torrijos Avenue at Pedregal, telephone 266-1111; and David, Chiriquí, telephone 775-2247.

RETAIL

Gran Morrison– a dynamic national institution

The Gran Morrison Department store chain and Servicio de Lewis: a part of the lives of all Panamanians for 77 years

"They have it in Gran Morrison". "I'll pass by Gran Morrison on my way home." Phrases like that, spoken countless times by Panamanians illustrate how much of an institution the Gran Morrison chain has become in the Republic.

The Gran Morrison chain is a subsidiary of the well-established company Servicio de Lewis, wholesalers of books, magazines, stationary and a range of goods so diverse that it makes you wonder how, even in the computer age, they can keep control of their stock, the variety of which is embodied in their slogan, "Variety, culture, beauty".

The business was founded in the 1920's by Mr. Glenn Lewis. It started as a small, but profitable film-developing shop on "J" Street in downtown Panama City.

Gran Morrison's credit card.

Celebrating its 77th anniversary, Gran Morrison is Panama's largest and most diverse chain of department stores. The chain currently has five branches strategically located close to the capital's tourist hot spots. Gran Morrison stores are in Vía España, in the heart of the banking and hotel district; Punta Paitilla; El Dorado Mall and Los Pueblos shopping center, a few minutes from Tucumen International Airport. Casa Zaldo , another store of the group, is located in the district of Santa Ana.

Both Panamanians and tourists can find almost everything in the store's 14 departments, from birthday cards and tourist videos on Panama, to designer clothes and best-sellers. Gran Morrison boasts the largest selection of CD's in the nation, featuring hits by national and international artistes, from salsa and merengue, to rock and baroque and offers excellent price promotions and sales throughout the year.

The store's handicraft department,

"Casa de Artesanías", offers an ample selection of souvenirs from all regions of the country, including dresses made by the Ngobe-Buglé indians of the province of Chiriquí, pottery from the province of Herrera, authentic Panama straw hats from Coclé; carvings made from tagua (vegetable ivory) and cocobolo wood by Darién's Emberá-Wounaan indians, and molas, the famous reverse appliqué cloth squares designed and produced by the Kuna Indians of the San Blas archipelago.

Gran Morrison's three clothing departments offer well-known international brands for all ages and styles. Gran Morrison is also the leading importer and retailer of books and all of their branches have large book departments with thousands of volumes in both Spanish and English. The magazine's section rivals that of any department store in the U.S., featuring a broad range of topics.

The stores are also famous for their office and school supply departments,

including English and Spanish text books and dictionaries. Special emphasis is placed on artists' supplies, which includes canvases, pencils, brushes, oils, acrylics and water colors. Other popular departments include toys, jewelry, and electronics.

In addition to its excellent-quality merchandise, Gran Morrison's source of pride is its friendly personnel and staff, which places high value on customer service and satisfaction. There is always someone willing to help you at Gran Morrison, attending to even the smallest details.

Contact Gran Morrison at
Tel.: 212-1888
Fax: 212-1450
E-mail:sdli@lewiserv.com

Joyeria Mercurio offers famous names in jewelry and watches

The first thing that captures your attention at Mercurio Joyeros, is the Rolex watches —the largest selection you could find anywhere. More than 250 different watches are exhibited in beautiful displays that match a mural which Rolex artists made in Switzerland specially for Mercurio. To see these displays is like strolling through a fantasy world of the most famous and prestigious watches in the world...Rolex.

A look around the recently remo delled showroom of Joyeria Mercurio, one of Panama's leading jewellers, reveals that in these days of globalization, jewelry is following the trend towards international brand names. This is the main reason that Mercurio's shop, almost opposite the Santuario Nacional in the hotel and banking district of Panama City, has been enlarged by over 70 percent ... to accommodate separate displays for the big names.

Until a few years ago, jewelry was selected entirely on its own merits but nowadays, as they would choose beau-

tiful clothing, customers are seeking designer jewelry. One name much in vogue is BVLGARI and so, in boutique style, the famous Italian jewels have their own corner at Mercurio with its own distinctive display-furniture and showcases and the image that BVLGARI projects in capitals around the world.

Tiffany & Co, the prestigious jewelry house of the United States, established in 1837, and Mikimoto, the most important Japanese house for cultured pearls, founded by Kokichi Mikimoto in 1893 also have their own individual displays in the store.

For those clients who still choose their jewelry without regard to an international name, Mercurio craftsmen turn out exquisite pieces, as they have done since Joyeria Mercurio was founded in Panama's famous Avenida Central by Sr. Henry Sommerfreund in 1944. In 1977 he sold the business to the Jelenszky family, which has built the business into what it is today.

At Mercurio Joyeros, apart from Rolex, BVLGARI, Tiffany and Mikimoto, can also be found a large selection from houses such as Omega, Baume & Mercier, Technomarine and Michel Herbelin.

Mr. Carli Jelenszky, president of Mercurio affirms that in the 58 years since its foundation, the company has established a reputation second to none for quality and after-sales services.
Tel. 223-7326.

The American Chamber of Commerce & Industry of Panama

The American Chamber of Commerce & Industry of Panama (AmCham) is a non-profit association of businesses and individuals dedicated to strengthening the commercial ties between the Republic of Panama and the United States of America. Since its creation by a small group of Panamanian and American businessmen on October 31 1979, AmCham has grown to become an important independent voice in the development of entrepreneurial ideas in Panama.

The organization has dedicated itself to the dissemination of business and economic information on Panama for American and European enterprises interested in investing in

Installation ceremony of the Board of Directors, 2002.

Panama. It has lobbied tirelessly with both the Panamanian and United States governments on behalf of free and open commercial exchange between the two nations. Through its forums and speaker presentations, AmCham has improved communication and understanding between the North American and Panamanian companies that are members of the Chamber, fomenting a spirit of cooperation that has helped everyone.

AmCham Panama develops and publishes economic and business information for its members, with an eye towards benefiting the Panamanian economy. Its reports on national markets and investment opportunities have been of incalculable value to its members and other businesses looking for an entry into the Panamanian economy. It also publishes the monthly magazine Business Panama and an annual membership directory.

AmCham Panama is working with its members and the Government of Panama for the development of a free trade agreement between the United States and Panama, and for the establishment of a Free Trade Area of the Americas.

In April 2002, the American Chamber of Commerce & Industry of Panama signed the United Nations Global Compact, dedicating itself to the improvement of the nine principles of human rights, labor rights and the environment. AmCham Panama is also affiliated with the Association of American Chambers of Commerce in Latin America (AACCLA) and is a fully accredited member of the U.S. Chamber of Commerce in the United Sates of America.

Website: www.panamcham.com

Signing Ceremony-Global Compact of the United Nations, 2002. Martin Alvarez, Elizabeth Fong.

Golf tournament, 2002.

PETROLEOS DELTA
A local company that contributes to the development of Panama

On October 21st 1983 , Petroleos Delta, S.A acquired Gulf Petroleum´s assets in Panama. The new company kept the same high standards of quality and the philosophies of a multinational company and added the flexibility and the agressiveness of a local company.

As the leading distribution company of petroleum finished products, Delta is an example of the excellent performance and capacity of a Panamanian workforce managing the supply of top-quality products and services that go hand in hand with the high demands and challenges of a global economy.

Among the products that Petróleos Delta distributes throughout the Republic of Panama are:

Gasoline 91 octane
Gasoline 95 octane
Diesel – regular
Diesel – additive
Kerosene
Bunker
Asphalt – penetration and irregular
Jet fuel
Aviation gas

Also included is a complete and modern line of lubricants and greases that comply and surpass the most demanding norms of international quality.

At the present time, Petróleos Delta, S.A. has the most extensive network of gas service stations of Panama, with more than 130 points of sale, located in strategic locations throughout the country. These service stations offer quality products at the best prices with outstanding service. In the industrial sector, Delta provides services to more than 400 clients. Among them are various national and international airlines, companies dedicated to construction, farming, port activities and many other companies that offer goods and services, that form part of the principal structures of economic life of

our country.

Petróleos Delta's mission is to expand its participation in the petroleum products market in the following three areas: gas service stations, the industrial sector and the government sector, as well as supporting social benefit programs. Delta is conscious of its responsibility to the community, especially where the well-being of The Panamanian children is concerned. Publicity and promotional campaigns contain a high degree of social content to demonstrate the conviction of Petróleos Delta, S.A. towards helping solve the problems that affect Panama. The company also constantly supports national sports as an effective mean to bring out the national values that have brought so much glory to our country.

As a contribution to the eco-system, Petróleos Delta, S.A. has launched campaigns at the national level geared to create ecological awareness as a base for sustainable development. Delta has created projects focused on improving the quality of air with the support of entities such as ANCON and the Specialized Institute of Analysis of the University of Panama. These

programs are focused in lowering of the levels of atmospheric contamination. The Specialized Institute has air monitoring stations situated in different locations of the capital city and recently acquired a mobile monitoring station, sponsored by Petróleos Delta, S.A.

By the year 2003 Petróleos Delta, S.A. will proudly reach its 20th year of existence as a company formed with Panamanian capital that has experienced a solid and sustained and continuing growth in its operations. As an example, it should be mentioned that in the periods from 1983 to 2002 the numbers of stations grew from 70 to more than 130. Industrial and commercial accounts grew from 95 to more than 400.

Petróleos Delta, S.A. is a subsidiary of Empresa General de Inversiones, S.A., along with Banco General, S.A. and Compañía Istmeña de Seguros, S.A..

The head office of Petróleos Delta is located at Miguel Brostella Avenue, Centro Comercial Camino de Cruces, Telephone: 260-6333, Fax: 260-6225, Web page: www.petrodelta.com

INSURANCE

NATIONAL UNION
FIRE INSURANCE
COMPANY OF
PITTSBURGH, PA.

How insurance helps a nation's progress

The staff (l to r seated): Rigoberto Chavarría, Marketing Manager; Armando Guillén, Claims Manager; Ed Mena, General Manager; (l to r standing): Aleyda de Perivancich, Human Resources Manager; Luis Della Togna, Personal Accident Manager; Melissa de León de Perez, Systems Manager; Rita Molina de Medina, Commercial Lines Manager; Melissa Vasquez de Moutran, Personal Lines Manager; Ariana de Rosario, Accounting Manager.

How much does the development and progress of a nation depend on insurance? A great deal, according to the executives of AIG National Union Fire Insurance Company of Pittsburgh, PA which has operated in Panama for over fifty-five years.

An example of this is the comprehensive gamut of products and services that the company offers in the marketplace to insure and protect the financial stability of some of the most important companies and individuals in Panama. These include policies to protect companies directors and officers from litigation. The company also provides protection to the financial center, and has made a significant contribution to the growth, over the last few decades, of the banking and maritime industries. AIG National Union also offers some of the most comprehensive Accident & Health and Auto policies in the industry.

The National Union Fire Insurance Company of Pittsburgh, PA forms part of AIG, the American International Group which is one the largest and most profitable companies in the world with over $400 billion in assets, 81,000 employees, and operations in over 130 countries in the world.

Forbes Magazine recently announced its annual global 500 ranking of the worlds largest public companies, with AIG making an impressive third place appearance. The ranking consists of a formula that incorporates sales, profits, assets, and market value. Reuters indicated in July 2002 that AIG is one of just nine U.S. companies that still enjoy "triple A" ratings from Standard & Poors and Moody's, two leading credit rating agencies. This gives AIG National Union Fire Insurance Company, as a branch office, the highest rating of any general insurance company in the Panamanian market.

AIG has the highest ratings and is one of the world's most innovative companies, well positioned to capitalize on opportunities on behalf of its clients throughout the global marketplace. While AIG's products and services have changed over the years with the needs of its customers, the AIG core values of integrity, quality service, financial strength and responsive leadership will never change.

With the backing of this gigantic enterprise AIG National Union Fire Insurance Company of Pittsburgh, PA is entering a dynamic phase in Panama. As General Manager Ed Mena said in a recent press interview: "Panama is a solid market. There are many very good companies here and ample scope for development. Our position in the market from now on is going to be more aggressive because we know we are in a superbly competitive position".

The company's Panama office is in the American International Building. 50 St. and Aquilino De La Guardia St, 4th Floor. P.O. Box 718, Zona 1, Rep. of Panama. Tel.: (507) 263-9666. Fax: (507) 223-9677. www.aig.com

American International Building, Panama

Compañía Nacional de Seguros, S.A.
45 years distinguishing Panama

Because of the surge of commercial activity which the construction of the Panama Canal (1904-1914) brought to Panama, many insurance companies were established in the early days of the Republic. Some of these companies were financed with Panamanian capital, while others were representatives of prestiglous international firms.

These companies were necessary in a country which had become the crossroads of the world, to protect valuable real estate, instalations, companies and individuals both Panamanian and the many foreigners in the new "country of transit".

Around the mid 1950s the government regulated the activities of these companies with law #17 of August 22,1956, and this caused many to close their doors. This left a vacuum in the market which three Panamanian entepeneurs decided to exploit. Mr. Gabriel De La Guardia, Mr. Leonel Moses and Mr. A.B. Remmington formed a new company, Compañia Nacional de Seguros, S.A. (CONASE)

CONASE was founded on June 1, 1957 and on 1998 joined forces with "Primer Banco de Ahorros" (PRIBANCO), making up the "Primer Grupo Nacional " (PGN). In July 2000 and after many months of negotiations the shareholders of PGN agreed to merge with "Banco del Istmo, S.A." to form the "Primer Banco del Istmo, S.A." (BANISTMO).

As a consequence of the merger of "Primer Grupo Nacional" with "Banco del Istmo" further mergers were decided on, with the "Compañia de Seguros Chagres, S.A." and "Compañia Nacional de Seguros, S.A.", which took place on December 31, 2000, thereby creating an insurance company of major solidity, strength, growth, vision and a high grade of competence that benefits customers, shareholders and partners.

The new CONASE offers more variety of insurance products with a value in endorsed premiums from December 31, 2001 of more than US$45 billion, with assets surpassing US$107 billion and a net worth of US$61 billion.

In September of 2002 the total insurance market amounted to US$264.7 billion, which represents a 3% increase compared to the previous year.

However, 65% of the total premiums is controlled by four companies all of which are owned by Panamanian shareholders.

Today, CONASE holds fourth place in billing premiums in the Panamanian market. Its portfolio contains 22% of fire insurance, 17% automobile, 7% life and the rest in other lines of business. The company continues to design new products to meet customers' expectations.

The company has branch offices in the provinces of Herrera, Veraguas and Chiriqui, which in recent years have made their presence felt strongly in that area.

Aware that the principle asset of any insurance enterprise is the loyalty of its customers and agents, CONASE is in the process of planning future growth, making plans to revitalize existing resources, and to continue to work as a team.

The CONASE offices are located in 50th Street, Building #62 Telephone: (507) 205-0300 P.O. Box: 0816-01085, Panama, Republic of Panama.

British American Insurance Company

Member of the CL Financial Group operating in 21 countries

The British American Insurance Company was founded in the Bahamas in 1920. In 1934 it joined the American McMillan Group of Companies, presided over by Laurence F. Lee.

Early in the 1950s the company launched an expansion program aimed at what were then British colonies, mainly in the Caribbean but later continuing to Africa, the Far East, the Mediterranean and Central America.

In 1967 operations in the Republic of Panama were initiated. In those days only industrial life policies were sold. In 1977 Monthly Debit Ordinary products, known as "MDO" were launched in the Panamanian market in amounts of $3,000.00 to $20,000.00 and premiums paid monthly instead of weekly. In 1985 the company ventured into the line of ordinary insurance after acquiring the portfolio of American Capital, first with traditional policies and later with an innovative universal life plan with totals of $50,000 and above.

In 1998 the British American Insurance Company became a member of the CL Financial Group with the purpose of forming a strategic alliance between the two companies.

CL Financial Group is an important conglomerate in Trinidad and Tobago which operates all over the Caribbean and South and Central America. The Company has assets of more than $1.5 billion with an administrative office in Fort Lauderdale which has allowed diversification in industries and geografic localization.

At the present time, the CL Financial Group consists of more than 70 companies, operating in 21 countries around the world offering a range of services which include: insurance, medical services, real estate, electrical generation, manufacturing, communications, financial services, commerce, sciences and agriculture.

Today, British American Panama has five agencies located in Panama, Colon, Chitre and David, offering insurance policies for life, savings, personal accident, health and an innovative retirement plan known as flexible premium annuity, supported by an administrative personnel which offer rapid and efficient service to its client from its home office located in the mezzanine of the Vallarino Building on 52nd Street and Elvira Mendez.

British American Insurance Company has evolved into a huge business poised to grow even bigger and always with the primary objective of the complete satisfaction of its customers.

Tel.: 269-0515 • fax: 269-0790
E-mail: britishp@cwpanama.net

Administrative Personnel in front of the main office, located in the mezzanine of the Vallarino Building between 52nd Street and Elvira Mendez

INSURANCE

ASSA Insurance Company, S.A.

A powerful Panamanian group now looking beyond national boundaries

ASSA head office.

The company which today is known as ASSA Insurance Company S.A., one of the most powerful in the industry, founded in 1982, grew as a result of various mergers and acquisitions which take its history back as far as 1937.

Recent acquisitions in the mid 90s of Metropolitana de Seguros de Vida S.A. , Real Panameña de Seguros, S.A. and Wico Compañía de Seguros placed ASSA in a position to offer the finest insurance and financial services in the republic.

ASSA pays particular attention to the individual needs of its clients and to this end, the company is divided into various departments such as: Consumer and Corporate Department, Claims Department, Branch Offices, Production and Engineering Department.

Like the rest of the insurance industry world-wide, ASSA Compañía de Seguros, S.A. was put to the test in 2001 by the terrorist acts of September 11 in the United States. ASSA's management responded swiftly and professionally to meet the threats posed by the escalation of risk factors and the new game rules which confronted the industry after the collapse of the Twin Towers in New York.

The reaction to changes which globalization has imposed on the market as well as the above-mentioned historical events would not have been possible without the vast experience of the company's president, Stanley. Motta and the staff of 317. For that reason, the company has traditionally spent 58% of its eight-number administrative costs in salaries, benefits, loans and staff training. As of December 31, 2001, ASSA's actual solvency was $ 99,441,608, actual liquidity was $ 106,669,267 and the Shareholders equity was $ 71,708,787. Based on the figures published on December 31, 2001, ASSA Compañía de Seguros, S.A. owns:

a) 11.2 more in margin and 5.5 more in liquidity than required.

b) 2.0 more in margin and 1.1 more in liquidity than the minimun required of all the insurance companies of the country.

For the convenience of its clients ASSA has branches in David, Chitre, Colon, Santiago, Chorrera and two in Panama City — El Dorado and Los Pueblos. All branches except in Santiago have the capacity to issue policies immediately and the branches in El Dorado and David settle claims and issue cheques.

For some time the company has been expanding its presence within the Panamanian market both in insurance and financial services in general. Now, ASSA is studying the possibility of expansion into regional markets. To facilitate this process they attained an A-classification (Excellent) with the renowned A.M. Best. The engineering department is also certified under the prestigious ISO 9001-2000 classification.

The head office of ASSA Compañía de Seguros S.A. is located in the ASSA building, Nicanor de Obarrio Ave. (Calle 50) between Calles 56th and 57th Streets.

Compañía de Seguros

P.O.Box 5371, Zona 5
Panama, Rep. De Panama
Telephones: 269-0444/269-0443
Fax: 263-9234/263-7453
Internet: http://www.assanet.com

The Corporate University

An innovative company offering training programs for corporations

In the fast-changing environment of the business world in these first years of the new century it is impossible for companies and the people who work for them, no matter how much experience they posess, to compete effectively in the market without using their resources in an intelligent manner.

Ongoing training is essential, and to meet this need, The Corporate University (Universidad Corporativa) was founded in 1999 with headquarters at building 215 at the City of Knowledge. It is not a university in the traditional meaning of the word but is a company specializing in creating and distributing training programs for corporations.

These programs can be with conventional methods such as classroom style teaching; by manuals or special projects; or with virtual aids, coded TV, programs, radio or internet, always using the latest technology.

Following their motto "The Power of organized knowledge" the primary object of the company is to stimulate the creation of "corporate universities" within their client corporations dedicated to in-house training according to the philosophy of the corporation.

According to the executive director The Corporate University Enrique Pizarro Duran, many executives fail to fulfil their mission and realize the objectives of the firms they work for. For these cases, The Corporate University offers a broad range of training packages especially prepared for different

Directors of The Corporate University: Enrique Pizarro Durán, Nuria Vanegas Rodriguez, María Fernanda Rios Navarro.

ages especially prepared for different types of employee and in different areas of work: commercial, management, supervisory, secretarial, and specialized and general labour. Banks, consulting firms, co-operatives, industrial companies, telecomunications and tourism entities are among the principal clients of The Corporate University.

The faculty of The Corporate University comprises a staff of experts in various specialties such as instructional design, multimedia, development of facilitators (trainers) and management training. They all offer workshops using the latest teaching and motivation techniques.

The Corporate University, a company comprising 100% Panamanian capital is one of the first Panamanian companies to expand abroad by means of franchises. To date it has franchises operating in San Jose, Costa Rica; Managua, Nicaragua; Tegucigalpa, Honduras; San Salvador, El Salvador; Guatemala City and Mexico D.F. Franchises also operate nationally in Colon and David.

According to Mr. Pizarro the company is proud of the recent entry in to the important Mexican market and expects to be the biggest educational franchise company in the Spanish speaking world by 2005.

With the new concept it has introduced to Panama, Corporate University has been able to strengthen its position with a network of alliances with other schools and universities, non-profit organizations and technology compa-

nies. It has also developed a diverse range of teaching aids and methods, utilizing magazines, radio programs and meetings; as well as an impressive library of instructional and technical material such as electronic books, and manuals on multimedia which cover specific needs in all the fields of business administration.

UNIVERSIDADCORPORATIVA.COM

Universidad Corporativa:
Ciudad del Saber, Edificio No. 215
Clayton, Panamá
Teléfono: (507) 317-0535
Fax: (507) 317-1149
www.universidadcorporativa.com

The International School of Panama, a nonprofit private school

Celebrating 20 years of Excellence in Education, 1982-2002

The International School of Panamá (ISP) was founded in 1982 for the purpose of offering high-quality education in English to members of the international community residing in Panama City, Republic of Panama and Panamanians interested in an international education. ISP is a private, independent, non-profit institution which provides instruction for 600 students from Pre-Kinder through the 12th grade. The student body represents forty countries.

The school's international administration and faculty is committed to developing each student's full learning potential. The school community attempts to engender joy and excitement in the learning process. Each student is treated as a unique individual within the context of his or her academic, cultural and personal background.

Since its beginning with 43 students in one building, the school has grown to more than 600 students in grades junior kindergarten through twelfth. The facilities consist of 44 air-conditioned and spacious classrooms, laboratories for art, computers, and science, a library / media center, administrative offices, counseling office, infirmary, and a student union. The eight-hectare site includes outdoor play areas, a track and field, and a gymnasium.

ISP is approved by the Ministry of Education in Panama. It is a member of the International Baccalaureate Organization, and it is accredited by the Southern Association

of Colleges and Schools. It has affiliation with the International School Association for Advancement of International Education, The Inter-Regional Center for Curriculum, and the Association of American Schools in Central America.

The school is located in Cerro Viento, on the Golf Club Road. Tel. 266-7037, 266-7862., 266-9532, fax: 266-7808, e-mail: isp@isp.edu.pa webpage: www.isp.edu.pa

EDUCATION

Catering to the new communities in the reverted areas

Since the former U.S. army bases with their extensive housing zones reverted to Panama, Panamanian families have been moving in to create new residential areas which need an infrastructure of services and facilities, one of the most important of which is schools.

Panama Clayton Academy, at the former Fort Clayton, is a nursery school and kindergarten which caters to the young and growing community there and in the neighboring areas of Albrook, Balboa, Corozal and Diablo.

The school is housed in two three-storey building with five classrooms, one for each kindergarten age (2,3,4, and 5) and a another room for games. The complex also houses a reception hall, library, kitchen, computer room, sickbay, a room for special classes and offices for academic administrative and psychological management. Ample parking and green areas with safe and healthy games for the children add to the ideal environment of the academy.

The prospectus of the Panama Clayton Academy states that its mission is to stimulate and develop the potential of each child.

The personnel of the school comprises qualified and dedicated professionals. The academic management is in the hands of Lorena Puello, administration is the responsibility of Olga de Pinilla. The head of the psychology department is Gloria de Benavides. Teachers, assistants and administrative personnel all work as a team for the wellbeing of every child who attends the academy.

All new entrants are given a psychological evaluation which aids staff to foster social skills, language, independence, motor skills and courses to nurture intelligence and intellectual capacity. To aid this process, special classes are given in swimming folklore, ballet, theatre, self expression, karate, art and handicraft.

The academy's Baby Gymnasium also has special equipment and a program for expectant mothers, offering physical and psychological preparation before and after birth, including intra-uterine stimulation.

The nursery school functions with different levels of attention according to the needs of the child and every child is watched over and directed at all times.

Panama Clayton Academy
Calle Agramente, Casa N° 507 A-B
Telefax: 317-0992 / 317-0993
pca@lgperfiles.com

Oxford International School
Developing each student's full potential

Oxford International School was founded in 1987 in response to the growing need to provide both the international and local communities with a global education at par with Panama's growing importance as an international center.

The school is a private, non-sectarian, politically neutral, day school committed to developing each student's full learning potential, through the use of modern teaching methods. The school offers a global education with an international emphasis. Each student is stimulated to acquire a world view academically, socially, culturally, and ethically.

Through positive reinforcement, the staff recognizes and rewards students' efforts, fostering their development as it allows them to explore new areas, thereby promoting a sense of satisfaction and enthusiasm about learning.

Each student is treated as an individual within the context of his academic, cultural and personal background. Parents participate actively in the instruction of their children, and while doing so allow them to benefit academically and socially.

The academic program is designed to develop each student's full learning potential. A strong elementary and secondary multicultural program conducted in English is integrated with the host country's (Panama) curriculum. Specialist teachers provide classes in art, phy-sical education, computer science, and foreign languages. The school utilizes international resources available through the community to broaden and enrich its program.

A low teacher-to-student ratio ensures that students receive the individual attention which educational research indicates is an important factor in promoting learning.

The pre-school program is rich in activities aimed at promoting the development of the child as an individual. Classes are taught entirely in English. The children work in small groups under the guidance of a teacher and a teacher's aide. The program is organized into themes of interest to the child.

The elementary school program emphasizes the development of attitudes and concepts, mathematical and computer skills, and the student's ability to communicate orally and in writing, both in English and in Spanish. The program also seeks to instill self-confidence and emphasizes family and community integration.

A well-rounded high school program prepares students to continue on at local or international universities whether their future interests lie in the field of business, science or the humanities. Oxford International high school graduates receive a typical American high school diploma or a classic diploma accredited by the Ministry of Education, or both simultaneously. The School is accredited by the Northwest Association of Schools, Colleges and Universities.

The main campus is centrally located on Ave. Federico Boyd and Vía España. Tel: 265-6422, fax: 265-7446, e-mail: oxford@ois.edu.pa

UNIVERSIDAD LATINA DE PANAMA

A serious commitment

Universidad Latina, (Latin University), which was founded in 1991 is now housed in a new building on Via Ricardo J. Alfaro which is a source of strength and pride. From its inception, the univeristy has been known for keeping it curriculums right up to date in all its courses and for its real commitment to higher education in Panama.

The academic activities of the university began on Jan 13, 1992 in its main campus and its regional campus in David in the province of Chiriqui.

Later, responding to the great acceptance of the university by students and the academic world, two new branches were opened— in Santiago, Veraguas on September 7, 1992 and in Chitre, Herrera on January 17, 1994.

At the same time, in the interest of offering the best study alternatives to the young people of Panama, Universidad Latina opened, as a priority course, its Faculty of Health and Medical Science on September 26, 1994. Its motto "a serious commitment" is applied to all its courses—undergraduate, postgraduate, masters and doctorate.

Faculties comprise: Education Science, Law and Political Science, Administrative Science and Economics, Tourism, Computer & Telecomunications Science, Communication Science, and Health and Medical Science .

Currently it is the university with the most courses approved by the Republic of Panama and is a leader in Panama and in Central America. Its programs are known for combining technical training with practical and theoretical work, using advanced techniques at all levels, which sets it apart from the rest.

Universidad Latina's staff of qualified professionals keep up-to-date all the time and maintain strict and coherent policies in teaching their courses.

The new building incorporates advanced technology, a large and comfortable library, a cafeteria, computer rooms. As well as having an institute of the English Language, English is incorporated at an advanced level in all the courses. The university also has a office for legal counselling available to students and the public. The Faculty of Health & Medical Science is located at Ave. Justo Arosemena.

Apartado Postal 87-0887 Zona 7
Panamá.
Tel.: 230-8600   Fax: 230-8605
E-mail: web@ns.ulat.ac.pa
Website: www.ulat.ac.pa

Ride the historic Panama Canal Railway

There is a great deal of romance wrapped-up in a railroad. Famous trains: the Orient Express immortalized by Agatha Christie, Paul Theroux's epic journey on China's "Red Rooster" are classics among thousands of stories and films inspired by railroad settings. The Panama Canal Railway has a romantic history as rich and exciting as any other railroad in the world.

Nostalgia and romance abound when the train winds through Panama's lush tropical rainforests, rolls past the former U.S. Southern Command Headquarters and follows the route of the famous Panama Canal. All this while

ships carrying the world's commerce sail alongside the tracks that made the building of the Panama Canal a reality.

But that is only part of the story. For the rest we must go back in time to the first half of the 19th century when Panama was but a province of Colombia. Panama City was not much more than the walled city of the Spanish Conquistadores and the City of Colon on the Caribbean side was the tiny settlement called Aspinwall located on a swampy coast.

The Panama Railroad was born when a group of New York businessmen saw the need for a route from the East

Coast to the West Coast of the United States that would be easier and safer than the long overland journeys through harsh lands and territories protected by Indians. The California Gold Rush was the final spur to action and the railroad was established in 1849 on a landfill in the mangrove swamps where the city of Colon today stands.

The First Transcontinental Train of the Americas crossed the Isthmus of Panama in January of 1855. This was 13 years before the golden spike linked the Central Pacific and Union Pacific railroads at Promontory, Utah.

Before Promontory, the Panama

The track crosses Gatun Lake on a causeway which runs alongside the famous Panama Canal.

Railroad had hauled $750 million worth of gold bound from California to the US East Coast. Rate: One quarter of one percent of the value of each shipment.

More than 400,000 gold-fevered adventurers paid a fare of $25 in gold for a one-way ticket. For those who could not afford the high fare, the railroad charged them $5 for the right to walk across the Isthmus on the railroad's right-of-way.

In a later era, the railroad played a key role in the founding of the Republic of Panama thanks to the manager of the Colon Terminal who purposely disabled a train loaded with Colombian troops who were trying to get to Panama City to quell the independence rebellion.

Today, all of this history is available for all to experience by purchasing a ticket for a journey aboard the famous Panama Railroad.

Thousands of tourists who come to Panama are now riding the train from ocean to ocean and re-living the experience of those dreamers who used the route to get to California during the Gold Rush.

The present-day Panama Canal Railway Company is a partnership between Kansas City Southern and MI-Jack Products. They have recently re-built the entire track and facilities and brought in new rolling stock and equipment. The passenger coaches, originally built in 1955 have been painstainkingly refurbished at great expense to re-create the elegance and luxury of the grand era of railroading. Lush carpeting, exotic wood paneling, brass lamps, galleys and an open-air observation deck transport the passenger to a time when railroad travel was the only way to go. Of course, air-conditioning has been added to make the experience not quite as realistic and a bit more comfortable than in our

Panama Canal Locks, lake, big ships and rainforest. There is a lot to see from the picture windows of the comfortable passenger cars.

forefathers' day.

As cruise ships have begun to visit Panama in greater numbers, tour directors have been quick to recognize the potential of this unique train ride. The breathtaking route follows the course of the Panama Canal and offers passengers the opportunity of seeing the Canal up close and allows them to appreciate the rich flora and fauna of Panama.

The train glides past Miraflores and Pedro Miguel Locks of the Canal, along the Gaillard Cut through the Continental Divide, the digging of which was a gigantic feat of engineering and ingenuity that cost many lives. The track penetrates thick jungle, past Barro Colorado Island, the Galapagos-like wildlife refuge operated by the Smithsonian Institute. A causeway carries the track right across a large section of Gatun Lake, once the largest man-made lake in the world under whose placid surface lie the remains of villages and the workings of the valiant French

pioneers who tried in vain to build a sea-level canal before the Americans bought them out and took over the monumental feat.

Although the beauty and history of this wonderful railroad captivates the imagination, the key objective of the owners in investing $78 million in the born-again railroad is to provide a "land-bridge" complementing the Panama Canal in moving freight across the Isthmus of Panama.

Containers are double-stacked on flatcars and make the journey from Ocean to Ocean in a mere hour and a half. The railway is adding a new dimension to the multimodal cargo carrying capacity of the Isthmus. It offers the World's maritime community an efficient, high volume, in-bond logistics tool with significant economic benefits.

Altogether the historic railroad has assumed a new and vital role in the life and progress of the Republic of Panama. A role which began over 150 years ago and which will continue well into the new millennium.

Fully renovated coaches are masterpieces of elegance. Insert shows a detail of one of the beautiful paintings which adorn the air conditioned coaches.

The Panama Canal Railway Company's real muscle— double-stacked containers speed from coast to coast.

Detail from a 19th century lithograph when the train carried "fortyniners" to the California gold rush.

Amazing Facts: Did you know?

• That at $295 a share, the Panama Railroad was at one time the highest-priced stock on the New York Stock Exchange?

• That the PRR was the most expensive (per mile) railroad ever built? It cost 8 million dollars and took 5 years to build.

• That in 1913 the Panama Railroad hauled 2,916,657 passengers and transported 2,026,852 tons of freight across the Isthmus; at this time it was reported to have the heaviest per-mile traffic of any railroad in the world

• That at US$25.00 in gold, for 47 and a half miles, the PRR was the most expensive railroad (per mile) to travel?

• That more than 12000 people died in the construction of the Panama Railroad?

• That disposing of the dead was becoming such a problem, that the Railroad started "pickling" the bodies in barrels and selling them to medical schools? The proceeds were then used to build a hospital for the Railroad.

• That the Panama Canal would have been impossible to build without the Panama Railroad?

Photos: Bob Johnston

PANAMA CANAL RAILWAY COMPANY
P.O Box 2669, Balboa, Ancón,
Republic of Panama
Tel: 317-6070. Fax: 317-6061   info@panarail.com

Hotel El Panamá

Icon of the Republic and still a five star leader

In 1946, Panama was a city of under a million souls; a relatively tranquil town with little of the hustle and bustle of today. During that year a group of far-seeing businessmen bought 60 hectareas of land in El Cangrejo from a Panamanian lady residing in Paris.

They bought the land for the laughable price of 10 or 15 cents per square meter. The president of the Republic at the time was Enrique Jimenez who, to close the deal, asked the purchasers to donate part of their extensive plot for a state university.

He also asked that they sell 15 acres of the best land to Hoteles Interamericano at an equally ridiculous price of 50 cents per meter, so they say. And that was the corner reserved for what would be the number one hotel of that time- the Hotel El Panama.

The architect was North American Edward D. Stone, whose notable buildings such as General Motors in New York, a part of the Museum of Modern Art and US embassies in India and Belgium, had brought him fame.

Stone and his associates made a very important decision at the start. They decided to use the tropical climate of Panama city and not fight it. The hotel is a masterpiece of cross-ventilation, utilizing the hundreds of rooms as "funnels" for the prevailing north east winds from the Atlantic or their counterparts from the Pacific to the south.

This technique applies especially to the lobby which has no doors or windows which, apart from the breeze, gives it a fine sense of space.

The opening of the hotel in 1951 was a spectacular event such as Panama City had never seen before-- and Architect Stone won a medal of honor for "The building of the year" at an exhibition of the Architectural league of New York.

Such topflight U.S. magazines as Life, Holiday, Vogue, Harper's Bazaar and Fortune devoted many pages to the hotel, often with models posed in front of the hotel's sharply classic angles, amid its tropical shrubbery or beside the swimming pool.

The hotel was immediately, and has remained, Panama's premier social center, a symbol of the country's history, her tourism and her image abroad.

When it opened, the hotel was almost on the outskirts of the city. The city grew and now the five-star Hotel el Panama is in the very heart of the banking and hotel area on a large compound in surroundings of tropical beauty.

Its 330 rooms include suites, junior suites, luxury executive suites and pool cabins. Two exclusive executive floors offers special services for business travellers. The pool is vast and spectacular and the casino is the biggest in the city. Shops, a spa and gym, heliport, cafeteria, gourmet restaurant, pool bar and executive bar are some of the hotels other facilities.

Hotel El Panama is the only hotel in the city with its own convention center which has 14 salons of different sizes and an exhibition center (named after Vasco Nuñez de Balboa, discoverer of the Pacific Ocean) with a capacity for 5,500 people in concert, ideal for big events and shows.

The five-star El Panama Hotel Also lives as a happy memory for thousands of satisfied visitors who have found it a home-away-from-home and social centre for their visit.

They will remember the luxuriant gardens, the gigantic pool, the elegant and comfortable restaurants and bars, the exciting night life, the casino, the shops and, above all, the outstanding and courteous service and attention of the staff.

Hotel
★★★★★
EL PANAMA
Convention Center, Golf & Casino

Tel.: (507) 215-9000   Fax:(507) 223-6080
vintl@elpanama.com   www.elpanama.com

Copa Airlines

New fleet, plaudits for punctuality, greatest growth in the world

Copa Airlines, Panama's flag carrier, can well be considered one of the most successful companies of the Isthmus in the last century.

In mid - 2002 the airline announced it had ordered up to 12 New Generation 737 Boeing aircraft. This included a firm order for six planes and the right to buy six additional 737 aircraft. The firm order includes two 737-800 and four 737-700 - a fact that demostrates the airline's commitment to the growth and renovation of its fleet. The deliveries are scheduled to begin in October, 2003.

The company entered the 21st century flying to 29 destinations in 19 countries of North, Central and South America and the Caribbean.... a great achievement for a company which began only 55 years ago.

Compañía Panameña de Aviacion S.A. (COPA) was founded in 1947 by a visionary group of Panamanians with the technical and financial help of Pan-American Airways. The first flights, in Douglas C-47 planes, linked Panama City with David and Bocas del Toro.

In 1960 the company made its first international flights to San José, Costa Rica and modernized its fleet with AVRO 748 and Electra 188 planes, although it wasn't until 20 years later (1980) that Copa abandoned all its local routes and dedicated itself exclusively to the international routes which it possessed in those days, offering regular passenger and cargo services.

The last decade of the 20th century was one of great growth for the company which established its 'Hub of the Americas' in the Tocumen International Airport. In 1998 the U.S. airline Continental Airlines acquired 49% of the shares of the Panamanian company, forming a strategic alliance which resulted in a system of interconnecting airline routes between the United States and Latin America as well as shared benefits in the One Pass frequent flyer program

Copa's hub at Tocumen International Airport.

and world-wide access to the President's Club. Along with all these benefits, in 1999 the Panamanian flagship airline launched a new corporate image, changing its name to Copa Airlines.

Careful organization on the part of Copa's management and 2,250 employees has resulted in a high percentage of punctuality (90.72%).

In February 2002, Copa Airlines was recognized as the most punctual airline

operating in Mexico City's International Airport during the year 2001. Copa rated 10% higher than more than 40 other commercial and cargo airlines, both national and international.

Holiday Inn Panama has everything for the travelling businessman

Holiday Inn, the world's number one hotel chain has a well-earned reputation as a leader in quality, guest services and communications.

Holiday Inn Panama, a luxury business hotel catering to international travellers, opened its doors in the heart of Panama's banking and financial center in January 2000 with the latest information technology readily available to facilitate business transactions for the travelling businessman.

The hotel offers 150 guest rooms on 11 floors, 112 deluxe rooms and 38 suites.

Each room offers online internet service 24 hours a day, two telephone lines with direct national and international dialling, coffee machine with prestigious brands, voice mail, spacious bathrooms, iron and ironing board, 26 inch color TV and rigorous security system. The 38 suites have a comfortable living room, spacious terrace, executive desk, fax machine on request and a kitchenette/dining room.

One of the outstanding features of the hotel is a complete Internet Cafe and Business Center. Coffee, and tea service are available to "executives-on-the-go" as are all essential services such as fax, scanner, video conferencing, digital cameras and 24-hour online service. "Ciber Masters" are on hand to offer specialized assistance.

Meeting rooms with capacity for up to 200 people are available for business meetings or special events. Each meeting room has capacity for 10 telephone lines, and the latest multimedia equipment is available for presentations. Professional meeting planners will assist you in all the details.

"La Galeria" restaurant, as its name suggests, is an art gallery which in addition to a superb international menu, offers support to Panamanian's art. New exhibitions are showed very often. Sports Bar Memories is a place where you and your friends will enjoy pleasant moments watching your favorites sports.

For you relaxation and physical fitness, the hotel has a swimming pool and fully equiped gym. Ample parking space and a heliport ensure hassle-free transport for the most discerning guest. A gallery of modern boutiques completes the list of comforts on hand for the busy executive.

Holiday Inn faithfully promises to extend its best service and personalised attention, exceeding the highest expectations of guests with a staff which is supremely capable and highly motivated.

Newspaper serves Panama's growing commercial activities

Founded 21 years ago, Panama's biligual English-Spanish weekly transport and commercial newpaper, The Bulletin, is a well-established chronicle of the development of Panama as an international maritime center.

The Bulletin is a key source for the latest trend in ports, business and Panama Canal activities. It has covered such stories as the development of Manzanillo International Terminal, Panama's first private port complex; the departure of a giant Far Eastern shipping line to a port competing with Panama, then the same company's return to build its own port; the privatization of the port of Balboa and Cristobal and the acrimonious comments of a foreign government whose chosen company missed out; the way in which taxes which the Government tried to impose on the Colon Free Zone began to cause its slow demise until they were removed and it rapidly began to boom again.

The Bulletin keeps a watch on all aspects of commerce and business and reports on the most interesting trends in all economic sectors, not only in Panama, but often in neighboring areas of Latin America.

The Bulletin also carries all shipping arrivals and departures from Panama ports and airline schedules through the Tocumen International Airport.

The publication's totally independent editorials often highlight and, where warranted, criticize, to the discomfort of some, what it perceives to be trends against public or business interests.

Please contact us at: 223-6967, 223-6494, or e-mail: elboletin@cwpanama.net

AGROINDUSTRY

CAFE DURAN

At the great moments of the Republic, Café Duran was there

In celebrating 95 years of Café Durán, the company is proud to remember how many moments through history have been lived while enjoying the stimulation and comfort of a good cup of coffee.

Café Durán was founded in 1907, three years after the republic was founded and seven years before the inauguration of the Panama Canal. From those early days on all citizens in the new nation enjoyed the unequaled flavor of this coffee brand which was born with the new nation and grew along with it.

Mr. Esteban Durán Amat, pioneer of the now-famous company, started his business around the town of Gorgona on the Pacific coast Initially, he bought coffee from the local farmers and after roasting and grinding the beans, he sold the coffee in small bags made from newspaper as was the custom then.

Also, the construction of the canal was getting under way with the help of more than 24,000 laborers who in spite of the hard work and an unforgiving climate, would always take a break from the job at hand to savor a good cup of Café Durán, which Esteban made sure was available to them.

Café Durán was also the coffee of choice in high places. The new republic, under the command of Doctor Manuel Amador Guerrero, gave birth to the first constitution through long and intensive debates during which a good cup of Café Durán could not be missing. Since

Blooming coffee tree.

Café Durán cultivations.

Ripening cherry coffee .

AGROINDUSTRY

Café Durán roasting plant.

Warehouses for the final product.

then presidents without a doubt, have made their contribution to improve the country, while making a Café Durán break indispensable in their daily agendas.

While Panama was developing as a new nation and the canal was under construction, Café Durán moved its headquarters to a small warehouse situated on 16th Street right in the center of the city. From there coffee was delivered from house to house and from cafeteria to cafeteria. This early

A modern plant with the latest technology.

marketing initiative took a supreme effort on the part of a great family, 100% Panamanian, who since then, has demonstrated for five generations that "it is always time for a good cup of coffee".

History books, of course, only recount important events for the progress of the new nation. But, it is easy to image that in everyday life, Café Durán was an important element in all those moments in which a good cup of coffee helped to savor exciting events and revive the spirits.

A steaming hot cup of coffee was always present on the work tables of the different National Assemblies that ratificd the constitutions of 1941, 1946 and 1972. The unequaled flavor of Café Durán was present at the celebrations of the Torrijos –Carter Treaty in 1977, for which today we give thanks that the national territory is sovereign and the canal is ours, as much ours as our Café Durán.

Along with political events in the republic there were also great developments in the economy, commerce, industry, banking, culture and sports: boxers, such as "Mano dc Piedra" Durán, Jockeys such as Laffit Pincay, Baseball Players such as Mariano Rivera, song writers and singers such as Ruben Blades, painters such as Alfredo and Olga Sinclair and Poets such as Ricardo Miró have brought

glory to our country, always willing to give the best of themselves and always relying on a good cup of Café Durán.

Numerous events have written the history of this young and beautiful nation; unforgettable moments such as the inauguration of the Bridge of the Americas, The Santo Tomas Hospital, The National University The "Normal de Santiago", The Universidad Santa María La Antigua among others, have set guidelines in our country and, like Café Durán, have given us an unequaled feeling of greatness.

Our folklore, together with Café Durán is also an important part of our pride in being Panamanian. From the fundamental roots born of our patriotism "the pollera" was born, a dress of unrivalled beauty, of mischievious coquetry and intense femininity.

Finally, we must remember that historical day, December 31st, 1999, when Panamá assumed total control of the canal and its territory; a moment which the people celebrated with a warm cup of Café Durán , lending a taste of true nationalism and independece .

In its 95 years, Esteban Durán Amat, S.A. has been a pioneer in the coffee industry providing a livelihood to more than 40,000 persons and being a leader in the care of the eco-system .

In every moment that is lived with a cup of Café Durán, there is something more than an aroma of tradition: there is effort, hard work, a will to give and a flavor of patriotism that is part of our being.

AGROINDUSTRY

Varela Hermanos, S.A.
Fine rums and spirits, family tradition and technology

The history of Varela Hermanos, S.A. dates back to 1908 when Don José Varela Blanco, a young Spanish immigrant, established in Pesé the San Isidro Sugar Mill, the first sugar mill in the recently formed Republic of Panama.

The town of Pesé, established in the mid XVIII century, is located in a fertile valley in the center of Panama, and the main activity of Its population of about 10,000 people is the cultivation of sugar cane.

The offices of Varela International (Zona Libre).

Following the wishes of his three eldest sons, Jose Manuel, Plinio and Julio, Don Jose began in 1936 the distillation of alcohol from sugar cane juice for the production of distilled spirits. From the very beginning he was recognized for the extraordinary quality of his products.

Since then, Varela Hermanos, S.A. has kept the leadership of the domestic distilled spirits industry, and today produces approximately one million cases per year, which accounts for 90% of the domestic distilled spirits market. The company has over 700 permanent employees, whose functions range from sugar cane harvesting to the sale and promotion of the finished products.

The main agro-industrial installations of the firm are located in Pese, which include 800 cultivated hectares, which produce approximately 50,000 tons of sugar cane per year. During the harvest season, over 500 people, including part time workers, are employed to cut, transport, mill and distill the sugar cane juice.

At the Don Jose distillery, a modern installation which opened in 1976, the industrial process starts with the milling and extraction of the sugar cane juice. This juice is then fermented and distilled

in a 4 column system, which results in an extra neutral alcohol, used exclusively to produce Seco Herrerano, the company's best selling product, recognized as the national drink of Panama.

During the rainy season, the alcohol distillation operations continue, starting from sugar cane molasses; this alcohol is used to produce other brands, particularly Ron Abuelo and Ron Cortez for the local and export market.

To produce these rums, all the way from the fermentation with yeast developed in our laboratories, to the aging in small white oak barrels, a perfect marriage of state-of-the-art technology and a rich tradition is achieved, which results products of unsurpassable quality.

Today, almost a century after Don Jose started operations in Pesé, a third generation, following the same family tradition, directs Varela Hermanos, S.A. the leading producer of distilled spirits in Panama. With a solid production infrastructure, and the passion and dedication of the entire workforce, the company is preparing to create a stronger presence in the international market as exporters of fine rums and spirits.

Tel.: 217-3777   Fax: 217-6046
www.varelahermanos.com

Cane cutter.

The plant.

The warehouse in Pesé.

Grupo Calesa

The most important agro-industrial group of Panama, leader in the technological development of agriculture and the agro-industrial sector

In the early days of the Republic, the Chiari family began farming in Natá in the province of Coclé, concentrating on cultivating sugar cane and breeding livestock. By January 1918, Don Rodolfo Chiari Robles had begun production of sugar and a few years later founded the Compañía Azucarera La Estrella, S.A. (CALESA); a powerful company with solid investment and sound technology. The company became the most important pillar in the development of the province, offering work to thousands of people directly and indirectly in the manufacture of Azucar La Estrella, a high quality product which is appreciated daily in every Panamanian home. The company's motto is: "Sweeten your life" with La Estrella.

The sugar mill Ofelina, also in Natá, where the products of La Estrella are manufactured, was the first sugar mill of our country to meet all the international norms required to certify its products under the quality of HACCP, a seal of approval for the exports which CALESA makes every year.

Because of his love for the land, his faith and his trust in the country and based on hard and honorable work, Don Rodolfo Chiari and later his sons Rodolfo Chiari R., Roberto F. Chiari R., and Ricardo A. Chiari R. continued over the years to make new investments in the agricultural sector. This led to the establishment of new consortiums such as Ganadera Industrial, S.A., founding company and promoter of Grupo Industrias Lácteas, and in Grupo Calesa formed by Compañía Azucarera La Estrella, S.A. and the following companies:

Compañía Ganadera de Coclé, S.A. (GANACO), was formally esta-

Grupo Calesa installations, located in the district of Natá, along the Interamerican Highway.

blished in August of 1951 and dedicated to the breeding, and commercialization of cattle and pigs. It was the first company in the country to import pure-bred Holstein dairy cattle, specializing later in beef cattle.

Industrias de Natá, S.A. (INASA), was formally established in July of 1959, dedicated, under the well-known brand LARRO, for the manufacture of pellet and extruded feed for animal consumption for the local and export market. Products include feed for shrimp, fish, poultry, horses, cattle, pigs, goats, rabbits and pets. INASA was the pioneer company in the manufacture of specialized food for aquaculture in our country, a field in which it is an undeniable leader, becoming a pillar of development in this important exporting sector of Panama.

Central de Granos de Coclé, S.A., (CEGRACO), was formally established in July 1986, dedicated to the cultivation, processing and commercialization of grains, particularly of rice, with its leading brands: Del'Oro, Premier and Predilecto. CEGRACO operates many rice farms in different areas of the county such as Alanje, province of Chiriquí; Bayano, province of Panama; Santa Rita, province of Herrera, and Natá, province of Coclé. CEGRACO supplies more than 12% of all the rice consumed by Panamanians and is in the process of exploring the development of new added-value products with which to grow in the local and foreign market.

Camaronera de Coclé, S.A. (CAMACO), formally established in July of 1990 is dedicated to the aquaculture of shrimps in tanks for export. CAMACO is proprietor of the most important shrimp farm in the district of Natá which has approximately 1200 hectares of ponds. This company is a regional leader in the development of up-to-date technologies in shrimp farming, in the establishment of closed cycles of production of larvae in its two larvae production centers and in the development of its own genetic lines of disease-resistant shrimp with the help of local and foreign consultants.

Semillas de Coclé, D.S. (SECOSA), formally established in July of 1993, is primarily dedicated to the pro-

duction, processing and commercialization of certified seeds particularly of rice for national cultivation. The company operates extensive and modern facilities in the district of Natá. Through strategic alliances in investigation and development it will continue expanding its products to ensure that producers can obtain better and better yields and the best results that the climate and soil conditions of our country can offer.

Central de Abastos, S.A. (CASA), formally established in August of 1995, is dedicated to the representation and distribution of national and international brands, especially agricultural products. Some of the brands that it represents are ProKura (Pro-bio vitamins), INVESA (veterinary products), Joosten Products (dairy substitutes), Dex Ibérica (vitamins and minerals), Duo Farms (equipment for pig farms), CONSERFRIO (equipment for the conservation of controlled temperature of grains). In addition the company represents an extensive variety of equipment, accessories and raw materials both in Panama, as well as increasingly in Central America and the Caribbean.

Through its financial, corporate, managerial and technological strength the group of companies that form Grupo Calesa has developed strategic ties with different first class national and international research and investigative centers. This enables the group to penetrate further into the local and international markets, in the fields of bio-technology, agricultural production, brand and market development, etc. This is the manner in which these companies are preparing to confront the challenges of the 21st century and continue as the undeniable leader of the agricultural and agro-industrial sector of Panama.

During approximately 85 years of existence, Grupo Calesa has actively contributed to the development of our country becoming a major generator of income through exports, as well as a source of indirect and direct employment particularly in the rural areas where the majority of its agricultural, agro-industrial and commercial activities take place. As always, Grupo Calesa continues to create new avenues of growth and will continue to develop strategies to further

CIA. GANADERA DE COCLE, S.A.

participate in the global markets. To that end and in harmony with its trajectory and history, Grupo Calesa is in a continuous process of development and modernization.

For more information about Grupo Calesa you may write to: P.O. Box 8404, Zona 07, Panama, Republic of Panama; visit: http://www.grupocalesa.com; or contact through:
info@grupocalesa.com

Administrative Offices:
Panamá tels: 236-1711/1150,
Natá tels: 997-4321/4163.
Sales: Panamá: 236-1380
Natá: 997-6700
Chiriquí: 774-3731

Lists and Data
Associations and Organizations

Foreign Countries

Alliance Francaise, Tel: 223-7376, 223-5792 alianza@afpanama.org

Chinese Association of Panama, Tel: 262-8499

Panamanian-German Chamber of Commerce and Industry, Tel: 269-9358 ihkd@cableonda.net

Spanish Chamber of Commerce, Tel: 225-1487 caespan@cwpanama.net

Chinese Cultural Center of Panama, Tel: 236-0255 jesusosacar@hotmail.com

Bolivarian Society of Panama, Tel: 212-0431

Colombian Civic Society, Tel: 265-1604

Hindu Civic Society, Tel: 260-4212/ 213-2366

Cuban Society of Panama, Tel: 264-4192

Hindu Society of Panama, Tel: 236-2366

Business Professional and Industrial Associations

American Chamber of Commerce and Industry of Panama, Tel: 269-3881, Web page: www.panamcham.com

APROSAC Association, Tel: 263-3370

Banana Trade Association, Tel: 775-2366

National Banking Association, Tel: 226-7630, 263-7044, E-mail: abapa@bellsouth.net.pa

Panamanian Foreign Press Correspondents Association (ACOPEP)

Film Distributors Association, Tel: 263-9669

Panamanian Fishing Industry Association, Tel: 251-0317

National Teachers Association, Tel: 265-5450, Web page: www.multired.com/educa/asprorep

Panamanian Association of Restaurants and Related Activities, Tel: 236-7066

Colon Free Zone Users Association, Tel: 441-4244, E-mail: usuarios@auzonalibrecolon.com

National Association of Farmers, Tel: 261-1272

National Association of Poultry Farmers, Tel: 261-1272

National Association of Traders and Distributors, Tel: 236-2459 / 5968, E-mail: acoriopa@eveloz

National Traders Association, Tel: 269-7217, E-mail: losandes@cwpanama.net

National Association of Agricultural Supply Distributors, Tel: 261-1264, E-mail: andia@sinfo.net

National Association of Construction Material Suppliers and Retailers, Tel: 261-0921

National Association of Loan Operators, Tel: 236-9594, E-mail: anafi@sinfo.net

National Association of Cattlemen, Tel: 225-1236, E-mail: anagon@sinfo.net

National Association of Rice Millers, Tel: 261-4618, E-mail: analmo@sinfo.net

Panamanian Association of Odontology, Tel: 269-1603, E-mail: aop@aopan.org

Panamanian Insurance Agents' Association, Tel: 225-9475, E-mail: info@apadea.com

Panamanian Association of Business Executives, Tel: 227-3511, E-mail: apede@apede.org

Panamanian Exporters Association, Tel: 230-0169, E-mail: apex@cableonda.net

Panamanian Broadcasting Associations (APR), Tel: 225-2052/ 227-0953, E-mail: exitosa@psi.net.pa

Colon Chamber of Commerce, Tel: 441-7182, E-mail: cancolon@cwpanama.net

Panamanian Chamber of Commerce, Industry and Agriculture, Tel: 227-1233, Web page: www.panacamara.com

Panamanian Chamber of Tourism, Tel: 211-3268

Panamanian Maritime Chamber, Cristóbal, Colón, Tel: 264-7996 / 8158

Panamanian Construction Chamber, Tel: 265-2500, E-mail: finanzas@capac.org

Panamanian College of Public Accountants, Tel: 236-6571, 225-6651, E-mail: ccpap@sinfo.net

National College of Lawyers, Tel: 225-6371, E-mail: cna01@orbi.net

Latinamerican Confederation of Savings and Loan Cooperatives, Tel.: 227-3322, Web page: www.colac.com

Council of Rectors or University Representatives, Web page: www.pa/consejo/universidad.html
Panama-United States Business Council, Tel.: 269-0401
Industrial Federation of Food Handlers and Hotel Workers, Tel: 221-5985
International Confederation of Construction and Wood Workers , Tel: 229-2952, E-mail: orl@cableonda.net
Respiratory and Allergy Institute: Tel: 229-0634
Tommy Guardia National Geographic Institute: Tel: 236-2444, E-mail: eirodriguez@mop.gob.pa
National Cancer Institute, Tel: 262-8877
International Work Organization (OIT)
Panama Canal Pilots Association, Tel: 228-4868
Credit Society, Tel: 262-0787
LatinAmerican Investment Society, Tel: 210-1969
Panamanian Society of Engineers and Architects, Tel: 213-1909/223-7265

Religious

Panamanian Baptist Convention, Tel: 268-2186
Home of the Teaching Mothers, Tel: 231-2269, E-mail: madresm@cwpanama.net
Panamanian Baptist Camp, Tel: 264-5585,
E- mail:convencionbautistadepanama@hotmail.com
Panamanian Federation of Catholic Women, Tel:. 226-1658
Episcopal Church of San Cristobal, Tel.: 224-1014
Panamanian Bible Society, Vías España y Fdez de Córdoba, Tel.: 264-1000, E-mail: sbp@sinfo@.net
B'nai B'rith Benefit Society, Av 5 San Fco, Tel.: 226-8750/26-2585
Yan Wo Religious Society, Cl Carlos A Mendoza 34, Tel.: 262-1034
Center for Islamic Studies and Research. Ave. Meléndez 3.021 Colón. Tel: 445-4718

Civic and Charity

SOS Children's Village Association of Panama (KINDERDORF), Tel: 261-2987
Police Force Benefit Association, Tel: 228-7100/ 228-7052
White Cross Association, Tel: 445-2937/ 270-0232, E-mail: cruzblanca@tutopia.com
Light and Life Association, Tel: 262-1540
National Medical Association, Tel: 263-7622
National Association of Nurses, Tel: 225-4717, E-mail: anap@sinfo.net
Panama National Association of Scouts, Tel: 261-4036
Panamanian Family Planning Association, Tel: 314-0430/317-0429
Pro Children Association, Tel: 264-5653
House of Hope for the Rescue of Street Children, Tel: 232-7367, E-mail: cesperanza@cw.net.pa
20-30 Club of Panama, Tel: 270-2030, E-mail: dir2030@cableonda.net
Lions Club of Panama, Tel: 225-0721, E-mail:

panaleon@cwp.net.pa
Kiwanis Club of Panama, Tel: 232-628, E-mail : kiwanis@cwp.net.pa
Rotary Club Panama South, Tel: 226-2684
Panamanian Red Cross, Tel: 315-1388
Children's Hospital Volunteers, Tel: 227-6076
Faith and Happiness, Tel: 261-8712
Louis & Marthe Deveaux Benefit Foundation, Tel: 223-5514
Rotary Benefit Foundation, Tel: 270-0147
Frank Ullrich Foundation, Tel: 441-8805
María & Dámaso Mora Foundation, Tel: 221-6659
Mary Arias Foundation, Tel: 264-8344
Foundation for the Children of Darien, Tel: 264-4336
Panamanian Disabled Foundation, Tel: 264-5333, E-mail: fundproi@cwp.net.pa
Panama Girl's Home, Tel: 268-4156
Hogares Crea de Panamá, Tel: 227-2582
Goodwill Industries, Tel: 267-7716
Nurture Home, Tel: 232-6955, E-mail: nutrehogar@cwpanama.net
Caritas Panama, Tel: 262-3777,
E-mail: caritas@caritaspanama.pa
Ciudad del Niño, Tel: 317-0240/0241
Remar Panama, Tel: 229-9543
Ecuadorian Benefit Society, Tel: 262-1142
Spanish Benefit Society, Tel: 261-6838
Israeli Benefit Society, Tel: 225-5990

Environmental

ANCON (National Association for the Conservation of Nature), Tel: 314-0060 E-mail: ancon@ancon.org
Audobon Society of Panama, Tel: 224-4740   E-mail: info@panamaaudubon.org

Cultural

Lecturers Circle, Tel: 264-0524
National Group of Artistic Expression (GANEXA), Tel: 264-3961/223-9140
United Panamanian Teachers, Tel: 264-9205
Friends of the Afroantillean Museum (SAMAAP), Tel: 262-1668 E-mail: samaap@yahoo.com
Panamanian Society of Authors and Composers, Tel: 264-7664
Spanish Union Sports Club, Tel: 226-1504,
E-mail: sdccpanama@hotmail.com
Panamanian Football Federation, Tel: 228-2238

Sports

Balboa Yacht Club, Tel: 228-5794, E-mail: bycpma@bycp-ma.com
Horse Owners Club, Tel: 233-5437
Clayton Equestrian Club, Tel: 232-6272/6071

Yacht and Fishing Club, Tel: 227-0145 E-mail: cypesca@sinfo.
Hotel Coronado Club, Riding, Golf. Tel: 264-2863
Summit Golf Resort. Tel: 266-7436
Spanish Union Sports Club, Tel: 226-1504,
E-mail: sdccpanama@hotmail.com
Panamanian Football Federation, Tel: 228-2238

Recreational

El Carrizal Country Club, Tel: 225-4797,
E-mail: elcarrizal@sinfo.net
Panama Golf Club, Cerro Viento, Tel: 266-7777, E-mail: clubgolf@clubgolf.com.pa
Panama Executives Golf Club, Tel: 277-5858
Montaña Altos del Lago Club, Tel: 230-1158,
E-mail: mercadeo_ventas@hotmail.com
Union Club of Panama, Tel: 263-5233, E-mail: cunión@sinfo.net

Labor Unions and Trade Associations

Panamanian Workers Confederation. Calle 31 y Ave. Justo Arosemena. Tel. 225 02-93. Secretario General: Guillermo Puga.
Panamanian General Workers Federation. (FEGE-TRAB RP). Ave. B, San Felipe, 9-38 Tel. 262-02-37.
Food Handlers and Hotel Workers Association. Parque Lefevre, 826. Tel. 221-59-85, E-mail: fstrp.@inpanama.com
Workers Union Federation. Calle16, Santa Ana #9,Tel. 228-44-48.
Industrial Union. Vía Ricardo J. Alfaro.Tel. 230-01-69.
Clothing Manufacturing Workers Union. Vía. Fernández de Córdoba Tel.: 261-75-42.
Airline Workers Industrial Union. Frente a Plaza Carolina **Cía SIELAS.** Tel. 224-66-83, E-mail: sielas@sinfo.net

Typesetting and Grafic Arts Union. Ave. 6 Colón, 13-81. Tel. 262-97-51.
National Port Workers Union
Interamerican Center of Tax Administrators, (CIAT). Ave. Ramón Arias. Tel. 223-10-44, E-mail: ciat@ciat.org
Panama's Brewery Workers' Union. Calle 6 Río Abajo, Local 31A. Tel. 221-3848.

Varied

A.A. Alcoholics Anonymous, Central Offices of Public Services and Information Committee. Vía España Edif. Las Camelias, 5° piso, 502. Tel.: 263-9906 panamakevin.com
American Society: Urbanización Dos Mares, edificio Pacific Hills Torre 100, piso # 21. Tel.: 260-8619. E-mail: pierce@sinfo.net
Association of Thoroughbred Owners. Vía José Arango. Tel.: 233-17-73. E-mail: appucapac@cwpanama.com
Senior Citizens Association, Bethania, Calle Cartagena, Tel.: 229-20-20.
Panamanian Girl Guides Association. Calle 3 Perejil. Tel.: 225-56-53.
Light and Life Association. Calle 9, San Felipe. Tel.: 262-15-40.
National Association for the Conservation of Nature (ANCON). Calle Alberto Navarro. Tel.: 314-0060 E-mail: ancon@ancon.org
Panamanian Family Planning Association, (APLAFA), La loceria, Tel: 236-4428.
United Nations Information Center. Tel: 223-05-57.
Food Producers Society, S.A. (SOPAS) Vía. Simón Bolivar 130, El Cangrejo Tel.: 263-95-22.
E-mail: caféduran@cableonda.net
Who's New. Tel: 264-0567, stpanama@pobox.com

Foreign Embassies in Panama

Germany, Edif. World Trade Center, P.H., Calle 53, Urb. Marbella, Tel.: 263-7733, E-mail: germpanama@cwp.net.pa
United States, Cl 37 y Ave. Balboa, Tel.: 207-7000, E-mail: usembisc@cwp.net.pa
Argentina, Edif. Banco Atlántico, 7to piso, Cl. 50 y 53, Urb. Obarrio, Tel.: 264-6561
Bolivia, Cl. Eric A. del Valle, Casa #1, El Cangrejo, Tel.: 269-0274. E-mail: emb-bol-pan@cwpanama.net
Brazil, Edif. El Dorado, piso #1, Cl. E. Méndez Campo Alegre 24, Tel.: 263-5322, E-mail: embrasil@cwpanama.net
Canada, Edif. World Trade Center, piso 1, Cl. 53 E, Galería Comercial, Urb. Marbella, Tel.: 264-9731
Chile, Edificio Bankboston Piso 11, Vía España, Tel.: 223-9748, E-mail: chilepa@cwpanama.net
Colombia, Edif World Trade Center 1802, Cl 53 Urb. Marbella, Tel.: 264-9266/ 9513 E-mail: emcolpan @cwpana-ma.net
Korea, Cls. Ricardo Arias y 51-E, Campo Alegre, Tel.: 264-8203
Costa Rica, Ave. Samuel Lewis, Tel.: 264-2980, E-mail: embarica@cwpanama.net
Cuba, Frente al Parque Porras, Ave. Cuba y Ave. Ecuador, Tel.: 227-0359, E-mail: embacuba@cableonda.net
Equador, Cl 50 y 53 Marbela, Tel.: 269-0477
Egypt, Cl 55, El Cangrejo #15, Tel.: 263-5020
El Salvador, Ave. Manuel Espinosa Batista, Tel.: 223-3020, E-mail: embasalva@cwpanama.com
Spain, Frente al Parque Porras, Cl 33 y Ave. Perú , Tel.: 227-5122
France, Las Bóvedas, Plaza de Francia, Tel.: 223-7824, E-mail: ambafran@pan.gbm.net
Great Britain, Swiss Tower, piso #4, Cl. 53 Urb. Marbella,

Tel.: 269-0866, E-mail: britemb@cwpanama.net

Guatemala, Edif Altamira Piso 9, Vía Argentina, Tel.: 269-3406, E-mail: embaguat@cwpanama.nct

Haiti, Edif Grobman Piso 7, Cl. Manuel M. Icaaza, Tel.: 269-3443, E-mail: ambhaiti@c-com.net.pa

Honduras, Edif. Bay Mall, piso # 1, Local #12, Ave. Balboa, E-mail: ehpan@cableonda.net

India, Ave. Fdco. Boyd, Tel.: 264-2416, E-mail: indempan@cwpanama.net

Italy, Edif. Banco Exterior, # 25, Ave. Balboa, Tel.: 225-8948, E-mail: panitamb@cwp.net.pa

Jamaica, Edif. Seguros Simpson 1422, Ave. de los Mártires, Tel.: 228-3818, E-mail: geosimp@sinfo.net

Japan, Edif. Sede Propia, Cls. 50 y 60 E Obarrio, Tel.: 263-6155, E-mail: taiship2@sinfo.net

Lybia, Ave. Balboa y Cl. 32, 227-3342

Malta, Cl 54, Urb. Marbella, Duplex # 8, 264-9538

Mexico, Edif. ADR, piso# 10 Ave. Samuel Lewis y Cl. 58, E-mail: embamexpan@cwpanama.net

Nicaragua, Quarry Heights, 16, Tel.: 211-2113,

Santa Sede de la Nunciatura Apostólica, Punta Paitilla, Tel.: 269-2102, E-mail: embapan@sinfo.net

Paraguay, Edif. Venecia 5B, Cl. Juan XXIII Paitilla, Tel.: 263-4782

Peru, Edif. World Trade Center Piso 12, Cl. 53, Urb. Marbella, Tel.: 223-1112, E-mail: embaperu@pananet.com

Poland, Torre del Pacífico, Apt.# 10 A, Urb. Marbella , Tel.: 263-5097, E-mail: her@pananet.com

Republic of China, Torre HSBC, piso #10, Ave, Samuel Lewis, Tel.: 223-3424

Dominican Republic, Cl. 75 Este San Fco, Tel.: 270-3884

Rusia, Edif. Int'L Business Center, piso #10, Ave. Manuel Espinosa Batista, Tel.: 264-1408,
E-mail. emruspan@sinfo.net

Western Sahara Cl. Manuel Icaza y Ave. Samuel Lewis, Tel.: 263-2599, E-mail: embrasdp@cableonda.net

Uruguay, Edif. J Vallarino, piso # 5, Ave. Justo Arosemena y Cl 32, Tel.: 225-0049 E-mail: urupanam@sinfo.net

Venezuela, Torre Hong Kong Bank Piso 5, Ave. Samuel Lewis, Tel.: 269-1244,
E-mail: embavenezpan@cableonda.net

Vietnam, Cl. José Gabriel Duque, casa # 52, La Cresta, Tel.: 265-2551, E-mail: tranquocbe@yahoo.com

Foreign Consulates in Panama

South Africa, Edif. Aquarius, piso # 2, Cl. 47, Bella Vista, Tel.: 264-5971

Germany, Edif. Beta, 5to piso, Vía España 120, Tel.: 263-6311

Austria, Edif. World Trade Center, # 1401, Urb. Marbella, Tel.: 265-3855

Belgium, Vía Tocumen, La Pulida, Tel.: 217-3277, E-mail: cocige@grupoescope.com

Belize, Villa de las Fuentes # 1, Cl 22 C Norte, Duplex F-32, Tel.: 236-4132

Belize, Edif. Atlas #8, Colón, Cl. 13 y Ave. Central, Tel.: 227-1697, E-mail: vasquezluisantonio@hotmail.com

Bolivia, Cl. 14 y Ave. Roosevelt, Zona Libre, Colón, Tel.: 433-2000

Canada, Edif. World Trade Center, piso # 1, Galería Comercial, Cl. 53, Urb. Marbella, Tel.: 264-9731

Chile, Edif. Bank Boston, piso #11, Vía España, tel.: 264-4317, E-mail: chilepa@cwpanama.net

Cyprus, Cls. Manuel M Icaaza y 51E, Tel.: 264-4147

Colombia, Colón 2000, 2ndo piso, Colón Tel.: 441-8057, E-mail: conscolombia@cwpanama.net

Colombia, David: Tel.: 775-4616

Colombia, Edif World Trade Center, Cl. 53, Urb. Marbella, Tel.: 223-3535, E-mail: cnpanama@cwpanama.net

Colombia, Puerto Obaldía, Comarca de San Blas, Tel.: 299-9449

Korea (South), Cls. Ricardo Arias y 51 – E, Planta Bja Campo Alegre, Tel.: 264-8203

Costa Rica, Ave. 17 de Abril, finca # 6, Changuinola Tel.: 758-9128

Costa Rica, Cl. Gerardo Ortega, Tel.: 264-2937, E-mail: consulpma@cwp.net.pa

Cuba, Frente al Parque Porras, Ave. Cuba y Ave. Ecuador, Tel.: 227-5277, E-mail: conscuba@cableonda.net

Denmark, Vía Cincuentenario 28, Tel.: 270-0944, E-mail: nielsp@gourmar.com

Denmark, Edif. # 1103, Cristobal, : Ave. Roosevelt, Tel.: 441-4082/205-6759, E-mail: dankonsul@yahoo.co.uk

Equador, Cls. 50 y 53, Tel.: 264-7820, E-mail: conecuat@cableonda.net

Equador, Edif. PH. Plaza 2000, 6to piso, entre Cls 50 y 53, Urb. Marbella, tel.: 264-7820

El Salvador, Edif. Metropolis, 4to piso, Ave. Manuel Espinosa Batista, Tel.: 223-3020,
E-mail: embasalva@cwpanama.com

Slovania, Cl. 16, Casa # 62, San Francisco, Tel.: 270-1830, E-mail: invqeo@cableonda.net

Phillipines, Cl. 48 Bella Vista, Tel.: 264-1355, E-mail: mdr@ucre.net

Finland, Cl. 64 Oeste y Vía Simón Bolívar, Tel.: 279-9802

France, Cl. 10 y Ave. Roosevelt, Colón, tel.; 441-9902

France, Edif. Brencan, 1er alto, #11 David, Tel.: 775-2528, E-mail: mabson@hotmail.com

France, Las Bóvedas , Plaza de Francia, Tel.: 228-7835, E-mail: ambafran@pan.gbm.net

Great Britain, Swiss Tower, piso #4, Cl. 53, Urb. Marbella, Tel.: 269-0866, E-mail: britemb@cwpanama.net

Greece, Antiguo Edif. NCR, 3er piso, Ave. Manuel Espinosa

Batista, E-mail: greecepa@psi.net.pa

Guatemala, Vía Argentina, El Cangrejo, Tel.: 269-3406, E-mail: embaguat@cwpanama.net

Hungry, Cl. 64-E Vía Porras, Tel.: 229-1742, E-mail: willifu@cableonda.net

Indonesia, Cl. 73 y Ave. 4ta, Casa # 50, San Francisco, Tel.: 226-1655, E-mail: indonesia@cciglobal.net.pa

Iceland, Edif. Tagarópulos, Ave. Ricardo J. Alfaro, Tel.: 236-1616, E-mail: tagpma@sinfo.net

Italy, Edif. Banco Exterior # 25, Ave. Balboa, Tel.: 225-8948, E-mail: panitamb@cw.net.pa

Lebanon, Cl. 2 y Fort De Lesseps, Colón, Tel.: 441-8414, E-mail: conslib@sinfo.net

Luxemburg, Vía Transistmica, Cl. 64 Este, Urb. Los Angeles, Tel.: 279-9854

Morocco, Cl. 16 y Ave. Roosevelt, Colón, Tel.: 433-2222, E-mail: vpzlsa@vidapanama.com

Mexico, Edif. Malami, Cl. C- Norte y Ave. 1era Este, Opticentro Vega, David, Tel.: 775-4947, E-mail: lochsa@cwpanama.net

Nicaragua, Vía Panamericana, frente al Hotel Galeria, Santiago, Tel.: 998-4434, E-mail: rymsa1@sinfo.net

North America, Ave. Balboa y Cl. 39, Tel.: 207-7030, E-mail: panama_usconsul@state.gov

Norway, Cl. La Boca #796X, Balboa, Ancon, Tel.: 228-1103

Norway, Edif Comosa Piso 5, Ave. Samuel Lewis, Tel.: 263-1955

Norway, Edif. #1103, Cristobal, Tel.: 441-4177, E-mail: cb_fenton@cwp.net.pa

Low Countries, Cl. 50 y Beatríz M. de Cabal, Tel.: 264-7257, E-mail: consuladonl@cwpanama.net

Paraguay, Edif. Venecia, Cl Juan XXIII Paitilla, 263-4782

Peru, Edif. World Trade Center, piso # 12, Urb. Marbella, Tel.: 269-6641, E-mail: conperu@sinfo.net

Poland, Plaza Colón 2000, Ofic. # 49, Cl 12 y Paseo Gorgas, Colón, Tel.: 433-2024, E-mail: jpalermot@hotmail.com

Puerto Rico, Bay Mall Plaza, 5to piso, Ave. Balboa, Tel.: 269-2412, E-mail: ocpr@pa.inter.net

Czech Republic, Vía Max Jimenez, La Locería, Tel.: 236-1777, E-mail: panama@embassy.mzv.cz

Republic of China, Ave. Roosevelt y Cl. 8, Colón, Tel.: 441-3061, E-mail: congencn@cwpanama.net

Republic of Malta, Cl. Elvira Mendez, Tel.: 223-9401, E-mail: malteseconsulate@anorco.com.pa

Dominican Republic, Banco de Boston, piso # 5, Vía España, Tel.: 264-8630

Romania, Edif. Geminis, 3er piso, Apto. 6-B, Cl.Santa Rita, Urb. Obarrio, Tel.: 213-0568, E-mail: consrumaniapty@hotmail.com

Syria, Cl. 17 Zona Libre, Colón, Tel.: 447-1338, E-mail: consiria@marsamericalatina.com

Sweden, Edif. Galerias de Balboa, 1er piso, #18, Ave. Balboa, Tel.: 264-3748, E-mail: condsween@cwpanama.net

Switzerland, Cls. Victoria y 1, Miraflores, 261-1530

Thailand, Edif. BMW, planta baja, Cl. 50, Tel.: 270-5444, E-mail: cdejanon@fasa.com.pa

Trinidad y Tabago, Edif. Plaza 50, piso #3, Cl.50 y Vía Brazil, Tel.: 263-4105

Turkey, Ave. 8 Norte y Cl. 64 Oeste, Urb. Ind. Los Angeles, Tel.: 260-5533

Uruguay, Edif. J. J. Vallarino, piso # 5, Ave. Justo Arosemena y Cl 32, E-mail: urupanam@sinfo.net

Vietnam, Cl. José Gabriel Duque, Casa #52, La Cresta , Tel.: 265-2551, E-mail: tranquocbe@yahoo.com

Foreign Missions in Panama

Japan International Cooperation Agency, (JICA) – Edif. World Trade Center, 4to piso, Cl. 53, Urb. Marbella, Tel.: 264-9669, Web page: www.jica.go.jp/panama/index.htm

Interamerican Development Bank (BID), Edif. Torre HSBC, piso # 14, Ave. Samuel Lewis, Tel: 263-6944, E-mail: cofcpn@iadb.org

Latinamerican Export Bank (BLADEX), Edif. Bladex, Ave. Aquilino de la Guardia y Cl. 50, Tel.: 210-8500 Web page: www.blx.com

Coordination Center for the Prevention of Natural Disasters in Central America (CEPREDENAC), Edif. # 707, Ranger AV, Howard, Tel.: 316-0064,
E-mail: secretario@cepredenac.org

Water Center of the Humid Tropic for Latin America and the Caribbean (CATHALAC), Edif. 801, Ciudad del Saber, Clayton, Tel.: 317-0125, E-mail: cathalac@cathalac.org

Interamerican Center of Tax Administrators (CIAT) – Ave. Ramón Arias, Tel.: 265-2766, E-mail: ciat@ciat.org

Interamerican Tropical Tuna Commission, Edif. Sousa, piso # 2 Cl. 43 y Ave. Colombia, E-mail: ciatpan@cwp.net.pa

Panama – United States Commission for the Eradication and Prevention of the Screw Worm (COPEG) – Edif. #552 –C, La Boca, Balboa, Tel.: 314-0761, E-mail: gbg@copeg.org

Panama – United States Commission for the Aftosa Fever – Edif. #522-C, La Boca, Tel.: 314-0761, E-mail: gbg@copeg.org

Latinamerican Federation for Savings and Loans Cooperation (COLAC), Ave. Justo Arosemena y Cl. 44, Bella Vista, E-mail: csanchez@colac.com

Interamerican Institute for Agricultural Cooperation, (ILCA), Edif. #128, Ciudad del Saber, Cayton, Tel.: 317-0174, E-mail: iica@iica.org.pa

Smithsonian Tropical Research Institute, Ave. Roosevelt No. 401, Ancon, Tel.: 212-8000, Web page: www.stri.org

United Nations Children's Organization (UNICEF)- Edif # 131, Ciudad del Saber, Clayton, Tel.: 317-0257, Web page: www.unicef.org/panama

Food and Agriculture Organization of the United Nations,

(FAO) – Edif. #0760-A, La Boca, Balboa, Tel.: 228-5259, E-mail: fao-pa@fao.org

Organization of American States (OAS), Edif. # 813, Ciudad del Saber, Clayton, Tel.: 317-0557, E-mail: oea-pan@cwpanama.net

International Regional Organization for Plant and Animal Health (OIRSA) – Casa # 1012 AB, Cl. Hocker Dr., Clayton, Tel.: 317-0902, E-mail: oirsa@cwpanama.net

Panamerican Health Organization (OPS) and Health

Organization, (OMS)- Edif. # 261, Ministerio de Salud, Gorgas, Tel.: 262-0030, E-mail: pan.ops-oms.org

United Nations Development Progam (PNUD)- Edif. Central, piso # 1, Ave. Samuel Lewis y Cl. Gerardo Ortega, Tel.: 265-0838, E-mail: registry@undp.org.pa

Free Trade Area of the Americas (IXLCX)- Ceasar Park Hotel, Vía Israel y Cl. 77, San Francisco, Tel.: 270-6900, E-mail: info@ftaa-alca.com

Churches

Assembly of God. Calle 75, Este Urb. Betania, Club X 4344, Tel. 261-7660, E-mail: concilio@cwpanama.net

Casa de Oración Cristiana: Ave. Sta. Elena. Tel: 221-9479

Minor Basilica Don Bosco. Ave. 7, Central, 32-121. Tel: 227-4561, E-mail: basbosco@pty.com

Panama Baptist Convention. Diagonally opposite to the **Santuario Nacional ,** Ave   Samuel Lewis, Tel. 264-5585.

Salvation Army. La Boca Road #0792. Tel. 228-1109, E-mail: salvationarmy@ihpanama.com

Angelican Episcopal. Ancón , Panamá. Tel. 212-0062. E-mail: iepan@sinfo.net

Panama Evangelic Methodist. Vía España 2104. Tel: 224-51-84, E-mail: iempa@hotmail.com

United Evangelic. Calle 1, 34-56, Juan Díaz. Tel. 220-6801, E-mail: ieu@sinfo.net

Evangelic Quadrangle. Calle Q y Mariano Arosemena, Tel. 262-38-20, E-mail: iccq@cristored.net

First Isthmian Baptist Church. Cristóbal, 99 Colón. Tel. 445-12-37. E-mail: isthmian@cwpanama.net

Seventh Day Adventist Church. Ave. Gavilán,0844 Balboa. Tel. 228-42-37. E-mail: advenpma@cwpanama.net

Free Baptist Church. Calle Las Acacias Bethania. Tel. 261-73-94.

Church of Latter Day Saints. Cl. 51. Bella Vista, Tel.: 213-9411.

Metropolitan Cathedral of Our Lady of Assumption.

Ave. Central, Calle 7E, 7-30. Tel:262-3720.

Cristo Rey Church. Cls. 36 y 37 y Ave. Justo Arosemena Tel.: 225-3708

El Carmen Church. (Al lado del Hotel Panama). Tel:223-0360. E-mail: martinar@sinfo.net

Kol-Shearith, Israel. Ave. Cuba. Tel:225-4100.

La Catedral de Vida: Ave. Fernández de Córdoba. Tel: 261-8484

Lutheran Redemption. Balboa 830, Ancón. Tel. 228-9628.

Methodist MCCA.   Calle 16 Este. Tel. 262-88-49.   E-mail: iwesley@tutopia.com

Panama Baptist Mission. Balboa Bldg. #812 Tel. 228-27-43.

Greek Orthodox. Vía B Porras, 39. Tel. 223-45-72.

United Pentecostal. Urbanización Altos de las Montañas,44. Tel. 230-03-39. E-mail: hopkins@cwpanama.net

National Sanctuary. Ave. Ricardo Arango. Tel.: 223-0952

Shevet Ahim Synagogue, Cl. 44 Este, Vía Ricardo J. Alfaro. 27. Tel.: 225-5990

Baha'I Temple. Milla 8. Transístmica. Tel:231-1191. E-mail: panbahai@cwpanama.net

Hindu Temple. Via. J. Alfaro frente al Edificio Villa Gloriela. Tel:236-2366.

Churches of Christ: Llanos de Curundu. Tel. 232-8833

Media

Newspapers

Crítica Libre, Editora El Panamá América, Vía Ricardo J Alfaro, Tel. 230-7777, Web page: http://www.epasa.com/critica

Diario Chino El Expreso, Edif Don Manuel, Piso# 20-B, Cl. Miguel Brostella, El Dorado, Tel.: 236-3197, E-mail: expreso@cableonda.net

Editora Dominical: Cl. 80 1/2, Miraflores, Tel.: 229-7051, E-mail: noticronicapa@hotmail.com

El Diario Chino Latinoamericano: Centro Comercial Los Tucanes, Cl. Miguel Brostella, El Dorado, Tel.: 236-9803 E-mail: diariochino@cwpanama.net

El Panamá América, Vía Ricardo J. Alfaro, Tel. 230-7777, http://www.epasa.com

El Siglo, Calle 58, Urb. Obarrio, Tel. 269-3311, Web page: http://www.elsiglo.com

La Estrella de Panamá, Vía Transístmica y Frangipani, Tel. 227-0555, Web page: http://www.estrelladepanama.com

La Prensa, Ave. 12 de Octubre, Hato Pintado, Tel. 222-1222, Web page: http://www.prensa.com

Television

Channel 13, Telemetro Panamá, Calle 50, Tel. 210-6713, Web page: http://www.telemetro.com

Channel 2, Televisora Nacional S.A, Ave. Simón Bolívar, Tel. 236-2222. Web page: http://www.tvn-2.com.

Channel 29, Televisión Cristiana, Vía Ricardo J. Alfaro, Tel. 236-7824. E-mail: canalza@pty.com

Channel 4, RPC Televisión, Calle 50, Tel. 210-4100.

Channel 5, FETV, Ave. Ricardo J. Alfaro, Tel. 264-6555.
 Web page: http//: www.fetv.org

RCM Televisión, Channel 21, Edif. Bel Air, Vía Ricardo J. Alfaro Tel.: 360-0808,

Web page: http://www.mileniumrtv.com

RTVE, Radio y Televisión Educativa, Channel 11, Curundu, Tel.: 232-8100

Other Media

El Boletín, Cl. 55 El Cangrejo, Tel: 223-6494, E-mail: elboletin@cwpanama.net

El Visitante, Ave. Justo Arosemena y Cl. 42, Tel: 225-6638 http//: www.focuspublicationsint.com

FOB Zona Libre de Colón, Ave, Justo Arosemena y Cl. 42, Tel: 225-6638 http//: wwwcolonfreezone.com

Focus Panamá, Focus Publications (Int) S.A. Ave. Justo Arosemena y Cl. 42, Tel: 225-6638

http//: www.focuspublicationsint.com

Gaceta Oficial, Organo Informativo del Estado, Ave. Norte, Eloi Alfaro y Cl. 3, 3-12 San Felipe, Tel: 227-9600

Panorama Católico, Cl. 1 Sur, Carrasquilla, Tel.:229-7387, E-mail: panoramacat@cwpanama.net

Foreign Correspondents

(Source: Foreign Correspondents Association, Luis Miguel Blanco, 10/03/02)

24 horas – Colombia, Cléber David González, Tel.: 232-5180, E-mail: Adecori@cwp.net.pa

Agencia France Press (AFP) – Francia

Agencia Latinoamericana de Información (ALAI) Ecuador, Marcelina Samaniego, Tel.: 229-2952 6053, E-mail: marce@cableonda.net , marcela103@hotmail,com

Agencia Latinoamericana de Información (ALAI), Ecuador, Marcelina Samaniego, Tel: 229-2952, 229-1542, Cel.: 638-3445, E-mail: marce@sinfo.net

Agencia Mexicana de Noticias (NOTIMEX), Isar Angeles, Vicente Barletta, Tel.: 264-9146, E-mail: notimex@sinfo.net

Agencias Centroamericana de Noticias (ACAN-EFE) – España Fernado Ruiz Tel.: 223-9014, E-mail: diacan@sinfo.net

Agencias de Noticias Xinhau,República Popular de China, Fa Xing Xu, Tel.: 226-3726, Fax: 226-8648, Cel.: 673-0298, E-mail: xinhuapa@sinfo.net

Cadena Radial La Libertad, Colombia, Jairo Pentuz,

CBS Telenoticias – EEUU, David Salayandia, Tel.: 212-2170, E-mail: Salayan@pty.com, dsalayan@@hotmail.com

Central News Agency (CAN) Taiwan, Oscar Chung Tel.: 214-7526 6053, E-mail: edchen@pananet.com

China Times – Taiwan, Neal Kuo Tel.: 264-2480, E-mail: nealkuo@usa.net cleverdavid@hotmail.com

El Diario del Pueblo-China, Liu Hong,
E-mail: rmrbcaracas@cantv.net

El Mundo de los Negocios, Puerto Rico, Luis Pimentel, Tel: 223-7924, Cel.: 613-1119,

E-mail: lpimentel@cwpanma.net

Fairplay Publications / Time Magazine – EEUU, Michelle Labrut, Tel.: 264-1438, E-mail: mlabrut@cwp.net.pa

James Aparicio Tel.: 227-0621,
E-mail: jamespa@estrelladepanama.com

La Jornada-Mexico, Fernado Martínez, Tel.; 264-2737, E-mail: jornando@@sinfo.net

La Voz de los Estados Unidos de America, Judith de León, Tel: 207-7268

Prensa Latina (PL), Cuba, Gabriel Vega, Gustavo Robreño, Tel: 269-6053, E-mail: prela@sinfo.net

Radio Martí, EUA, Mayín Correa, Tel: 264-2231 6053, E-mail: mayincor@bellsouth.net.pa

Radio Red-Mexico, Adela de Coriat, Tel.: 613-0280, E-mail: adecori@cwp.net.pa

RCN TV- Colombia, Sara Guevara Itagaki, Tel.: 210-1716, E-mail: saraguev@yahoo.com

Reuters (Reino Unido), Alejandro Carbonell, Tel.: 264-2792 6053, E-mail: alexcarbo@hotmail.com, Tel: 223-7739

The Associated Express (AP) – EEUU Juan Zamorano Tel.: 269-4736, E-mail: jzamorano@ap.org , Tomas Munita, Tel.: 269-4736, 6053 E-mail: tmunita@ap.org

The Dallas Morning News-EEUU, Tod Robberson, Tel.: 264-8562, E-mail: robbersont@csi.com

The Miami Herald, and Los Angeles Times, Financial Times, Berta Ramona Thayer, Tel: 264-0794. 6053, E-mail: bertha@thayer.net

Toronto Star, George Thomas, Tel: 620-1115 6053, E-mail: gthomas06@hotmail.com

United Press (UPI), United States

Washington Post/ Los Angeles Times / Platts – EEUU, Berta Thayer, Tel.: 264-0794, E-mail: berta@thayer.net

Internet Services

Alianza Viva, Tel.: 206-3099, E-mail: ventas@alianzaviva.com, Webpage: www.alianzaviva.com

Bellsouth Internet, Tel.: 265-0400, E-mail: telemercadeo@bellsouth.com.pa,
Webpage: www.bellsouth.com.pa

Broadband Wireless Communications Corp., Tel.: 264-4134, E-mail: ventas@broadbandwc.com, Webpage: www.broadbandwc.com

Cable & Wireless, Tel.: 882-2227, E-mail: internet.ventas@cwpanama.net,
Webpage:www.cwpanama.net

Cableonda, Tel.: 206-7555, E-mail: attnclientes@cableonda.com, Webpage: www.cableonda.com

Charter Comunicaciones, Tel.: 223-4646, E-mail: ventas@c-com.net.pa, Webpage: www.c-com.net.pa

Convergence Communications, Tel.:210-1570, E-mail: infocci@cciglobal.net.pa, Webpage: www.cciglobal.net

Interdotnet, Inc., Tel.: 206-8000, E-mail: ventas@pa. inter.net, Webpage: www.pa.inter.net

Quick Internet, Tel.: 264-8861, Webpage: www.quick.com.pa

Panamanian Embassies and Consulates Abroad

(List supplied by the Department of Foreign Affairs of the Chancellery of the Republic)

ARGENTINA

EMBASSY: Avenida Santa Fe 1461, 5to. Piso, 1060 Capital Federal, Casilla
Correo 98 (1448) Suc. 48, Buenos Aires, Argentina.
Tel: (0054-11)4816-7384/ 0054-11-4813-8543
Telex: 22033 Nelco AR., Fax: (0054-11) 4814-0083
E-mail: epar@fibertel.com.ar
CONSULATES
• Buenos Aires: Ave. Santa Fé 1461, 5th Floor, C.apital Federal 1060,
Casilla Correo 98 (1448) Suc. 48 Buenos Aires, Argentina
Tel. 0054-11-4813-8543/ 4815-0726/ 811-1254
Fax:0054-11-4814- 0083. e-mail:
panaconsular@impsatl.com.ar, panama@ciudad.com.ar
• Mendoza: Paseo Sarmiento 49-9o, Depto. A, 5500 Mendoza, Tel y fax: 542-614-255-678
e-mail: comspanamza@servinet.com.ar
Tel part: 5426-14392262/ Cel.: 54-261-156501180

AUSTRIA

EMBASSY: Elisabethstrasse 4/5/3/9 A-1010 Vienna, Austria, Tel: (0043-1) 587-2347, Fax: (0043-1) 586-3080, Cable: Panaemba-Vienna, e-mail: mai@empanvvienn.co.at.
CONSULATES
•Salzburg: MorzgerstrasseBe 15, A-5020 Salzburg, Austria Tel: (0043-662) 82-36-42, Fax: 0043-662-82-3641

AUSTRALIA

CONSULATES
•Sydney: 39 Wardell RD, Earlwood Sydney NSW 2206 Australia. Tel: 02-95582500, 94408783.
E-mail: jjmodra@ozemail.com.au

BAHAMAS

CONSULATES
Nassau: P.O. Box. N0.7776, Nassau, Bahamas.
Tel: 001-242-362-4429, Fax: 001-242-362-4886
E-mail: dcm@mail.batelnet.bs

BELGIUM

EMBASSY: Av. Louise 390-392, 1050 Brussels, Belgium, Tel: (0032-2) 6490729 - 6492879 - 6494833, Fax: (0032-2) 6489216, E-mail: embajada.panama@skynet.be
CONSULATES
•Amberes: Meibrug 1-B/39, 2000 Antwerp, Belgium, Tel: (032)3-231-6961, Fax: (032)3-231-9969

BELIZE

EMBASSY: Headquarters in Mexico, Concurrently accredited in Belize, Horacio, Casa No.1501, Colonia Polanco,
Delegación Miguel Hidalgo, C.P. 11560, Mexico, D.F. Tel: (0052-5) 5557-2793/ 5557-6159, Fax: 0052-5395-4269
embpanmx@avantel.net, mbpanmx@mail.internet.com.mx
CONSULATES:
•Belmopan: Matus Brosther, Cover Central American Boulevard and Mahogany Streets, P.O. Box 494, Belize City, Belize, Central America.
Tel: 501-2-24551- 34862, Fax: 501- 2 - 34863

BOLIVIA

EMBASSY: Avenida Ballivian No. 1110, Esquina 17 de Colacoto, Casilla Postal 678. Tel: (00591-29) 79-2036/ 00591-2-8116981, Fax: (00591-29) 79-7290,
E-mail: empanbol@ceibo.enletnet.bo
CONSULATES
•La Paz: Calle Julio Patiño No. 1526 entre Calle 21 y 22 Colacoto Zona Sur, La Paz, Bolivar Zona 678, Tel. 00591-29-7972. E-mail: empabol@aceibo.entelnet.bo
•Santa Cruz de la Sierra: Barrio Urbari Calle Arruma, Casa 106, Casilla Postal 2148 Santa Cruz. Tel: 53-3236. Fax: 00591-3126923. E-mail: efescobar@hotmail.com
Bolivar No.545, 1er. Piso Santa Cruz, Bolivia
Casilla 595 Santa Cruz, Bolivia, Tel: 00591-33-331132/ 00591-33-349475,
Tel. resid. 340257, Fax:00591-1-37369391.

BRAZIL

EMBASSY: SHIS, QI 06, Conj. 11, Casa 18, Lago Sul. Cep 71620-115 Brasilia, D.F. Tel: (0051-61) 248-7423, Fax: (0051-61) 248-2834, Cel: (061)987-2718
e-mail: empanama@nettur.com.br
CONSULATES
•Brasilia: Cep.71620 115-Brasilia DF. Brazil. Tel: 0051-61-248-7423, Fax: 0051-61-248-2834. E-mail: empanama@nettur.com.br
•Río de Janeiro: Rua Figueiredo de Magalhaes, 122, Apto. 1002, Copacabana, CEP 22.031-010 Rio de Janeiro, Tel.casa:3834154, Tel: 0055-021-2255-9085 / Fax: 0055-021-2255-2012. Cel: 9147-8806. E-mail: panacon@acl.com
•Santos: Ave. Senador Fleijo 173 Alto, Cep.11055-501 Centro Santo. S.P. - Brazil Tel: 0055-13-32228722, Fax: 0055-13-32338247. E-mail: panacons@zaz.com.br
•Sao Paulo: Rua Ouvidor Peleja #85 Vila Mariana. Aptdo. 22 Cep. 04128-00 Sao Paulo–Sp-Brazil. Tel: 0055-11-3120-5482, Fax: 0055-11-2599959. E-mail: alpadel@hotmail.com
•Fortaleza: Rua Belhar 44, apto.502 Meireles. 60-160-110 Ceará, Fortaleza. Tel: (85) 268-3570. Fax: (85) 268-35.

CANADA

EMBASSY:130 Albert Street, Suite No. 300, Ottawa, Ontario Kip 564, Canada, Tel: (001-613) 236-7177, Fax: (001-613) 236-5775
E-mail: pancanem@travel-net.com
CONSULATES

•Montreal, Canada, 1425 Rene Levesque O. Bureau, 504, Montreal, Quebec, H 3G IT 7, Canadá· Telefax: 001-514-874 1929, Fax: 001-514-874 1947. E-mail: cgpm@generation.net
•Ottawa: 130 Albert Street, Suite No. 300, Ottawa, Ontario Kip 5 G4 Canada Tel: (001-613) 236-7177, Fax: (001-613) 236-5775
E-mail: pancanem@magma.ca
•Toronto: 881 St. Clair Ave. West 2 floor Toronto, Canada·, Ontario, Canada M6C 1C4, Tel: (416) 651-2350, (416) 780-0131 res. Fax: (416) 651-3141.
•Vancouver: 1112 West Pender Street, Suite 407 Vancouver, B.C. Canada V6E 2S1. Tel: (604) 682-6128/ 682-7128. Fax: (604) 682-0528. E-mail: info@panaconvan.com

CHILE

EMBASSY: Calle la Reconquista No. 640 Las Condes, Santiago, Chile, Casilla 27043, Correo 27. Tel: (0056-2) 202-6318. Cel: 569-238-2467/ 569-888-9932. Fax: (0056-2) 202-5439. E-mail: panaembchile@entelchille.net
CONSULATES
•Valparaiso: Calle Blanco #1623, Edif. Mar del Sur Torre 2, Ofic. 1103, Valparaiso, Chile. Casilla 1695. Tel: 56-032-591660/ 213592, Fax: 56-032-236-042, Cel. 221-0015

CHINA, REPUBLIC OF (TAIWAN)

EMBASSY: 6 Fl., No. 111 Sung Chiang RD., Taipei, Taiwan, R.O.C., Tel: (00886) 2-2509-9802, Fax:(00886) 2-2509-9801. E-mail:panaemba@iplus.net.tw, j-a-domingueza@excite.com
CONSULATES
•Taipe: 6 Fl., No. 111 Sung Chiang RD., Taipei, Taiwan, R.O.C., Tel: (00886) 2-2509-9802, Fax:(00886) 2-2509-9801. E-mail:panaemba@iplus.net.tw, j-a-domingueza@excite.com

COLOMBIA

EMBASSY: Calle 92 No. 7 – 70, El Chico, Santafé de Bogotá, Colombia, Apartado 90094 Tel: (0057-1) 257-5067 / 257-4452, fax: (0057-1) -257-5068.
Telex 45708 Exec Co., E-mail: empacol@cable.net.co
CONSULATES
•Barranquilla: Carrera 54 Na. 64-245, Local No.1, Edif. Camacol, Apartado Aéreo No. 50873, Barranquilla, Colombia, Telfax: 0057-5-360-1870 / 1872/ 1748.
• Bogotá: Calle 92 No. 7–70 El Chico Santafé de Bogotá, Colombia. Apdo: 90094. Tel: (0057-1) 2578-5067/ 257-5068, fax: (0057-1) 257-5068. E-mail: empacol@cable.net.co
•Cali: Calle 11 No. 4 - 42, Oficina 316, Apartado Aereo 68, Cali, Colombia, Tel: 00-572- 880-9590/ 28-73-1462, Fax:00-572-889-6706, Tel/Resid.(572)-6677586, Fax: 8896706. E-mail: quijano@emcali.net.co
• Capurganá: Tel: 0057-4-8243717, 0057-4-8243711, 0057-4-824-3093
•Cartagena: Dir. Centro, Plaza San Pedro, Claver No. 30-14 Cartagena, Colombia. Tel: 0057-566-655-1055. Fax: 0057-566-6735212/ 0057-5-655-0222. Casa 5756657455. Cel:

5737312415. E-mail: rafael.varela@decamercon.com
•Medellin: Torre empresarial Dann Av. Poblado Cr. 43a. No. 7-50A, Tel:0057-4-268-5477, Fax: 0057-4-352-2867. Cel. 0057-1-555-7770. E-mail: gusceper84@hotmail.com
•Monteria: Barrio El Recreo, Apdo Aéreo 488, Monterìa, Colombia
Tel: 0057-4782-850496/ 4782-850331/ 4782-850097
•San Andrés Isla: E-mail: brittonsonia@hotmail.com
• Santa Marta: Av. Libertador, No. 22-42 AP.01, Edif. Limay, Apdo Aéreo 570,
Santa Marta, Colombia. Tel: 005-954-4203183. Fax: 005-954-4203183.

COSTA RICA

EMBASSY: Barrio La Granja del Higueron De San Pedro, de Montes de Oca, San José, Costa Rica. Apto. Postal 103-2050. San Pedro de Montes de Oca.
Tel: (00506) 280-1570/ 281-2103/ 281-2442, Fax(00506) 281-2161. E-mail: vibusol@hotmail.com, empancr@racssa.co.cr
CONSULATES
•San José: San Pedro, Monte de Oca, Barrio La Granja del Higueron 200 metros al sur y 25 al Este San José, Costa Rica, Apartado 4441-1000,
Tel: (506) 281-2103/ 281-2104, fax(506) 281-2116. E-mail: panama@racsa.co.cr
• San Vito Coto Brus: Registro Civil de Chiriquí, Dirección Provincial, Río Sereno. Tel: 722-8013

CROATIA

EMBASSY: Tribaljska 11/1, 4100 Zagreb, Croatia. Tel: 0038-41-564-393.

CUBA

EMBASSY: Calle 26 entre 1er. y 3era, No. 109 Miramar, La Habana, Cuba
Tel: (0053-7) 204-0858, Fax: (0053-7) 204-1674, consulado. Tel: 204-1673/ 204-3421. Fax 204-9011. E-mail: panaembacuba@ip.etecsa.cu
CONSULATES
•La Habana: Calle 26 entre 1er y 3era. 109 Miramar, La Habana, Cuba. Tel: (0053-7) 24-0858. Fax: (0053-7) 24-1675. E-mail: panaembacuba@ip.etecsa.cu

CYPRUS

EMBASSY: Headquarters concurrently accredited in Israel, Calle Hei'Iyar No. 2 10, tercer Piso, Apto, 3 Kikar Hamedina, Apartado Postal 2093. Apartado Postal: 21260, Tel Aviv 61210. Tel: (00972-3) 69-60849 / 69-56711, Fax: 00972-3- 6910045
CONSULATES
•Nicosia: 8th Floor, Nicosia Tower Center 36, Byron Avenue. P.O. Box: 21341, 1506 Nicosia, Chipre. Tel: 00357-02-677000. Cable Panaconsul. Fax: 00357-02-359790. E-mail:

sarrilaw@spidernet.com.cy

CZECH REPUBLIC
EMBASSY: Headquarters concurrently accredited in Austria, Elizabethstrasse 4/5/4/10, A-1010 Vienna, Austria, Tel: (0043-1) 587-2347, Fax:(0043-1) 586-3080, Cable: Panaemba–vienna, E-mail embassy@empanvienna.co.at
CONSULATES:
•Praga: Korunni 63, 120 00 Praga 2, Rep. Czech, Tel: 420-2545509/ 420-2562273, Fax: 420-2545509.

DENMARK
EMBASSY: Embassy concurrently accredited with headquarters in Sweden, P.O. Box 555 47, 102 04 Stockholm, Sweden, Tel: (0046-8) 662-6535, Fax(0046-8) 662-8991
Horario de Oficina: 9:00 a 2:00p.m. (público): horas privada 2:00 a 4:00p.m.
E-mail: panaembasuecia@telia.com
CONSULATES
•Copenhagen: Amaliegade 42, 1256, Copenhagen K, Denmark, Tel: 45-33113399, Fax: 45-33324625
Postboks 427. DK-2500 Valbyy, Copenhagen, Denmark. Tel: 45-31-176806. Fax: 45-36-309822

DOMINICAN REPUBLIC
EMBASSY: Calle Benito Monción 255 Santo Domingo, Dominican Republic.Tel: 001-809-6883789, Fax: 685-3665, e-mail: emb.panama@codetel.net.do
CONSULATES
•Santo Domingo: Calle Bernardo Richardo #51, Alta, Gazcue entre Leonis de Ovando y Enrique y Henriquez, Santo Domingo, Dominican Republic, Tel: 809-688-1043 / 685-3533, Fax: 809-689-1273. Apartado Postal: 21604.
•Santiago de los Caballeros: Calle México No. 2 Villa Olga, Santiago, Dominican Republic. Tel: 582-0160/ 583-8418.

EQUADOR
EMBASSY: Alpallana No. 505 y Whimper Edificio Espro, Piso 6, Apartado Aéreo 17-07-9017, Quito Equador. Tel: (00593-2) 2508-856/ 2508857, Fax: (00593-2)-2565-234, E-mail: pmaemecua@interactive.net.ec, teranbas@interactive.net.ec
CONSULATES
• Quito:Alpallana No. 505 y Whimper Edificio Espro, Piso 6, Apartado Aéreo 17-07-9017, Quito, Equador. Tel: (00593-2) 2508-856/ 2508857, Fax: (00593-2)-2565-234, E-mail: pmaemecua@interactive.net.ec
•Guayaquil: Calle Tungurahua 502-A y 8 de Octubre. Tel: 005-934-455648. Fax: 005-934-455656. Aguirre 509 y Chimborazo, Edificio Balmoral S.A.,Piso 9, Oficina 901.
Apdo Postal 325, Guayaquil, Equador, Tel: 00593-4-512158, 00593-4-250094. Tel. casa. 00593-4-342875

EGYPT
EMBASSY: 4-A, IBN ZANKI St. / Apart. No. 3, P.O.Box 62 –Zamalek 11211, Cairo, Egypt, Tel: (0020-2)7361093/ 7361094/ 7366830. Fax:(0020-2) 7361092. Tel res. 7356913, E-mail: panaembcon@infinity.com.eg
CONSULATES
Cairo: P.O. Box 62–Zamalek 11211, Cairo, Egypt.

EL SALVADOR
EMBASSY: Buganbidea No. 21 Colonia San Francisco. San Salvador, El Salvador. Apartado (01)104, Tel: (005-03) 2980773, Fax (005 03) 278-0234,
E-mail: embpan@telesal.net
CONSULATES.
• San Salvador: Buganidea No.21. Colonia San Francisco, San Salvador, Apartado (01) 104. Tel: 005-03-298-0773. Fax: 005-03-278-0234, E-mail: embpan@telesal.net

FINLAND
EMBASSY: Embassy concurrently accredited headquarters in Sweden, Ostermalmsgatan 34/2tr., 114 32 Stockholm, Sweden, Tel: (0046-8) 662-6535, Fax(0046-8) 663-0407
P.O.Box 26 146, S-100 41, Stockholm, Sweden.
CONSULATES
•Helsinki: Undenmaankatu 4-6 E 19, 00120 Helsinki, Finland, P.O.Box 40, SF- 02631, Espoo 63, Tel-Fax: 00358-9-607097. Telex: 12469 KAUFO SF. undenmaankatu 4-6-E 19 S.F.00120 Helsinki 12.

FRANCE
EMBASSY: 145 Avenue de Suffren, 75015 París, France, Tel: (033-1) 45664244, Fax: (033-1) 45679943, E-mail: panaemba@worldnet.fr
CONSULATES
•Marsella: 11 Quai Dies Belges, 13001 Marsella, France, Tel: 33-0491-90-0584, fax: 33-0491-91-1026. Telex: 440-640 F Panamá. E-mail: panaconsmf@aol.com
1 Rue Freres Aillaud 13190 Allauch, France. Tel: 0033-91-68-1735.
•Paris: 145 Avenue de Suffren 75015 Paris, Francia. Tel: (033-1)45664244, Fax: (033-1) 45679943.

GERMANY
EMBASSY: Joachim-Karnatz-Allee 45 (3 OG)
10557 Berlin - Tiergarten,Tel: 0049-3020605811
Fax: 0049-3020605812, E-mail: panama@elg.lg.de
CONSULATES:
•Berlin: Joachim-Karnatz-Allee 45 (3OG). 10557 Berlin-Tiergarten
Tel. 0049-3020605811, Fax: 0049-3020605812
E-mail: panama@elg.lg.de
•Hamburg: Gansemark 44V 20534 Hamburg, Germany, Tel: 0049-40-343616, 40-307218
Fax: 0049-40-353-771

•Kiel: Schlossgarten,6–D-24103 Kiel, Germany
Tel: 0049-431-5199-733, Fax: 0049-431-5199-735
• Mainz: Viermorgenweg 4, D-55124 Mainz, Germany, RF
Tel:0049-06131473174 / 06131476872
Fax: 0049-6131-477580
• Munich: Nordlicher MunchserstR 31-33, Germany
82031 Munchen-Grunwald, Tel: 0049-89-6493205
Fax: 0049-89-6492789.

GREAT BRITAIN

EMBASSY: Panama House Mayfari 40 Hertford Street
London WIY Reino Unido. Tel: 0044-020-7493-4646, Fax:
0044-020-7493-4333.
e-mail: emb.pan@lineone.net
CONSULATES
Liverpool: Everitt & Co.LTD., 7 Queen Ave., Dale Street,
Liverpool L2 4TZ,Tel: 0151-236-4816. Fax: 0151-236-2221.

GREECE

EMBASSY: II Merarchias & Praxitelous, 185 35 Pireo 192
Grecia, Tel:003-01-4286441, Fax:003-01-4286448/ 0030-1-
42-86-449.
e-mail: embassyoan@hotmail.com
CONSULATES
•Pireo: 3,II Merarchias st. Praxitelous 192 185-35 Pireo,
Grecia, Tel: 003-01-42-86-441, Fax: 003-01-42-86-448.

GUATEMALA

EMBASSY: 10 A, Avenida 18-53, Zona 14, La Cañada,
Apartado 929 A- Reforma Zona 10, Guatemala, Guatemala,
Tel y Fax: 333-3885. E-mail: panguate@hotmail.com
CONSULATES:
• Guatemala: 10 A., Avenida 18-53 Zona 14, Larañada,
Apartado 929-A Reforma Zona 10, Guatemala, Guatemala.
Tel y Fax: 502-2-333-3885. Tel: 502-2-337-2445/2446.

GUINEA

EMBASSY: IIcadquarters in Egypt, concurrently accredited in
Guinea, 4-A IBN Zanki St. Apto. No. 3 P.O. Box: 62 - Zamalek
11211 El Cairo, Egipto. Tel: (0020-2) 736-1093/ 736-6830.
Fax:0020-2-736-1092.E-mail:panaemba.con@infinity.com.eg

HAITI

CONSULATES
•Puerto Principe: Delmas 60, Rue Stephen Casa #3,
Apartado: 15550- Pétion-Ville (W.I.) Tel: 509-1-257-0795/
509-1-256-0990.

HOLLAND

EMBASSY: Embassy concurrently accredited with head-
quarters in Belgium. Ave. Louise, 390-392, 1050 Brussels,
Belgium, Tel: 0032-2-6490729 / 6492879 / 6494833,
Fax: 0032-2- 6489216, e-mail: panameba@antrasite.be
CONSULATES
•Amsterdam: Eisdenstrant 10, 1066 L.K. Amsterdam,

Holanda, tel: 0031-20-69-7621 / 3776
•Aruba: G.M. de Bruynewijk #9 Savaneta Aruba. Telfax:
00297-85-843479. P.O. Box: 4143 Noord Aruba, Ant.
Holandes. E-mail: gaa.aua@setarnet.aaw
•Curazao: Maduro Plaza, Dokweg Z/N Curazao, Antillas
Holandesas, P.O.Box 3841, Tel: 599-9-37-1566, Fax:599-9-
37-2574.
•Rotterdam: Weena 723, 3010 AM Rotterdam, Holanda, P.O.
Box 29180, 3001 G.D., Rotterdam, Tel: 3110-413-8512/ 414-
3200, Fax: 3110-404-8243. E-mail: copanro@bart.nl

HONDURAS

EMBASSY: Colonia Palmira, Edificio Palmira, Segundo
Piso, (frente al Hotel Honduras Maya), Apartado postal 397,
Tegucigalpa, Honduras, Tel: 504 239-5508, fax 504-232-
8147. E-mail: ephon@hondudata.com
CONSULATES
•San Pedro Sula: Oficina Principal Banco FICOHSA,
Prolongación 3 ave. N.O, 16 Calle, Barrio Guadalupe, San
Pedro Sula, Honduras, C.A, Tel: 252-5350, Fax: 252-1251
•Tegucigalpa: Colonia Palmira, Edif. Palmira Segundo piso.
Apartado postal 397 Tegucigalpa, Honduras. Tel: 504-239-
5508, Fax; 504-239-8147.

HUNGARY

EMBASSY: Tglot U. 6/b. 2., 1118 Budapest Hungary, Tel:
0036-1- 4669817, Fax 0036-1- 4669817.
CONSULATES:
• Budapest: Tglot U. 6/b. 2 1119 Budapest, Hungary. Tel:
0036-1-4669817. Fax: 0036-1-4669817.

INDIA

EMBASSY: Chancery C-321, Defence Colony New Delhi
110-024, India. P.O. Box: 3168 Jor Bagh New Delhi- Fax:
00-91-11-4642350, Tel: 00-91-11-4642518/4627890
CONSULATES
• Mumbai/ Bombay: Ras Bussines Centre, Ram Nimi Bldg.
2nd Floor 8 Mandlik Road-Colaba, Mumbai 400-005, India,
P.O.Box 1976, Bombay, 400 001, Tel: 91-(22)282-5564/
2042108/ 2042110. Fax: 91-(22)2021933. E-mail: pcon-
sul@vsnl.com

INDONESIA

EMBASSY: World Trade Center, Building 13 Floor JL.
Jenderal Sudirman Kav 29-31 Jakarta, Indonesia 12920. Tel:
62-21-571-1867/ 62-21-570-0218. Fax: 62-21-571-1933. E-
mail: panacon@pacific.net.icl
CONSULATES
•Yakarta: World Trade Center,8 piso, JL. Jenderal Sudirman
Kav, 29-31. Jakarta 1290 INDO, Tel: 0062-21-5711867/0062-
21-5700218, Fax:0062-21-5711933

ISRAEL

EMBASSY: Calle Hei Be'Iyar No.10, Tercer Piso, Apto. 3
Kikar Hamedina, Tel Aviv 62093, Apartado postal 21260, Tel

Aviv 61210, Tel: 00972-3- 6069849 / 6956711, Fax: 00972-3-6910045. E-mail: panama@netvision.net.il
CONSULATES
•Haifa: Calle Hechalutz 21., P. O. Box 4071, Haifa 31040, Israel, Tel: 00972-4-8625265, Fax:00972-4-8624311.
•Jerusalem: 27 Moderchai Caspi 93549, Jersusalem, Israel, P.O.Box 3399, 91033 Jerusalem, Israel.

ITALY

EMBASSY: Viale Regina Margherta No. 239, Cuarto Piso, Interno 11, 00198 Rome, Italy, Tel: 0039-6-115660707, Fax: 0039-6-114407519.
e-mail: ambpanama@seq.it
CONSULATES
• Civitavechia: Vía Crescenzio No. 16 00053 Localita Santa Marinella
Civitavechia. Tel: 0039-0766-5330065. Fax: 0039-06-233224-024.
•Florencia: Vía Enrico Mayer No. 19, 50134 Firenze, Italy, Europa
Tel: 0039-055-473-904, Fax:0039-055-474-751
•Genova: 16122 Genova, Vía Assarotti 15/9, SCALA B, Tel: 010-83-91-786, Fax:010-83-93-024.
E-mail: paconsge@tin.it
•Milan: Vía Bagutta No. 3, 20121 Milán, Italy, 20121 Milán, Italy, Tel:0039-2-760-05220, Fax:0039-2-780-903.
• Napoles: Via G. Porzio Centro Direzionale Isola El 4-80143-Nápoles. Tel: 0039-081-6029540/ 6029541. Fax: 0039-081-606300448
•Turin: Vía Vittorio Amedeo II No. 6, 10121 Torino, Italy. Tel: 0115-660707. Fax: 011-4407519. E-mail: conspana@libero.it
•Venecia: Cannaregio 2009/B 30121 Venecia, Italy. Tel & Fax: 0339-0412750788.

JAMAICA

EMBASSY: 1 St. Lucia Avenue, Spanish Court, Office No.26, Kingston 5, Jamaica. Tel y Fax: (876) 960-1618. Tel: 968-2928.
E-mail: panaemba@cwjamaica.com
CONSULATES
• Kingston: 1 St. Lucia Avenue, Spanish Court, Office No.26, Kingston 5, Jamaica. Tel y Fax: (876) 960-1618. Tel: 968-2928.
E-mail: panaemba@cwjamaica.com

JAPAN

EMBASSY: Kowa International Bldg., Room 902, Nishi Azabu 4-12-24,
Minato-Ku, Tokyo 106-0031 Japón, Fax (computadora) 03-3499-3666, Fax: 813-5485-3548. Tel: 813-3499-3741 E-mail: panaemb@gol.com
CONSULATES
•Kobe:Yamamoto Bldg, 7th F1, 71 Kymomochi, Chuo-Ku, Kobe, 650 Japón, P.O.Box 43, Kobe Port, 651-01 Japón, Tel:

078-392-3361 / 62, Fax:078-392-7208
E-mail: pancosl-kj@ma.neweb.ne.jp
•Osaka: Furukawa Osaka Bldg, Nischi ñ Kan 6thOsaka, Shi, Japon, tel: 0081-6-347-1212

KOREA

EMBASSY: No. 4-Fl. Hyundai, Merchant Marine Bldg., 66, Cheokseon-dong, Jongro-Ku, Seúl, Korea Tel: (0082)- 734-8610/ 8611/ 8612, Fax: (0082) 734-8613. E-mail: panaemba@kornet.net
CONSULATES
• Seúl: 4o. Fl Hyundai Merchant Marine bldg.66, Cheokseon-dong, Jongro Ku, Seoul, Korea. Tel: 822-734-8610/ 822-734-8611. Fax: 822-734-8613. E-mail: panamemba@kornet.net
•Pusan: 309-901. Samick Beach Apt, Namchum-Dong, Suyoung-Gu, Pusan, Korea. Tel: 051-465-6147.

LUXEMBOURG

CONSULATES: Sede concurrente en Bélgica Ave. Louise, 390-392, 1050 Bruselas, Bélgica Tel.0032-2-6490729. Fax: 0032-2-6489216. E-mail: panaemba@antrasite.be

MALAYSIA

CONSULATES
•Kota Kinabalu, Sabah: 3ed. Floor, Wisma Parkasa, jalan Tanjung Lipal, 88800 Kota Kinabalu, Sabah, Malaysia, WDT 219 , 870 Kota Kinabalu
tel: 088-225-377/8, fax: 0688-259-554
•Kuala Lumpur: Agathis M9 SDN BHD.,1st. Fl., Industrial Park, Lot.2, Jalan Demajauan, Petaling Jaya 46200, Selandor Malaysia, tel: (03) 756-7848
fax: (03) 757-6482

MALTA

EMBASSY: Headquarters concurrently accredited in Italy, in the headquarters of Largo di Torre Argentina, II in 28 BIS 00186 Rome, Italy. Tel: 0039-6-68809764, Fax:0039-68809812.
e-mail:epss@iol.it
CONSULATES
•La Valleta: GM International Services, Limited, 147/1, St. Lucia Street, Valleta VLT 04, Tel: (+356)235341 (15 lines), Fax:(+356) 220101.

MOROCCO

CONSULATES:
•Rabat: 25 rue Abou Rayane Al Falaki Casablanca, Morocco. Tel: 00212-376-3672/ 00212-235-1578/ 00212-234-1905. Fax: 00212-2-660303. E-mail: jaidi@casanet.net.ma

MEXICO

EMBASSY: Horacio, Casa No. 1501 Colonia Polanco, Delegación Miguel Hidalgo. C.P. 11560, México D.F. Tel: (0052-5) 5557-2793/ 5557-6159. Fax: 0052-5395-4269. E-

mail: embpanmx@avantel.net
CONSULATES
•Guadalajara: Calle Donato Guerra No. 25 interior 17 entre Pedro Moreno y Morelos Código Postal 44100. Guadalajara, Jalisco, México. Tel-Fax: 0035-86-8907. E-mail: abdiel50@hotmail.com
•Monterrey: Monte Viminal # 202, Colonia fuentes del Valle Garza García, Nuevo León 66220, Tel: (8) 335-5965, Fax: (8) 318-673941. Tel: 318-673940.

MONACO
CONSULATES: 15 BD Louis II (Narte Carlo Star 67) Monte Carlos MC
Principado de Monaco. Tel: 0037-7678-630425.

NICARAGUA
EMBASSY: Reparto Mántica del cuartel General de Bomberos, 1 cuadra abajo casa No. 93, Managua, Nicaragua, Apartado No. 1, Tel: 266-2224, Fax: 266-8633
e-mail:embdpma@hotmail.com
CONSULATES:
•Managua: Reparto Mántica del cuartel General de Bomberos, 1 cuadra abajo casa No. 93, Managua, Nicaragua, Apartado No. 1, Tel: 266-2224, Fax: 266-8633
e-mail:embdpma@hotmail.com

NORWAY
EMBASSY: Headquarters concurrently accredited in Sweden, Ostermalmsgatan 34/2tr., 114 32 Stockholm, Sweden, Tel: 0046-8-662-6355, Fax: 0046-8-663-0407
P.O.Box 26 146, S-100 41 Stockholm Sweden.
CONSULATES
•Oslo: Akergaten 18 N-0158 Oslo, Norway, Tel. 47-22-427600. Fax 47-22- 421858

NEW ZEALAND
CONSULATES:
•Auckland: Shorthland Street, Auckland New Zealand. P.O. Box: 2062. Tel: 64-9-379-8550, Fax: 64-9-379-8449. E-mail: gthwaite@iprolink.co.nz

PARAGUAY
EMBASSY: Calle Piribeduy No. 765 Casi Ayolas, Asunción, Paraguay, Casilla de correo No. 873, Tel: 443-522, Fax: 00595-21-446-192
e-mail:embapana@conexion.com.py
CONSULATES:
•Asunción: Calle 25 de mayo No. 865 Asunción Paraguay, Apdo postal: 793 Asunción Paraguay. Tel: 00595-21-444-534/ 491-199. Fax: 0055-21-446-192.

PERU
EMBASSY: Alvarez Calderon 738 San Isidro, Lima, Perú. Tel: 00511-441-3652. Fax: 00511-441-9323. E-

mail:linclark@amauta.rcp.net.pe
CONSULATES:
• Lima: Emilio Cavenecia 175, 4to.piso, Lima - Peru. Tel: 005114-264-2621. Fax: 005114-440-6592.

PHILLIPINES
EMBASSY: 10th Floor 2000 Tower, 1973 Talf. Avenue corner Pres. Quirino Avenue Malate, Manila, Phillipines. Central P.O. Box 493 (Main Office).Tel: 00632-521-1233/521-2790, Fax: 00632 521-57-55.
E-mail: panaembassy@greendot.comph
CONSULATES:
• Manila: Rua 501 Victoria Bldg. 4299 United Nationas Ave, Ermita Manila, Phillipines. Central P.O. Box 493 (Main Office) Tel: 0063-2-521-1233/ 0063-2-521-2790. Fax: 0063-2-521-5755. E-mail: panaembassyl@i-manila.com.ph

PORTUGAL
EMBASSY: Ave. Helen Keller # 15 Lote C, 4 Esq., Restelo 1400-97 Lisboa, Portugal. Tel: 00351-21-364-4576/4577, Fax: 00351- 364-4589. E-mail: panaconsulisboa@netc.pt
CONSULATES:
•Faro: Castelo Paraiso-Corotelo 8150 Sao Bras De Alportel Portugal. Tel: 00351-96-6778760. Fax: 289-843169.
•Lisboa: Ave. Helen Keller #15, Lote C. 4 13d 1400 Lisboa, Portugal. Tel: 00351-1364-2899. Fax: 00351-364-4589.

REPUBLIC OF CHINA (BEJING)
EMBASSY: 6-1-11Tayuana Diplomatic Compound, No.1 Dongzhimen Wai, Xin Donglu Chao Yang District, 100600, Beijing, Republic of China, Tel: 8610 6532-5981, Fax:8610 6532-6822, Internet: panachin@public3.bta.net.cn
CONSULATES
•Hong Kong: Room 1008, Wing On Centre 111 Connaught, Road, Central Hong Kong / G.P.O. Box 75 Hong Kong, Tel: 852-2545-2166, Fax: 852-2543-4614 E-mail: jpereira@netvigator.com

ROMANIA
CONSULATES
•Bucarest: Bulevard Lasca Catargiu 24-26 SC. A, AP. 4 sector 1, Bucarest, Rumania. Tel: 0040-1-650-6309.

RUSSIA
EMBASSY: Moskfilmosraya No. 50, Moscú, Tel y Fax (007-095) 956-0729 / 956-0730 e-mail:empanrus@aha.ru

SAUDI ARABIA
CONSULATES
Arabia Saudita: P.O. Box 30367 Jeddah 21477 Saudi Arabia Tel: 636-4153, Fax: 608-0190, E-mail: aksaeedco@hotmail.co

SINGAPORE

EMBASSY: 16 Raffles Quay No. 41-06, Hong Leong Building, Singapore 0104
Tel: 0065-221-8677, Fax: 224-0892, E-mail: pacosin@pacific.net.sg

SOUTH AFRICA

EMBASSY: 832 Duncan Street Brooklyn Pretoria, 0181, South Africa. Tel: 27-12-3622778/9. Fax: 27-123622629. E-mail: ptyembsa@infotech.co.za

SPAIN

EMBASSY: Caludio Coello 86, 1o, 28006, Madrid, Spain, Tel: 0034-91-576-7668, Fax: 0034-91-576-7161, Sección Consular Tel: 91-7668, Fax: 0034-91-435-4923. E-mail: panaemba@teleline.es, Fax: 0034-91-435-4923.
CONSULATES
•Barcelona: Paseo De Gracia No.20, 4o. 1o, 08007, Barcelona, Spain., Apdo. No. 36119, C/Valencia 231,08007 Barcelona, Tel: 3493-302-0073, Fax: 3493-302-6350
•La Coruña: Avenida de Perulerio, 8, 1o-Drecha B. Apdo. 15011, La Coruña, Spain, Tel: 0034-981-251542, Fax: 0034-981-251542.
•Las Palmas de Gran Canarias: Calle Juan Rejon # 42, 1.izq. Apdo. 35008, Las Palmas, Gran Canarias, Spain, Tel: 0034-928-463307, Fax:0034-928-463317
•Madrid: Claudio Coello 86,1, 28006, Madrid, Spain, Tel: 0034-1-576-5001, Fax:0034-1-576-7161
•Málaga: Paseo de Miramar, 35-4o.A, Portal, 1, 29016, Málaga, Spain. Apdo. 6047, 29080 Málaga, España, Tel: 3495-221-3397, Fax: 3495-2299389
•Sevilla: Plaza Alfonso de Cossio No. 1, 6to. C-8, Sevilla 41004, Spain, Tel: 677-654-541, E-mail: panaconsul sevilla@ole.com
•Valencia: Calle Alicante 19-1-3, 46004 Valencia, Spain,Tel. y Fax: 34-963-106-390, 34-963-106-384, E-mail: panamaccv@rctcmail.cs
•Vigo: Via Hispanidad No.75, II Izquierda Oficina #1, Código Postal 36203, Vigo, Spain, Tel y Fax: (34986) 41-8465.
•Santander: La Venera S/N Bareyo Cantabria P.O. Box: 5004-39080, Santander, Cantabria, Spain. Tel. Ofic.:600-08-83-79. Fax: 942-363482, E-mail: jmhpp@mundivia.es

SRI LANKA

CONSULATES:
oColombo: 99 1/6 Harbour View Apts. 16th lane College Street Aluthmawatha 71-Road Colombo 15 Sri Lanka. Tel: 94-1-431782, Fax: 94-75333057. E-mail: susanthaj@slt.lr

SWEDEN

EMBASSY: Ostermalmsgatan 59, 114 50, P.O.Box. 55547, 102 04 Stockholm, Sweden.Tel: 0046-8-662-6535, Fax: 0046-8-662-8991.

SWITZERLAND

EMBASSY: Headquarters in France, 145 Avenue de Suffren, 75015 París, France, Tel:0033-1-45664244, Fax:0033-1-4567-9943, e-mail panaemba@worldnet.fr
CONSULATES
•Switzerland: 72 Rue De Lausanne, 1212 Geneva, Switzerland, Tel: 002-738-0318 / 0388
Fax: 0041-22-738-0363
•Lugano: Vía Degli Amadio, 1, 6900 Lugano, Switzerland, tel: (0041-91)233-837 73651 235-358
•Zurich: Loewenstrasse No.40 Piso 4, 8,023 Zurich, Switzerland, Tel:0041-1-225-1414, Fax:0041-1-225-1489., Villa Falkenstein Schanzengasse 22, Ch-8001 Zurich, Switzerland. Tel: 0041-1-261-334/ 0041-1-261-1177. Fax: 0041-1-261-2163.

THAILAND

EMBASSY: 14 Saracin Bldg. 7Floor, Surasak Roud, Silom, 10500. Bangkok, Thailand, Tel. y Fax:2-237-9008/9009, E-mail: ptybkk@ksc.th.com

TRINIDAD Y TOBAGO

EMBASSY: Highsquare Bldg., Suite No. 6, LST. Level, 1-Adere Street, Queen's Park West, Port Spain, Tel: 001-809-623-3435 / 3436, Fax:001-809-623-3440.
e-mail: embapatt@wow.net

TURKEY

CONSULATES
•Istambul: Kubilay Sitesi-Acar Sok Mimoza Apt. 26 D, 4, Tarabya 80880, Istambul Turkey, Tel: 90-1-244-6981, Fax:90-1-531-3820.
•Trabzon: Isekele COD No. 45, Trabzon, Turkey, Tel: 0090-462-321-1235/ 0090-462-326-6456. Fax: 0090-462-321-9859.-

URUGUAY

EMBASSY: Edificio Coimbra, Calle José Martí 3295, (Esq. Pedro Berro) Oficina 501, Apartado Postal 12071, Montevideo 11300, Tel. y fax: 00598-2-708-0206. E-mail: empauru@netgate.com.uy

UNITED ARAB EMIRATES

CONSULATES
•Dubai: P.O.Box 2121, Dubai, E.A.U., Tel: 00971-4-263319, Fax: 00971-4-263315

UNITED STATES OF AMERICA

EMBASSY: 2862 McGill Terrace N.W. Washington, D.C. 20008, Tel: 001-202-483-1407, Fax:001-202-483-8413 / 8416, Priv. Direct: 202-234-0247,
E-mail: embajador@panaembadc.org
CONSULATES
•Atlanta, Georgia: 225 Peachtree St. NE, South Tower Suite

50 3, Atlanta, GA, 30303, Tel: 404-522-4114, Fax: 404-522-4120, Cel: 678-6436131. E-mail: pma_altconsulate@hotmail.com
•Baton Rouge, Louisiana:
•Chicago, Illinois: 3930 North Pine Grove Ave. No.903 Chicago, Illinois 606-13-3357, Tel: 001-773-933-7736, Fax: 001-733-933-0442. 1310 n. Ritchie Court, # 28C, Chicago Illinois 60610. Tel: 001-312-266-2770, Fax: 001-312-266-2447. P.O. Box: 174, Wambegan 11 60079. Tel: (847) 816-3365/1854.
•Cleveland, Ohio: 31300 Tuttle Drive, Bay Village, Ohio, Cleveland 44140, Tel: (440) 835-8671, (440) 871 7199
•Detroit, Michigan
•Philadelphia, Pennsylvania: 124-Chestnut Street, Philadelphia, P.A. 19106, U.S.A., Tel: (215) 574-2994, Fax (215)625-4876. E-mail: cgralpmaph@msn.com
•Honolulu, Hawaii: Bill Brophy A. C/D ZI Si Century Ughting 1325 SO. Beretania St. Honolulu, Tel: (808) 521-5043.
•Houston, Texas: 24 Greenway. Plaza, Suite 1307, Houston, Texas 77046
Tel 713-622-4451 o 4459, Fax 713-622-4468. E-mail: panama1@winstarmail.com. Tel: 713-622-4451. 13302 Barryknoll Lane, Houston, Texas 77079, USA, Tel: 001-713-461-4802, Fax:001-713-461-7455.
•Los Angeles, California: 3137-W.Ball R. Suite 104, Anaheim California 92804, Los Angeles, California, Tel. (714) 816-1809, Fax (714) 816-1809. E-mail: panamadaly@aol.com
•Miami, Florida: 2801 Ponce De Leon Bldv. Suite 1050, Coral Gables, Florida 33134. Tel: (305) 447-3700, fax: (305) 447-4142, Cel: 318-9064. E-mail: cohenmanuel@aol.com
•New Orleans, Louisiana: 1324 World Trade Center # 2 Canal St. , New Orleans, Louisiana 70130, Tel: 504-525-3459, 504-525-3458, fax: 504-524-8960. E-mail: consul@consulateofpanama.com
•New York, New York: 1212 Ave. of the America, 10 th Floor N.Y., N.Y. 10036, Tel: 212-840-2450 / 51, 713-622-4459, fax: 001-212-840-2469, E-mail: rgdf2001@aol.com
•San Diego, California: C.T. Mouritzen, Cónsul, 2552 Chatsworth Blvd., S.Diego, Calif. 92106 o1351,
Tel: 001-619-225-8144/ 001-619-222-5700, Fax: 001-619-222-0201

•San Francisco, California: Flood Bldv. 870 Market, Street, Suite 551, San Francisco, CA. 94102, Tel: 415-391-4268, Fax: 415-391-4269
e-mail: panama@pacbell.net, 870 Market Street Flood Building, Suite 551-553, S.F., CA. 94102. Tel: 001-415-221-5699, 001-415-221-4773, 208 Glenvien Drive, San Francisco, California 94131. Tel: 001-415-648-3164.
•San Juan, Puerto Rico: 225 Calle Tulip, Courtyard, Suite 5, San Juan 00926-5950 San Juan, Puerto Rico. Tel: (787) 789-2003. E-mail: conpapr@microjuris.com
•Tampa, Florida: 1101 Channelside Dr. #279 Tampa, Florida 33602 USA, Tampa, Florida. Tel: 001-813-831-6685, fax: 001-813-254-3492
• Washington: 2862 McGill Terrace N.W. Washington, D.C. 20008. Tel: 001 (202) 483-1407, Fax: 001 (202) 483-8413. E-mail: fm@panaembadc.org, 22 Fox Run-East Sandwich, Massachusets 02537, E.E.U.U. Tel-Fax: 001-508-888-7311.

VENEZUELA
EMBASSY: Calle La Guairita, Edif. Los Frailes, Piso 6, Oficina 6-A. Chuao. Apdo, 1989, Caracas, 1010a, Carmelitas, Caracas, Venezuela
Tel: 0058-2-992-7058, Fax: 0058-2-9928107.
CONSULATES
•Maracaibo: Tel.Ofic: 0058-0416-6660867. E-mail: avivar01@cant.net
Res. Gran Tepuy, Apto. 9-A, Ave. 22 entre C/70 y C/71 Maracaibo, Estado Zulia Rep. Bolivariana de Venezuela

VIETNAM
CONSULATES
•Ho Chi Ming: 7a. Le Thanh Ton St. Dist. 1-Ho Chi Ming City, Vietnam Tel: 84-8-8250334, Fax:84-8-8236447

YUGOSLAVIA
EMBASSY: Headquarters concurrently accredited in Hungary, 1118 Budapest - Hungary, Tel: 0036-1-4669817, Fax: 0036-1-4669817
CONSULATES•Zagreb: Tribaljska 11/1, 4100 Zagreb, Yugoslavia, tel: 0038-41-564393.

GOVERNMENT ENTITIES

MINISTRIES
Ministry of Canal Affairs, Edif. PH Plaza 2000, 5to piso, Cl. 50, tcl: 263-4545, Web page: www.acp.gob.pa
Ministry of Commerce and Industry, Edif. Plaza Edison, piso # 2y 3
Ministry of Agriculture and Fisheries—MIDA, Altos de Curundu, tel: 232-6254, Web page: www.mida.gob.pa
Ministry of Economy and Finance, Vía España y Cl. 52, tel: 269-4133, fax: 264-7755. Web page: www.mef.gon.pa (Hacienda y Tesoro: Página Web: www.hacienda.gob.pa y

Ministry of Planning and Political Economy—MIPPE: Web page: www.mippe.gob.pa)
Ministry of Education, Cárdenas, Ancón, Tel.: 317-6118, Web page: www.educación.gob.pa
Ministry of the Government and Justice, Ave. 7 Central, 2-24, Tel: 212-2000, fax: 212-2106, Web page: www.gobiernoyjusticia.gob.pa
Ministry of Youth, Women, Family and Minors, Edif. Edison Plaza, Vía Ricardo J. Alfaro, tel: 279-0701, fax: 279-0665

Ministry of the Presidency, Ave. 3, Tel: 227-9600, Web page: www.presidencia.gob.pa

Ministry of Public Works, Curundu, tel: 232-5333, fax: 232-5776, Web page: www.mopgob.pa

Ministry of Foreign Affairs, Altos de Ancon, Edif. # 88 Tel: 211-4200, Web page: www.mire.gob.pa

Ministry of Health, Edif. # 261, Ancón, Gorgas, E-mail: salud/s@cwpanama.net

Ministry of Labor, Vía Ricardo J. Alfaro, 279-0051, fax: 279-0602, Web page: www.mitrabs.gob.pa

Ministry of Housing—Edif. Plaza Edison, piso# 4, Ave. Ricardo J. Alfaro, Web page: www.mivi.gob.pa

AUTONOMOUS AND SEMIAUTONOMOUS INSTITUTIONS

Municipality, Panama City, Ave. B, tel: 212-9600, fax: 262-4580, Web page: www.sinfo.net/alcaldia/ or www.alcaldiapanama.gob.pa

Municipality, San Miguelito, Cl. P. San Miguelito, Tel.: 274-0730

Legislative Assembly, Plaza 5 de Mayo, tel. 212-8300, fax. 262-5165

National Association of the Environment (ANAM), Edif. # 804, Albrook, Tel.: 315-0257 Web page: www.anam.gob.pa

Interoceanic Region Authority—ARI, Edif. 1220 Amador, **Panama Canal Authority**, Edif. Admnistración, Balboa, tel: 228-0357, 263-6354, Web page: www.pancanal.com,

Transportation Authority (ATTT), Vía José Agustín Arango, El Cruce de Juan Díaz, tel: 290-0547, fax: 290-0516

Panama Maritime Authority, Diablo, 232-5100, fax: 232-5597, Web page: www.amp.gob.pa

Agriculture Development Bank—BDA, Ave. de Los Mártires y Cl. L, tel: 262-0266, fax: 262-1713, Web page: www.bda.gob.pa

National Mortgage Bank, Ave. Balboa y Cl.40, tel: 227-0055, fax: 225-6906

Mortgage Bank, Edif. Peña Prieta, piso # 6, Ave. Balboa Tel.: 227-3770, fax: 227-2327.

Banco Nacional de Panamá, Vía España y Cl. 55, tel: 263-5151, fax: 223-3205, Web page: www.banconal.com.pa

National Bingo, Cl. J. B. Sossa, tel: 228-3215, fax: 228-1498

Caja de Ahorros, Vía España y Cl. Thais de Pons, tel.: 205-1551

Social Security, Edif. Bolívar, tel: 261-7555, fax: 261-2208, Web page: www.css.org.pa

Free Competition and Consumer Affairs Commission—CLICAC, Cl. 50 y 57, tel: 265-3555, fax: 265-3511, Web page: www.enteregulador.gob.pa, Vía Fernández de Córdoba, tel: 261-1313, fax: 229-6229

Comptroller General's Office, Avenida Balboa y Federico Boyd, tel: 210-4359 Fax: 210-4355, Web page:

www.contraloria.gob.pa

Postal Services—COTEL, Ave. Central y Cl. 33 Calidonia, tel: 225-2830, fax: 225-2671 E-mail: felixpardo67@hotmail.com

Supreme Court of Justice, Edif. # 224, Cl.L, primer piso, tel: 262-7158, fax: 262-5956 Web page: www.sinfo.net/orgjup

Attorney General's Office, Edif. Don Camilo, Calle 50, tel: 214-9835, fax: 214-9839, Web page: www.defensoriadelpueblo.gob.pa

Civil Aviation Office, Edif. 805, Albrook, tel: 315-1622, Web page: www.aeronautica.gob.pa

General Customs Office, Curundu, Edif. # 1009, tel: 232-6277, fax: 232-6494, Web page: www.aduanas.gob.pa

Urban and Residential Sanitation Municipality, Carrasquilla, tel: 229-3327

Immigration and Naturalization, Ave. Cuba y Cl. 28 y 29, Tel.: 227-1448, Fax: 227-1227

Public Services Regulator, Edif. Discount Bank & Trust Co.,

Fondo de Inversión Social (FIS), Ave. 3, a un costado de la Presidencia, tel: 207-9000 Web page: www.fis.gob.pa

IDAAN (Instituto de Acueductos y Alcantarillados Nacionales)-, Vía Brasil, tel: 223-8640

IFARHU (Instituto para la Formación y Aprovechamiento de los Recursos Humanos), Vía España, tel: 269-6666, fax: 263-6101, Web page: www.ifarhu.gob.pa

INAC (Instituto Nacional de Cultura) INAC, Plaza de Francia, tel: 228-4362

Agriculture Marketing Institute—IMA, Cl I. J. Zarak, Vista Hermosa 69, tel: 261-6898 Web page: www.mida.gob.pa/ima

National Sports Institute—INDE, Ave. José Agustín Arango, tel: 217-2333, fax: 217-3007 ISA

National Institute for Professionals —INAFORP, Vía Tocumen, tel: 266-1333, fax: 266-2602, Web page: www.inaforp.edu.pa , E-mail: relacionespublicas@inaforp.edu.pa

Instituto Panameño Autónomo Cooperativo—IPACOOP, El Paical, Urb. Los Angeles, tel: 236-4411, fax: 260-5712, E-mail: ipacoopdp@cwpanama.net

Instituto Panameño de Habilitación Especial-IPHE, Camino Real, Bethania, tel: 261-0500 E-mail: iphespecial@cwpanama.net

Panamanian Institute of Tourism (IPAT), Vía Israel, San Francisco, tel: 226-7000, fax: 226-4849, Web page: www.ipat.gob.pa

National Lottery, Avs. Perú y Cuba, entre Cls. 31 y 32, tel: 227-4666, fax: 227-7257 Web page: www.loterianacional.com.pa

Public Ministry, Ave. Perú y Cl. 33, Tel.: 227-1114, E-mail: inforelp@panama.c-com.net

National Police, Curundu, Ancón, tel: 232-5577, fax. 227-2036, Web page: www.policia.gob.pa

Policía Técnica Judicial—PTJ, Ancón, tel: 262-6077

Procuraduría de la Admistración, Ave. Perú y Cl. 33, tel: 225-3350, fax: 227-5536, Web page: www.procuraduria-admon.gob.pa
Public Registry, Cl 50, tel: 263-3000, Web page: www.policia.gob.pa, E-mail: relpo@cwp.net.pa
SINAPROC Sistema Nacional de Protección Civil
Superintendency of Banks, Ave. Samuel Lewis, tel: 206-7800, Web page: www.superbancos.gob.pa
Electoral Tribune, tel: 225-5569, Página Web: www.tribunal-electoral.gob.pa

Univeristy of Panama, El Cangrejo, tel: 263-6133, Web page: www.up.ac.pa
Colon Free Zone, Calle 16, Colón, tel: 445-1033, Web page: www.zonalibredecolon.com.pa

Universities

UNIVERSIDAD LATINA DE PANAMA: Tel. 230-8600/6185, Fax: 230-8605, http://www.ulat.ac.pa, latina-esl@ns.ulat.ac.pa
UNIVERSIDAD LATINA: (Chiriquí), Tel. 774-3737, Fax: 774-8821 Cl Central, David, Chiriquí, (Santiago) Tel.: 998-5412, Fax: 998-6402, (Chitré) Tel: 996-1179, Fax: 996-2146.
UNIVERSIDAD DEL ISTMO: Tel. 227-8822, Fax: 227-8831, http://www.uistmo.edu, Ave. Justo Arosemena.
UNIVERSIDAD DEL ISTMO (Chiriquì), Tel. 775-2535, Fax: 774-7758, Avenida Domingo Díaz, Edif. Salamanca, David, Chiriquì
ULACIT: Tel. 224-5377/ 5677, Fax: 224-0318, calle 54 Carrasquilla, Antigua entrada Club de Golf, e-mail: aadmision@ulacit.ac.pa, http://www.ulacit.ac.pa,
UNIVERSIDAD CATOLICA SANTA MARIA LA ANTIGUA (USMA): Tel. 230-8200/8300, Fax: 230-3593, Vía Ricardo J. Alfaro/ Tumba Muerto, www.usma.ac.pa, e-mail: websmaster@usma.ac.pa
USMA (Colón), Tel. 441-4932
USMA (Chiriquí), 775-3284
USMA (Los Santos), 966-9111/9393
UNIVERSIDAD INTERAMERICANA DE PANAMA: Tel. 263-7787, Fax: 263-3688. Ave. Manuel Espinosa Batista, Antiguo Edificio de Cemento Panamá, www.uinteramericana.ed, e-mail: info@vip.edu.pa
ITEA JUNIOR COLLEGE (Universidad Politécnica de Panamá), tel. 264-9624, Cl 30 y Av. Cuba, Panam·
COLUMBUS UNIVERSITY (Panamá), Tel. 263-3888, http://www.columbus.edu, Cl. 50 Panamá, e-mail: columbus@columbus.edu
COLUMBUS UNIVERSITY (Chitré), Tel. 996-8825, Fax: 996-8002 Calle Julio Botello, final a un costado del Colegio José Daniel Crespo, Chitré.
COLUMBUS UNIVERSITY (David) Tel. 775-8068/ 774-7134, Fax: 774-5782, Plaza Oteima, Calle "D" Norte y Ave. 2da. este Daniel, David, Chiriquí
COLUMBUS UNIVERSITY (Santiago), Tel. 998-3091, Fax: 998-3090, Calle 1o. de diciembre, a un costado de la Loteria Nacional, Santiago, Veraguas
NOVA SOUTHEASTERN UNIVERSITY, Tel. 315-1395,

Fax: 315-1396 , Albrook #869, Panamá, www.nova.edu, e-mail: rroman@nova.edu
UNIVERSIDAD INTERAMERICANA DE EDUCACION A DISTANCIA DE PANAMA, (UNIEDPA): Tel. 227-2902, Fax: 227-5565, e-mail: uniedpa@cwp.net.pa, Cl. 38 Sur, Bella Vista, Panamá
FLORIDA STATE UNIVERSITY: Tel: 314-0367/ 0368, Fax: 314-0366, calle Ernesto J. Castillero #1033, La Boca, Balboa, Ancón Panamá, e-mail: fsupanama@mailer.fsu.edu www.fsu.edu/panama
UNIVERSIDAD DE LA PAZ: Tel. 228-0049, telefax: 228-0050 Balboa, Panamá
UNIVERSIDAD METROPOLITANA: Tel. 727-6325, Paso Canoa, Chiriquí, Panamá.
INCAE: Tel. 264-3253, e-mail: incaepty@sinfo.net, Ave. Samuel Lewis, Panamá
QUALITY LEADERSHIP UNIVERSITY: Tel. 210-1464, Cl. 50, Panamá
UNIVERSITY OF LOUISVILLE: Tel. 264-0777, Fax: 264-7962, www.louisville-panama.com, e-mail: reclutar@louisville-panama.com
UNIVERSIDAD ABIERTA Y DISTANCIA DE PANAMA: Tel. 227-7242, Telefax: 227-7243, Ave. Perú, Panamá.
UNIVERSIDAD AUTONOMA DE CHIRIQUI: Tel. 775-1114, David, Chiriquí
UNIVERSIDAD DE PANAMA: Tel. 263-6133, http://www.up.ac.pa, Urbanización El Cangrejo, Panamá
UNIVERSIDAD DE PANAMA: Tel. 445-2567, Fax: 445-5857, Arco Iris, Colón
•**Centro Regional de Azuero:** Tel: 996-4712, Fax: 996-5910,
•**Centro Regional de Coclé:** Tel: 997-9642, Fax: 997-8260
•**Centro Regional de Los Santos:** Tel: 994-7399, Fax: 994-8080,
•**Centro Regional de Veraguas:** Tel: 958-5569, Fax: 958-7622,
•**Centro Regional de Panamá Oeste:** Tel: 253-5058, Fax: 253-2114,
•**Centro Regional de San Miguelito:** Tel: 267-8960, Fax: 267-1885.
UNIVERSIDAD TECNOLOGICA DE PANAMA: Tel.

263-8000, Fax: 264-9149, http://www.utp.ac.pa, Ave. M E Batista, Panamá
Tel. 775-4563, Urb. Lassonde, David, Chiriquì
Tel. 473-0377, Residencial Davis, Colón
•**Centro Regional de Azuero,** Tel. 966-8219, Fax: 966-9255
•**Centro Regional de Bocas del Toro:** Tel: 758-8373, Fax: 758-7490
•**Centro Regional de Coclé:** Tel: 997-9600, Fax: 997-9182
•**Centro Regional de Colón:** Tel: 473-0249, Fax: 473-0337
•**Centro Regional de Chiriquí:** Tel: 774-3016, Fax: 774-6843
•**Centro Regional de La Chorrera:** Tel: 244-0377, Fax: 244-1917
•**Centro Regional de Veraguas:** Tel: 999-3991, Fax: 999-3244

UNIVERSIDAD ESPECIALIZADA DE LAS AMERIC-AS (UDELAS): Tel: 315-1024, Albrook, Edif. 806-808, Panamá, Tel. Colón: 473-0221, David: Tel:775-3717, Santiago: Tel: 998-5540.
UNIVERSIDAD LATIOAMERICANA DE COMERCIO EXTERIOR: Tel: 223-5777, Telefax: 213-1792, Calle Alberto Navarro, Panamá.
UNIVERSIDAD PANAMERICANA: Tel: 265-0641/ 0638. Fax: 265-0638, El Cangrejo, Panamá.
UNIVERSIDAD DE TECNICAS DE LA COMUNICA-CION: Tel: 265-2434, Fax: 265-2432, Ave. Ma. E. Batista, Panamá.

Libraries and Information Centers

•**Caritas de Panamá,** #437-A, Ave. Frangipani, Tel.: 262-3777, E-mail: caritas@caritaspanama.org
•**Biblioteca José Agustín Arango,** Casa Museo, Banco Nacional de Panamá. Cl.34 y Ave. Cuba, Tel: 225-0640
•**Biblioteca José Antonio Susto,** Lotería Nacional de Beneficiencia, Tel: 207-6800 ext. 1009, Web page: www.loterianacional.com.pa
•**Biblioteca José María Pinilla,** Cl. 50 y Vía Porras, Tel.: 226-5138
•**Biblioteca Nacional Ernesto J. Castillero,** Parque Recreativo "Omar," San Francisco, Tel: 221-5965, Web page: www.binal.ac.pa
•**Biblioteca Pública Escolar Eusebio A. Morales,** Cl. L. Ave. Central, Centro de Documentación, Tel: 262-4777
•**Biblioteca Pública Mateo Iturralde,** Cl. 2 Central, Colón, tel.: 441-0722
•**Centro de Estudios Latinoamericanos CELA,** Centro de Documentación, Casa # 23, Cl. 55, El Cangrejo,Tel.: 223-0028, E-mail: celaja@pty.com
•**Centro de Estudios y Acción Social de Panamá (CEAS-**

PA), Vía Cincuentenario #84, Tel: 226-6783, fax: 226-5320, E-mail: padiadmon@cwpanama.net
•**Centro de Información Naciones Unidas,** Cl. Gerardo Ortega y Samuel Lewis, frente Edif. Comosa, 1er. Piso, Tel: 223-0557, fax: 223-2198, Web page: www.cinup.org
•**Centro de Recursos Informativos,** Edif, Torre Miramar, Ave. Balboa y Cl. 39, Tel.: 207-7100
•**Centro Latinoamericano de Periodismo (CELAP), Biblioteca Manuel Borbón,** Centro Comercial Aventura, El Dorado, Tel: 236-6181/83/9 , Web page: www.celap.net
•**Instituto Centroamericano para la Administración y Supervisión de la Educación (ICASE),** 5to piso, Facultad de Humanidades, Universidad de Panamá, Tel.: 264-2586, E-mail: icase@ancon.up.ac.pa
•**Instituto Cooperativo Interamericano,** La Pulida, Pueblo Nuevo, Tel.: 224-6019, E-mail: ici.pa@cw.panama.net
•**Instituto Smithsonian de Investigaciones Tropicales,** Ave. Roosevelt # 401, Biblioteca, Tel: 212-8113, Web page: www.siris.si.edu

Museums in Panama City

Anthropological Museum, Reina Torres de Araúz, Plaza 5 de Mayo. Tel: 262-8338. Exhibits a fine collection of pre-colombian art.
Afro-Antillian Museum, Calle 24 y la Avenida Justo Arosemena. Tel: 262-1668. Open Tuesday - Saturday from 8-30 a.m. to 3-30 p.m.. Exhibits photography, domestic and artistic objects of the Afro-West Indian group that helped build the Canal.
Natural Science Museum, Avenida Cuba entre las Calles 29 y 30. Tel: 225-0645. Open Tuesday – Saturday from 9.00 a.m. to 3.30 p.m.. Exhibits geology, paleontology, mammals, reptiles y other species of the fauna, as well as the Panamanian flora.
Panamanian History Museum, Palacio Municipal, in front

of Parque Catedral in Casco Viejo (Colonial Panama) Tel: 228-6231
Religious Art Museum,Casco Viejo (Colonial Panama) in an 18th century chapel, next to the Church and Convent of Santo Domingo where the "Arco Chato" is. Remains open from Tuesday to Saturday from 8-30 a.m. a 4-30 p.m. Tel: 228-2897
Panama La Vieja Museum, Artisan market of Panamá Viejo, Open Monday – Sunday from 9:00 a.m. to 5:00 p.m. www.panamaviejo.org
Contemporany Art Museum, Calle San Blas, Ancon y Avenida de los Martíres. Open from Tuesday – Sunday from 9:00 a.m. to 5:00 p.m. Exhibits art by national and reknowed international artists. Offers a workshop in serigraphy and

framing, as well as concerts, conferences and expositions. Tel: 262-3380, 262-8012 www.mac.panama.org

Canal Museum Interoceánico, Plaza de la Independencia (Plaza Catedral), San Felipe. Open Tuesday – Sunday from 9-30 am to 5-30 p.m.. Tel: 211-1649 www.museodelcanal.org

Banco Nacional Museum, Calle 34 y Avenida Cuba. Exhibits a fine collection of coins and stamps dating back to the 16th century.. Tel: 225-0640

Other Museums in the country

Museum of History and Tradition of Penonomé, Open Tuesday – Saturday from 9 a.m.to 12:30 p.m. and 1:30 p.m. to 4:00 p.m. Sunday from 9:30 to 12:00 p.m. Calle San Antonio , Penonomé, Provincia de Coclé, Tel. 997-8490.

El Caño Archaelogical Park, Open Tuesday – Saturday from 9 a.m.to 12:30 p.m. and 1:30 p.m. to 4:00p.m. Sunday 9:30 a.m. to mid-night. El Caño, Natá, Provincia de Coclé, Tel. 987-9352. Dedicated to exalt the indigenous culture of Cocle. José D. de Obaldía History and Art Museum, Calle 8, Davíd, Provincia de Chriquí. Tel: 775-7839.

San Pablo History Museum el Nuevo, Provincia de Chiriquí. Tel: 775-7918.

Herrera Museum, Open Tuesday – Saturday from 9 a.m. 12p.m. and 1:30 p.m.to 4 p.m. Sunday from 9:30 a.m. 12p.m.. Julio Arjona Ave. y Calle Manuel M. Arjona, Chitré, Province of Herrera,. Tel. 996-0077.

Colonial Religious Art Museum, Open Monday – Friday from 8:30 a.m. to 4:30 a.m. Iglesia de Santo Domingo, Parita, Provincia de Herrera

Nationality Museum, Open Tuesday – Saturday from 9 a.m. to 12:30 p.m. and 1:30 p.m. to 4 p.m., Sunday from 9:30 a.m. to 12p.m.. Calle José Vallarino , Los Santos, Provincia de Los Santos.

Belisario Porras Museum, Dedicated to the life of Dr. Belisario Porras, three times president of the republic. Las Tablas, Provincia de Los Santos. Tel: 994-6326.

Manuel F. Zarate Museum Open Tuesday – Saturday from 10 a.m. to 4 p.m., Sundays from 2 p.m. to 4 p.m. Guararé, Provincia de Los Santos. Tel. 994-5644.

Principal Theaters of the City

Ancón Theater Guild, Ancón, tel. 212-0060/24.

Teatro Aba, Urb. Los Angeles Bethania, Tel.: 260-6316

Teatro Anayansi, Centro de Convenciones Atlapa, tel: 226-7000

Teatro Balboa, Balboa Canal Zone, tel: 228-0327, 262-1952

Teatro En Círculo, Herbruger, Ave. 6C Norte, Urb.

Herbruger, tel. 261-5375 tcirculo@sinfo.net

Teatro La Cúpula, El Cangrejo, tel. 223-7516

Teatro La Huaca, Centro de Convenciones Atlapa, tel: 226-7000

Teatro Nacional, Cl. 3 Catedral y Ave. B, tel: 262-3525

Art Galleries

Art Americas, Ave. Aquilino de la Guardia, Tel.: 214-9612 www.arteamericas.net

Bernheim Gallery, Calle 50, Edif. Madison, tel: 223-0012, fax: 223-0009 bernheim@psi.net.pa www.bernheim.com

Enmarcados La Acuarela, Vía Porras, Tel.: 226-2467

Enmarcados Liner Gallery, Cl. 50 y 56, tel: 269-7029

Frames & Gallery, Cl. 50 y Vía Cicuentenario, Tel.: 270-7502

Galeria Arteconsult, S.A., Ave. Manuel Espinosa Batista, Tel: 269-1523, artecons@orbi.net

Galeria Artegma, Ave. Samuel Lewis, Tel.: 263-3816; Camino Real Bethania, Tel.: 236-6740

www.galeriaartegma.com

Galeria y Enmarcados Habitante, Cl. 48 y Cl. Uruguay, tel: 264-6470

Imagen, Cl. 50, tel: 226-2649, fax: 226-8989 imagen@pty.com

Legacy Fine Arts, Ave. Balboa, Calle 50 Este, Tel.: 265-8141, legacy@sinfo.net

Marcorama, Ave. Ramon Arias, tel: 223-5001, fax: 223-5002; Ave. Balboa, Tel.: 269-0643; El Dorado, Tel.: 260-5846 imagen@pty.com

Marquetería Dalí, Cl. Israel, tel: 226-1018

Banks

EXPLANATORY NOTE: The information for these lists was obtained from reports by the Panama Banking Superintendency as of mid 2002. Amounts are expressed in thousands of dollars.

BANK WITH GENERAL LICENCE BY TOTAL

ASSETS (MARCH 30,2002).

BANCO LATINOAMERICANO DE EXPORTACIONES, S.A. (Latinoamérica/ Panamá), tel. 263-6766, fax 269-6333, http://www.blx.com

Activos (Assets): $4,860.923

Préstamos(Loans): $314,301
Depósitos (Deposits): $75,845
BANCO NACIONAL DE PANAMA (Panamá), tel. 263-5151, fax 269-0091, http://www.banconal.com.pa
Activos (Assets): $3,369,985
Préstamos(Loans): $1,460,938
Depósitos (Deposits): $2,575,175
PRIMER BANCO DEL ISTMO, S.A. (Panamá), tel. 270-0015, fax 270-1667, http://www.banistmo.com.
Activos (Assets): $ 2,955,548
Préstamos(Loans): $ 1,418,219
Depósitos (Deposits): $ 1,959,875
BANCO GENERAL, S.A. Y SUBSIDIARIAS (Panamá), tel. 265-0303, fax. 265-0210, http://www.bgeneral.com
Activos (Assets): $2,394,542
Préstamos(Loans): $1,297,546
Depósitos (Deposits): $1,629,618
BANCO CONTINENTAL DE PANAMA, S.A. Y SUBSIDIARIAS (Panamá), tel. 215-7000, fax. 215-7134, http://www.bcontinental.com.
Activos (Assets): $ 1,237,673
Préstamos(Loans): $ 642,611
Depósitos (Deposits):$ 713,033
HSBC BANK USA, tel. 263-5877, fax. 263-6009, http://www.hsbc.com
Activos (Assets): $ 1,206,077
Préstamos(Loans): $ 844,118
Depósitos (Deposits): $ 753,002
DRESDNER BANK LATINOAMERICA (Alemania), A.G, tel. 263-5055, fax 269-1877, http://www.dbla.com
Activos: (Assets): $1,188,464
Préstamos(Loans) $95,529
Depósitos (Deposits):$ 218,645
CAJA DE AHORROS (Panamá), tel. 205-1000, fax 269-3674, http://www.cajadeahorros.com.pa
Activos (Assets): $ 907, 773
Préstamos(Loans):$ 510, 016
Depósitos (Deposits):$ 586, 039
BANCO BILBAO VIZCAYA ARGENTARIA S.A. (Panamá) tel. 227-1122, fax. 227-3663, http://www.bbvapanama.com
Activos (Assets):$ 852,287
Préstamos(Loans):$506,686
Depósitos (Deposits):$328,574
CITIBANK, N.A. (E.U.), tel. 210-5900, fax 210-5901, http://www.citibank.com/panama/
Activos (Assets): $805,856
Préstamos(Loans): $ 598,544
Depósitos (Deposits): $ 467,995
BANQUE SUDAMERIS (Italia), tel. 207-0300, fax. 227-5828, http://www.sudameris.com.pa
Activos (Assets):$ 768, 316
Préstamos(Loans): $ 19, 581
Depósitos (Deposits):$ 149, 708
BANCOLOMBIA (PANAMÁ), S.A. (Colombia), tel. 263-6955, 263-1138, http://www.bancolombiapanama.com
Activos (Assets):$ 754,809
Préstamos(Loans):$ 795
Depósitos (Deposits):$ 87

GLOBAL BANK CORPORATION Y SUBSIDIARIAS (Panamá), tel. 269-9292, fax. 264-4089, http://www.globalbank.com.pa
Activos (Assets):$575,906
Préstamos(Loans):$ 418,111
Depósitos (Deposits):$ 390,197
BANCO INTERNACIONAL DE COSTA RICA, S.A. Y SUBSIDIARIAS (Costa Rica), tel. 263-6822, fax. 263-6393, http://www.bicsapan.com
Activos (Assets): $ 524, 010
Préstamos(Loans): $ 41, 237
Depósitos (Deposits):$73, 868
THE BANK OF NOVA SCOTIA (Canadá), tel. 263-6255, fax. 263-8636
e-mail: scotiabk@sinfo.net
Activos (Assets):$ 474,737
Préstamos(Loans):$ 305,082
Depósitos (Deposits):$33,724
BANCO ATLÁNTICO (PANAMÁ), S.A. (España), tel. 263-5366, fax. 269-1616, http://www.batlantico.com.pa
Activos (Assets):$ 418,129
Préstamos(Loans):$277,054
Depósitos (Deposits):$153,253
MULTI CREDIT BANK, INC. Y SUBSIDIARIAS (Panamá), tel. 269-0188, fax. 264-4014 e-mail: mcbank@pan.gbm.net
Activos (Assets):$ 413,074
Préstamos(Loans):$294,194
Depósitos (Deposits):$ 205,371
BANKBOSTON, N.A. (E.U.), tel. 265-6077, fax. 265-7400, e-mail: bkboston@sinfo.net
Activos (Assets):$ 396,271
Préstamos(Loans):$ 315,533
Depósitos (Deposits):$207,658
BANCO MERCANTIL DEL ISTMO, S.A. (Panamá), tel. 263-6262, fax. 263-7553, http://www.banistmo.com
Activos (Assets):$ 367,448
Préstamos(Loans):$ 237,406
Depósitos (Deposits):$ 159,481
BANCO PANAMERICANO S.A. (PANABANK) Y SUBSIDIARIAS (Panamá), tel. 263-9266, fax. 264-5357, http://www.panabank.com
Activos (Assets):$ 333,914
Préstamos(Loans):$203, 674
Depósitos (Deposits):$ 249,895
CREDICORP BANK, S.A. (Panamá), tel. 210-1111, fax. 210-1037, http://www.credicorpbank.com, e-mail: credi@sinfo.net
Activos (Assets):$ 283,700
Préstamos(Loans):$175,602
Depósitos (Deposits):$180,365
TOWERBANK INTERNATIONAL, INC. Y SUBSIDIARIAS (Panamá), tel. 269-6900, fax. 269-6800, e-mail: towerbank@towerbank.com, http://www.towerbank.com
Activos (Assets):$ 282,709
Préstamos(Loans):$ 88,886
Depósitos (Deposits):$106,721
BNP PARIBAS PANAMA, S.A. (Francia), tel. 264-8555, fax. 263-6970
Activos (Assets):$ 267,114

Préstamos(Loans):$ 175,593
Depósitos (Deposits):$136,916
BANCO ALIADO, S.A. (Panamá), tel. 263-9777, fax. 263-9677, e-mail: bkaliado@panama.phoenix.net
Activos (Assets):$ 265,883
Préstamos(Loans):$ 126,529
Depósitos (Deposits):$ 182,102
BANCO UNO (Guatemala), tel. 223-5333, fax. 223-5338, e-mail: banexger@sinfo.net
HTTP://www.bancouno.com.pa
Activos (Assets):$ 256,968
Préstamos(Loans):$ 44,461
Depósitos (Deposits):$ 69,461
BANCO DO BRASIL, tel. 269-1444, fax. 269-1716, http://www.bb.com.br
Activos (Assets): $ 239, 449
Préstamos(Loans): $ 229
Depósitos (deposits):$ 1,798
LLOYDS TSB BANK Plc. (Inglaterra), tel. 263-6277, fax. 264-7931
Activos (Assets): $ 237,705
Préstamos(Loans): $ 122,358
Depósitos (Deposits): $50,072
BANCAFE (PANAMA) S.A. Y SUBSIDIARIA, (Colombia) tel. 264-6060, fax. 263-6115, http://www.bancafe-panama.com
Activos (Assets):$ 210,555
Préstamos(Loans):$102,500
Depósitos (Deposits):$57,910
BAC INTERNATIONAL BANK , INC. (Nicaragüense), tel. 213-0822, fax. 269-3879, http://www.bacbank.com.
Activos (Assets): $ 203,146
Préstamos(Loans): $ 38,829
Depósitos (Deposits): $ 30,783
THE DAI-ICHI KANGYO BANK, LTD. (Japón), tel. 269-6111, fax. 269-6815
Activos (Assets):$ 202,153
Préstamos(Loans): $ 1,895
Depósitos (Deposits): $ 2,445
THE INTERNATIONAL COMMERCIAL BANK OF CHINA (China), tel. 263-8108 fax: 263-8392, e-mail: icbcpmpm@pananet.com
Activos (Assets):$ 178,265
Préstamos(Loans):$ 88,967
Depósitos Deposits):$ 93,482
BANCO SANTANDER (PANAMA), S.A. (Colombia), tel. 263-6577, fax. 263-7534, e-mail: santander@sinfo.net
Activos (Assets):$ 160,076
Préstamos(Loans):$ 40,553
Depósitos (Deposits):$ 248
WALL STREET BANK, S.A. (Panamá), tel. 227-8775, fax. 225-3702
Activos (Assets):$ 151,639
Préstamos(Loans):$ 4,768
Depósitos (Deposits):$ 76,308
BANCO TRASATLANTICO, S.A. (Panamá), tel. 269-2318, fax. 269-4948
Activos (Assets):$ 149,222
Préstamos(Loans):$ 55,958

Depósitos (Deposits):$103,295
BANCO DE BOGOTA, S.A. Y SUBSIDIARIA (Colombia), tel. 264-6000, fax. 263-8037, e-mail: banbogo@sinfo.net
Activos (Assets): $ 138,320
Préstamos(Loans):$ 3,939
Depósitos (Deposits):$ 2,932
KOREA EXCHANGE BANK (Korea), tel. 269-9966, fax. 264-4224, e-mail: keb@sinfo.net
Activos (Assets):$ 123,135
Préstamos(Loans):$ 20,047
Depósitos (Deposits)$ 14,197
BANCO PANAMEÑO DE LA VIVIENDA (BANVIVIEN-DA), S.A. (Panamá), tel. 227-4020, fax. 227-5433, e-mail: bpv@pty.com
Activos (Assets):$ 121,241
Préstamos(Loans):$ 81,252
Depósitos (Deposits):$101,252
GNB BANK (PANAMA), S.A. Y SUBSIDIARIAS (Colombia), tel. 269-9333, fax. 264-1285 e-mail: gnbbank@sinfo.net
Activos (Assets):$ 88,601
Préstamos(Loans):$ 17,914
Depósitos (Deposits):$ 63,772
BANK LEUMI LE-ISRAEL, B.M. (Israel), tel. 263-9377, fax. 269-2674, e-mail: leumi@sinfo.net
Activos (Assets):$ 85,194
Préstamos(Loans):$ 78,100
Depósitos (Deposits):$ 70,107
BANK OF CHINA (China), tel. 263-5522 fax: 223-9960, e-mail: yinxn@bank-of-china.com
Activos (Assets):$ 84,805
Préstamos(Loans):$ 5,705
Depósitos (Deposits):$ 15,538
METROBANK, S.A. (Panamá), tel. 223-1666, fax. 223-2020, e-mail: metrobank@pananet.com
Activos (Assets):$ 79,773
Préstamos(Loans):$ 34,997
Depósitos (Deposits):$ 54,363
BANCO UNIVERSAL, S.A. Y SUBSIDIARIA (Chiriquí), tel. 775-4394, 774-2308
Activos (Assets):$ 52,327
Préstamos(Loans):$ 34,933
Depósitos (Deposits):$ 38,919
BANCO FEDPA, S.A, tel. 263-3235, fax. 263-1153
Activos (Assets):$ 38,709
Préstamos(Loans):$ 27,325
Depósitos (Deposits):$ 34,688
ABN AMRO BANK N.V. (Holanda), tel. 263-6200, fax. 269-0526, e-mail: abnamro@sinfo.net
Activos (Assets):$ 13,221
Préstamos(Loans):$ 200
Depósitos (Deposits):$ 12,263
MI BANCO, S.A. (Panamá), tel. 229-7001, fax. 229-6774
Activos (Assets):$ 6,405
Préstamos(Loans):$ 2,319
Depósitos (Deposits):$ 1,614
Banks with international licence by total assets (March 30, 2002)

SOCIETE GENERALE (Francia), tel. 264-9611/ 264-0295, e-mail: sgpanama@panama.phoenix.net
Activos (Assets):$ 826,351
Préstamos (Loans):$ 293,618
Depósitos (Deposits):$ 317,220
BNP PARIBAS (Francia), tel. 264-8555, fax. 263-6970, e-mail: bnpsuc@sinfo.net
Activos (Assets):$ 814,387
Préstamos(Loans):$ 175,593
Depósitos (Deposits):$ 136,916
BANCO DE LA PROVINCIA DE BUENOS AIRES (Argentina), tel. 227-2167 fax: 227-8378, e-mail: bpbama@pananet.com
Activos (Assets):$ 697,871
Préstamos(Loans):$ 84,649
Depósitos (Deposits): $ 159,704
POPULAR BANK & TRUST, LTD. (Rep. Dominicana), Calle Aquilino de La Guardía, Edificio Banco General piso 20, tel.: 269-4993, fax: 269-1309
Activos: (Assets): $ 581,867
Préstamos(Loans): $ 248-066
Depósitos (Deposits):$ 366,001
BANCO DE LA NACION ARGENTINA (Argentina), tel. 269-4666, fax. 269-6719, e-mail: lan@sinfo.net
Activos (Assets):$ 319,242
Préstamos(Loans):$ 143,234
Depósitos (Deposits):$ 211,817
BANCO ALEMAN PLATINA, S.A. (Alemania), tel. 223-8005, fax. 269-0526, e-mail: baplatina@pananet.com
Activos (Assets):$ 291,913
Préstamos(Loans):$ 146,603
Depósitos (Deposits):$ 207,041
BANCO DE OCCIDENTE (PANAMA), S.A. (Colombia), tel. 263-8144 / 269-3261, e-mail: boccipan@pty.com
Activos (Assets):$ 219,238
Préstamos(Loans):$ 21,699
Depósitos (Deposits):$ 204,776
BANCO BCT (PANAMA), S.A. (Costa Rica) Torre BAC, Calle Aquilino de La Guardía, tel.: 269-9565, fax: 269-9563, hhtp://www.bct.fi.cr
Activos (Assets):$ 169,016
Préstamos(Loans):$ 162,524
Depósitos (Deposits): $ 127,091
BANCREDITO (PANAMA), S.A. (República Dominicana), tel. 214-9613/ 223-2977, fax: 264-6781, e-mail: bancred@sinfo.net
Activos (Assets):$ 143,930
Préstamos(Loans):$ 28,934
Depósitos (Deposits):$ 51,516
BANESCO INTERNACIONAL (PANAMA), S.A. (Venezuela), tel. 269-7421, 264-9342
Activos (Assets):$ 127,318
Préstamos(Loans): $ 47,534
Depósitos (Deposits): $ 121,707
BANCO AGRICOLA COMERCIAL EL SALVADOR, S.A. (El Salvador), tel. 263-5762, fax. 263-5626, e-mail: bac-salv@pan.gbm.net
Activos (Assets):$103,347
Préstamos(Loans):$
Depósitos (Dcposits):$ 107,470
DISCOUNT BANK AND TRUST COMPANY (Suiza), tel. 269-4011, fax. 269-6266
Activos (Assets):$ 79,141
Préstamos(Loans):$ 2,452
Depósitos (Deposits): $ 5,097
BANCO DE CREDITO (PANAMA), S.A. (Colombia), tel. 214-9713, 214-9715, e-mail: bancrepa@sinfo.net
Activos (Assets):$ 61,059
Préstamos(Loans):$ 28,934
Depósitos (Deposits):$ 51,516
BANCO DEL PACIFICO (PANAMA), S.A. Y SUB-SIDIARIA (Ecuador), tel. 263-5833, fax. 263-7481, e-mail: bpacificopanama@pacifico.fin.ec
Activos (Assets):$ 55,125
Préstamos(Loans):$ 27,297
Depósitos (Deposits):$ 36,898
BANCO DEL CENTRO, S.A. (Venezuela), tel. 223-5062, e-mail: lsombrano@bancodelcentro.com
Activos (Assets):$ 35,396
Préstamos(Loans):$ 16,752
Depósitos (Deposits):$ 25,601
AUSTROBANK OVERSEAS, S.A., tel. 269-5275, 269-5372
Activos (Assets) $ 36,912
Préstamos (Loans) $ 8,182
Depósitos (Deposits) $ 25,194
BANCO DE FINANZAS (INTERNATIONAL), S.A., tel. 223-9524, 223-8425
Activos (Assets):$ 27,429
Préstamos(Loans):$ 17,169
Depósitos (Deposits):$ 24,001
ATLANTIC SECURITY BANK (Perú), tel. 215-7311, fax. 215-7323, e-mail:
Activos (Assets):$ 19,782
Préstamos(Loans):$ 16,895
Depósitos (Deposits):$ 14,519
INTERBANK OVERSEAS LTD. (Perú), tel. 265-7300, fax. 223-3333, e-mail: ysoo@pan.gbm.net
Activos (Assets):$ 16,278
Préstamos(Loans):$ 15,370
Depósitos (Deposits):$ 12,537
INTERNATIONAL UNION BANK, S.A. (Venezuela), tel. 263-4623, 263-9985
Activos (Assets):$ 3,450
Préstamos(Loans):$ 1,309
Depósitos (Deposits):$ 234

BANKS WITH REPRESENTATION LICENCE, SOURCE SUPERINTENDENCIA DE BANCOS DE LA REPUBLICA DE PANAMA (2002)

AMERICAN EXPRESS BANK, Ltd. (E.U.A.), tel. 263-5555
BANCO GENERAL (OVERSEAS), Inc. (Panamá), tel. 264-737, 265-0227
BANK HAPOALIM, B.M. (Israel), tel. 263-7222, 263-7647
NORFOLK AND HAMPTON BANK (Panamá), tel. 263-5955, 215-7134
COMMERCIAL BANK (GRAND CAYMAN), Ltd., tel. 263-6066, 263-5305
FIRST UNION NATIONAL BANK, N.A. (E.U.A.), tel. 269-7345, 269-7435.

Panama in Figures

A concise reading of the economic pulse of the country

Sources: Statistics and Census Bureau, Office of the General Comptroller; Panama Canal Authority; International Monetary Fund; Ministry of Commerce and Industry; Superintendency of Banks

POPULATION

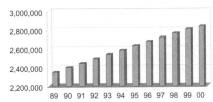

▲ Inhabitants

Average population growth during the 90s was 1.76%, a substantial reduction compared with 2.6% for the previous ten years.

FERTILITY AND BIRTH RATE

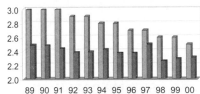

☐ Fertility (children per woman)   ■ Birth Rate (per 100 inhabitants)

Showing a decrease in the last ten years, Panama's fertility rate is one of the lowest in Latin America.

LABOR FORCE

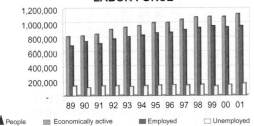

▲ People   ■ Economically active   ■ Employed   ☐ Unemployed

A steady growth has been registered in the economically active labor force, but the unemployment rate has remained above 10%.

ENROLMENT

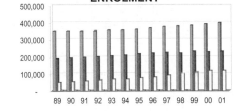

▲ Students   ■ Elementary   ■ Secondary   ☐ University   ☐ Other

The opening of private centers of higher learning in the last decade has contributed to a stable growth in university enrolment.

INSURED POPULATION

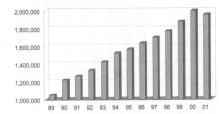

▲ People

Between 2000 and 2001 a sharp drop reflected a rise in unemployment.

HEALTH INSTITUTIONS

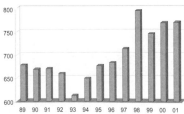

▲ Hospitals

There was an increase in hospitals between 1993 and 1998, and a sharp fall in 1999 and a later growth in the last two years.

CATTLE

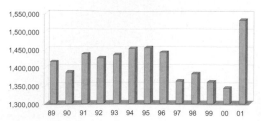

▲ Heads of cattle

After a decline between 1996 and 2000, a rise in the number heads of cattle occurred in 2001, mostly because of the rising exports to Central America.

HOG PRODUCTION

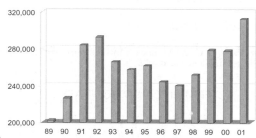

▲ Hogs

After a constant decline between 1992 and 1997, there was remarkable growth subsequently.

SHRIMP CATCH

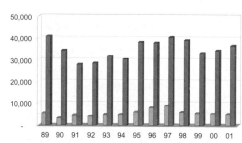

Quantity (thousands of kilos) ■ Amount (thousands of balboas)

After a stable growth between 1991 and 1997, shrimp catch decreased between 1998 and 1998, due to "white spot" disease, but recovered in the last two years.

COFFEE

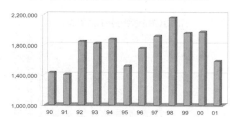

▲ Processed quintals

Coffee production has seen its cyclic ups and downs in the past years. It reached a maximum of 307,247 quintals in 2001.

POULTRY

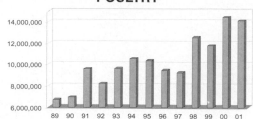

▲ Poultry

This vibrant industry has seen steady growth since 1991. The province of Panama contributes to 53.4% of national production.

INDUSTRIAL FISHING

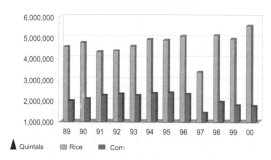

Quantity (thousands of kilos) ■ Amount (thousands of balboas)

With the exception of 1996 and 1999, industrial fishing maintained a steady growth in the last 10 years.

RICE AND CORN

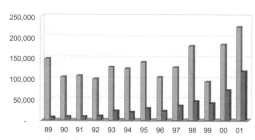

▲ Quintals Rice ■ Corn

While rice annual harvest between 1990 and 2000 grew 17.3% due to better returns per hectare, corn production dropped 9.8%, mostly because of a reduction in cultivated lands.

SUGARCANE PRODUCTION

▲ Short tons

Sugarcane cultivated lands in 2001 fell 5,303 hectares from 1991. However production increased in the same period by 13.1%.

CONSTRUCTION

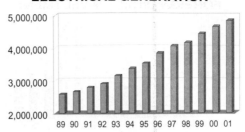

▲ Millions of balboas

After a fall between 1996 and 1998, the construction sector has seen an increase in the last three years, due to strong investment by the public and private sectors in mega-projects.

ELECTRICAL GENERATION

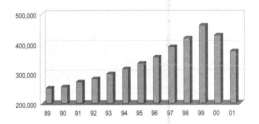

▲ Thousands of kilowatts-hour

Electrical production grew continually in the last 10 years. Panama produces the majority of its electricity through hydroelectric plants, a cheap and environmentally friendly process.

ELECTRICAL GENERATION BY SOURCE

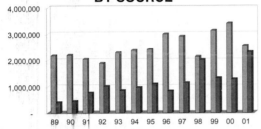

▲ Thousands of kilowatts-hour   ■ Hydroelectrical   ■ Thermal

In 1998 a dramatic fall of hydroelectrical generation, due to the El Niño phenomenon, required a bigger share of thermal generation.

TELEPHONES

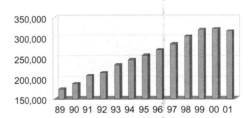

▲ Active Telephone Lines

The rise in mobile telephony and the effects of the economic crisis lessened the continuous growth in active telephone lines in Panama.

ROADS AND HIGHWAYS

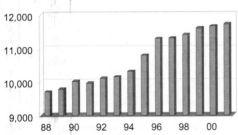

▲ Kilometers

The accelerated growth of roads and highways between 1994 and 1996 diminished in the last 5 years to a yearly average of 3.27%.

AUTO CIRCULATION

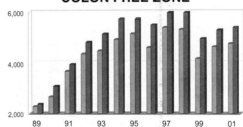

▲ Autos

The number of autos peaked in 2000, but fell in 2001, reflecting the global economic crisis.

BANKING SYSTEM

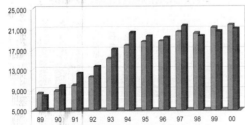

▲ Millions of Balboas   ■ Productive Assets   ■ Liquid Liabilities
Since 1990 the banking system saw steady growth.

COLON FREE ZONE

▲ Millions of Balboas   ■ Imports   ■ Re-exports
The last decade has seen relatively steady growth although activity fell in 1999 mostly due to political instability (Venezuela and Colombia).

FOREIGN DIRECT INVESTMENT

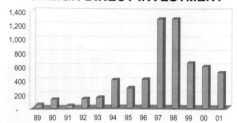

▲ Millons of Balboas

Foreign Direct Investment increased, due in part to the recent privatization of public utilities, laws to protect investors and fiscal incentives.

FOREIGN TRADE

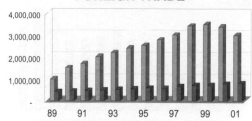

▲ Thousands of Balboas ■ Imports ■ Exports

Due to Panama's service-based economy and its lack of a strong export base, imports continue to be a greater part of the trade balance than exports.

GOVERNMENT INCOME AND EXPENSES

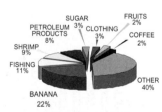

▲ Thousands of Balboas ■ Income ■ Expenses

In the past decade the government's income and expenses have shown fairly consistent growth.

PUBLIC SECTOR DEBT

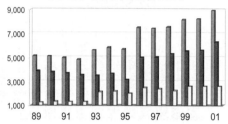

▲ Thousands of Balboas ■ Public Debt ■ External Debt □ Internal Debt

A sharp rise in public debt occurred in the last 6 years, most of it external debt.

EXPORTS YEAR 2000

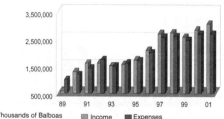

A prolonged labor strike in 1998 and the European Union ban on Latin America banana imports have affected exports badly. This product is the most important of Panama's exports.

GROSS DOMESTIC PRODUCT

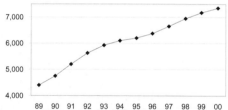

▲ Millions of Balboas (at 1982 prices)

After a large fall due to the political and economical turmoil of the late eighties, GDP rebounded and continued a steady rise, an average annual rate of 2.88%.

CANAL TRANSITS

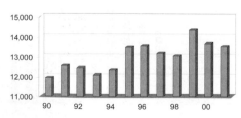

▲ Ocean going transits

In fiscal year 2001, Canal ship traffic was 13,492.

CANAL TOLLS REVENUE AND COMMERCIAL CARGO

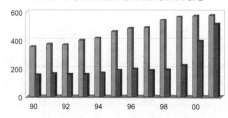

■ Tolls revenue (millions of Balboas) ■ Commercial cargo (million long tons)

Tolls revenue registered a constant increase in the last 10 years, due to the rate increase in 1997, the admeasurements rule change to cover on-deck container carrying capacity and the increase in average vessel size.

Panama in Figures
In more detail

POPULATION OF THE REPUBLIC BY PROVINCE (THOUSANDS)

Year	Total	Bocas del Toro	Coclé	Colón (1)	Chiriquí	Darién	Herrera	Los Santos	Panamá	Veraguas
1911	336.7	22.7	35.0	32.1	63.4	9.0	25.0	30.1	61.9	59.6
1920	446.1	27.2	45.2	58.3	76.5	10.7	29.0	34.6	98.8	66.6
1930	467.5	15.9	48.2	57.2	76.9	13.4	31.0	41.2	114.1	69.5
1940	622.6	16.5	55.7	78.1	111.2	14.9	38.1	49.6	173.3	85.0
1950	805.3	22.4	73.1	90.1	138.1	14.7	50.1	61.4	248.3	107.0
1960	1,075.5	32.6	93.2	105.4	188.4	19.7	61.7	70.6	372.4	131.7
1970	1,428.1	43.5	118.0	134.3	236.2	22.7	72.5	72.4	576.6	151.8
1980	1,805.3	53.5	140.9	162.5	287.4	26.5	82.0	70.3	809.1	173.2
1990	2,329.3	93.4	173.2	202.3	370.2	43.8	93.7	76.9	1,072.1	203.6
2000	2,839.2	89.3	202.5	204.2	368.8	40.3	102.5	83.5	1,388.4	209.1

(1) Until 1990, the data for Colon included the Kuna Yala Indian reservation; the 2000 census separates the population of Kuna Yala (32,446), Emberá (8,246) and Ngöbe Buglé (110,080), from the provinces of Bocas del Toro, Chiriquí, Darién and Veraguas.

ANNUAL POPULATION GROWTH RATE
(Per 100 inhabitants)

Año	Total	Bocas del Toro	Coclé	Colón (1)	Chiriquí	Darién	Herrera	Los Santos	Panamá	Veraguas
1920	3.17 %	2.03 %	2.86 %	6.85 %	2.11 %	1.98 %	2.60 %	1.58 %	5.25 %	1.24 %
1930	0.47 %	-5.57 %	0.66 %	-0.19 %	0.06 %	2.25 %	0.68 %	1.76 %	1.63 %	0.43 %
1940	2.76 %	0.39 %	1.38 %	3.01 %	3.56 %	1.04 %	1.97 %	1.78 %	4.05 %	1.92 %
1950	2.56 %	3.02 %	2.69 %	1.41 %	2.15 %	-0.18 %	2.71 %	2.11 %	3.59 %	2.28 %
1960	2.94 %	3.83 %	2.45 %	1.58 %	3.15 %	3.01 %	2.10 %	1.40 %	4.14 %	2.10 %
1970	3.06 %	3.12 %	2.54 %	2.6 %	2.43 %	1.50 %	1.74 %	0.27 %	4.76 %	1.52 %
1980	2.37 %	2.08 %	1.79 %	1.92 %	1.98 %	1.58 %	1.23 %	-0.30 %	3.44 %	1.33 %
1990	2.58 %	5.73 %	2.08 %	2.22 %	2.57 %	5.15 %	1.34 %	0.91 %	2.85 %	1.63 %
2000	1.65 %	3.16 %	1.06 %	1.19 %	1.2 %	3.12 %	0.55 %	-0.11 %	2.12 %	0.48 %

(1) Includes the Kuna Yala Indian reservation

GROSS DOMESTIC PRODUCT (GDP)

Year	Total in millions of dollars (1982)	Gross Domestic Product Per Capita (1) in $ of 1982	GDP Variation (%)
1988	4,320.7	1,876	-15.1
1989	4,388.2	1,868	-0.4
1990	4,743.6	1,979	5.9
1991	5,190.4	2,125	7.4
1992	5,616.1	2,257	6.2
1993	5,922.5	2,336	3.5
1994	6,091.3	2,359	1.0
1995	6,198.0	2,356	-0.1
1996	6,372.2	2,383	1.1
1997	6,657.5	2,449	2.8
1998	6,947.2	2,514	2.7
1999	7,169.9	2,552	1.5
2000 (P)	7,345.7	2,572	0.8
2001 (E)	7,365.2	2,542	-1.2

(1) Based on the estimated total population of the Republic of Panama by July 1st of every year, prepared with the figures of the National Population Census of 1990.
(P) Preliminary data
(E) Estimated data

GROSS DOMESTIC PRODUCT, ACCORDING TO ECONOMIC SECTOR AND 1982 PRICES: 1996-2001

Description	Gross Domestic Product at market prices (in Millions of dollars)					
	1996	1997	1998	1999	2000 (P)	2001 (E)
Agriculture and related	441.1	429.2	44,139.0	478.7	475.0	459.4
Fishing	73.9	85.7	105.6	80.2	93.0	112.9
Mining	7.2	13.6	16.7	19.3	18.0	15.7
Manufacturing industry	608.1	646.8	672.1	622.0	589.2	555.6
Electricity, gas and water	305.9	308.2	294.0	346.6	387.4	387.6
Construction	248.1	261.8	279.4	324.0	332.1	299.9
Wholesale commerce	1,166.9	1,273.5	1,297.8	1,252.0	1,271.3	1,247.7
Hotels and restaurants	100.9	107.7	133.3	117.8	121.8	120.2
Transport, communications, related	780.1	824.9	914.7	1,010.8	1,112.1	1,162.9
Financial mediation	725.4	729.2	809.4	913.5	938.2	945.3
Real estate activities						
Business and rental	879.2	908.8	937.2	981.3	1,019.0	1,047.9
Teaching	34.6	38.0	38.6	38.8	41.0	42.1
Social services and health	108.2	113.1	113.9	120.5	114.8	110.4
Other community activities						
social and presonal service1	62.5	174.9	184.7	198.3	185.4	190.1
Minus: Fees due to financial						
mediation services	246.9	276.0	336.7	406.4	435.3	441.8
Subtotal: Industries	**5,395.2**	**5,639.4**	**5,882.6**	**6,097.4**	**6,263.0**	**6,255.9**
Government services	665.3	690.6	711.3	721.3	729.2	762.7
Domestic services	55.2	57.0	58.9	60.3	62.6	63.7
GROSS AGGREGATE VALUE	**6,115.7**	**6,387.0**	**6,652.8**	**6,879.0**	**7,054.8**	**7,082.3**
Plus: Import fees	219.0	232.1	253.5	249.5	251.8	246.5
Plus: Transfer of value						
added tax (1)	37.5	38.4	40.9	41.4	39.1	36.4
GROSS DOMESTIC PRODUCT						
AT MARKET PRICES	**6,372.2**	**6,657.5**	**6,947.2**	**7,169.9**	**7,345.7**	**7,365.2**

(1) This refers to the percentage of the transfer of value added tax which, after deduction, is not registered in the values added tothe amount of tax paid directly with the purchase of taxable items, purchased by private houscholds.
(P) Preliminary data
(E) Estimated data

INDUSTRIAL PRODUCTION INDEX OF THE REPUBLIC, ACCORDING TO SECTOR: 1994-2001 (1992=100)

Industrial division	1994	1995	1996	1997	1998	1999	2000	2001 (P)
Global index	**110.3**	**111.1**	**111.0**	**117.3**	**121.8**	**117.0**	**111.2**	**123.9**
Food & drink production	106.8	107.7	109.3	118.2	128.2	119.5	116.2	161.9
Tobacco products	172.8	164.0	180.8	172.4	98.7	-	-	-
Manufacture of textile products	112.2	104.1	104.3	118.5	114.4	112.3	112.5	109.2
Clothing manufacture	86.2	83.2	75.4	67.2	63.0	49.0	42.9	32.5
Leather treatment and footwear manufacture	114.9	130.2	106.9	97.5	88.0	84.4	70.0	60.1
Production of timber and related products	112.8	96.6	85.6	93.2	86.1	84.5	57.8	57.6
Manufacture of paper and related products	118.4	119.3	108.6	101.1	90.9	83.1	72.7	74.0
Editorial and printing activities	112.0	116.3	105.7	106.4	134.1	136.8	131.1	120.7
Petroleum products production	64.4	74.5	122.6	124.7	136.8	147.8	133.8	129.0
Chemical substances and products	110.9	115.5	107.9	108.1	107.4	97.9	93.0	73.1
Rubber and plastics	108.6	110.7	104.4	116.7	113.0	105.1	101.6	96.5
Production of other non-metal items	142.4	130.1	118.3	128.7	155.3	171.2	163.4	139.2
Metal productions	100.4	119.6	134.0	177.9	148.6	211.6	162.0	72.4
Manufacture of metal products, except machinery and equipment	117.3	122.7	123.5	140.4	167.4	165.0	173.8	195.8
Equipment and machinery production	127.0	145.6	108.8	125.6	175.5	189.5	132.2	77.4
Production of machinery and electrical appliances	147.2	142.9	170.1	171.7	143.2	58.7	61.8	43.7
Manufacture of medical, optical and precision instruments	111.9	114.8	109.4	119.8	104.3	102.7	133.3	152.4
Production of vehicle bodies	128.8	127.3	121.4	138.2	140.7	131.1	111.8	128.8
Production of other types of transport equipment	99.7	151.4	157.4	149.4	107.7	195.3	216.5	134.0
Furniture and manufacturing industries	114.1	101.4	96.2	109.6	121.9	103.2	91.3	61.2

Note: This refers to the trimester index average.
(P) Preliminary data for 2001 first quarter.

ELECTRICAL POWER GENERATION AND DISTRIBUTION IN THE REPUBLIC (GW-HOURS)

Year	Total	Hydro-electric	Thermal
1989	2,579.3	2,180.6	398.7
1990	2,660.0	2,212.6	447.4
1991	2,761.1	2,036.0	725.1
1992	2,840.5	1,891.1	949.4
1993	3,072.8	2,294.5	778.2
1994	3,284.5	2,390.9	893.6
1995	3,393.8	2,418.0	975.8
1996	3,758.0	3,003.2	754.8
1997	3,971.8	2,902.5	1,069.3
1998	4,114.1	2,139.3	1,974.8
1999	4,773.8	3,087.7	1,575.4
2000	4,885.0	3,416.6	1,468.4

Source: Public Utilities Authority of Panama

DIRECT FOREIGN INVESTMENT IN THE REPUBLIC
ACCORDING TO CAPITAL: 1996-2000 (in millions of dollars)

	1996 (R)	1997 (R)	1998 (R)	1999 (R)	2000 (R)
Direct investment	**415.5**	**1,299.3**	**1,296.0**	**652.4**	**603.4**
Panama Canal Commission	17.7	52.3	88.9	130.9	0.0
General license banks	154.2	159.6	42.1	-58.4	98.8
International license banks	12.0	28.8	-35.0	14.9	55.7
CFZ Businesses	77.9	103.8	173.7	206.7	162.6
Other companies	153.7	954.8	1,026.3	358.3	286.3
Stocks and other capital participation	**172.7**	**982.7**	**979.4**	**175.5**	**174.4**
Panama Canal Commission	0.3	-0.1	-0.1	-3.0	0.0
General license banks	32.4	78.1	38.2	-28.9	-10.4
International license banks	4.7	10.1	13.3	-2.9	54.5
CFZ Businesses	6.3	5.4	67.7	47.7	47.0
Other companies	129.0	889.2	860.3	162.6	83.3
Other capital	**132.7**	**222.1**	**162.6**	**374.8**	**287.4**
Panama Canal Commission	17.4	52.4	89.0	133.9	0.0
General license banks	121.8	81.5	3.9	-29.5	109.2
International license banks	7.3	18.7	-48.3	17.8	1.2
CFZ Businesses	29.0	81.3	-10.3	91.6	71.6
Other companies	-42.8	-11.8	128.3	161.0	105.4
Other capital	**110.1**	**94.5**	**154.0**	**102.1**	**141.6**
Assets vs direct investors	-12.8	-12.9	-84.9	-56.4	-51.3
CFZ companies	0.5	2.9	-67.2	-51.1	-45.3
Other companies	-13.3	-15.8	-17.7	-5.3	-6.0
Liabilities vs direct investors	122.9	107.4	238.9	158.5	192.9
CFZ companies	42.1	14.2	183.5	118.5	89.3
Other companies	80.8	93.2	55.4	40.0	103.6

Source: Statistics and Census Department, Office of the General Comptroller of the Republic
(R) Revised data.

ASSETS AND LIABILITIES OF THE NATIONAL BANKING SYSTEM
(In millions of dollars)

	Assets				Liabilities and Capital		
Year	Liquid	Productive	Other Assets (1)	Total	Liquid	Other	Capital & Reserve
1988	2,359.2	8,170.1	1,063.5	11,592.8	8,247.7	2,571.2	773.9
1989	1,876.7	8,305.6	991.4	11,173.7	7,830.0	2,603.1	740.6
1990	2,887.9	8,818.2	920.7	12,626.2	9,874.5	2,091.5	660.2
1991	4,522.1	9,908.1	840.8	15,271.0	12,276.7	2,229.1	765.2
1992	4,683.6	11,557.9	879.2	17,120.7	13,633.4	2,434.0	1,053.3
1993	5,337.3	15,174.9	864.5	21,375.8	17,072.6	3,058.9	1,244.3
1994	7,077.4	17,783.8	1,673.5	26,534.7	20,321.6	4,619.0	1,594.1
1995	6,597.4	18,578.5	1,573.0	26,748.9	19,650.6	5,319.2	1,779.1
1996	6,787.4	18,640.7	1,835.7	27,263.8	19,401.9	5,733.6	2,128.3
1997	7,932.1	20,481.1	1,321.9	29,735.1	21,692.1	5,571.2	2,471.8
1998	7,001.3	20,200.7	1,293.7	28,495.7	19,665.9	6,055.8	2,774.0
1999	7,055.9	21,312.5	1,226.8	29,595.2	20,596.1	6,145.3	6,585.0
2000	7,508.5	21,845.5	1,531.2	30,885.2	21,142.8	2,853.8	3,157.4

NOTE: The National Banking System includes general-license private and state banks.
(1) Includes fixed assets.
Source: Banking Superintendency of Panama

SECURITY SALES BY INSTRUMENT TYPE, SECTOR AND YEAR
(Thousands of dollars)

Year	Total	Stocks	Bonds
Banking and finance			
1996	167,220	9,220	135,000
1997	769,000	510,000	221,000
1998	623,030	63,030	399,000
1999	24,443,495	1,991,495	356,000
2000	340,500	321,000	10,000
Industrial			
1996	6,788	288	4,500
1997	41,000	-	41,000
1999	27,000	-	25,000
2000	10,000	-	10,000
Real Estate			
1997	4,000		4,000
1998	15,000		15,000
Utilities			
2000	30,000	-	30,000
Commercial			
1996	12,000	4,000	8,000
1997	39,600	5,600	30,000
1999	26,000	-	20,000
Forestry			
1996	34,900	8,400	26,500
1997	6,000	-	6,000
1998	3,300	-	3,300
1999	2,025	2,025	-
Agro-industrial			
1996	14,000		14,000
1997	32,000		27,000
1998	40,000		40,000
1999	26,500		21,500
2000	16,500		16,500

Source: Ministry of Commerce and Industry

INSURANCE INDUSTRY INDICATORS
(Billions of dollars)

Year	Company Assets	Premium income
1989	297.80	217.70
1990	305.90	152.40
1991	326.70	176.40
1992	346.90	203.50
1993	381.50	232.30
1994	417.40	259.60
1995	417.10	283.78
1996	461.06	299.70
1997	514.96	308.47
1998	564.58	339.67
1999	626.94	354.29

Source: Superintendency of Insurance and Re-insurance, Ministry of Commerce and Industry

CONSUMER PRICE INDEX PER GROUP IN PANAMA CITY
(1987 price index = 100) (a)

	1994	1995	1996	1997	1998
Total	**106.5**	**107.5**	**108.9**	**110.2**	**110.9**
Percentage variation	1.3	0.9	1.3	1.2	0.6
Food and drink	110.0	110.6	111.4	112.2	112.6
Clothing & footwear	111.5	110.0	109.0	106.8	108.2
Electric power	103.8	105.2	107.7	110.0	111.8
Home care	103.4	105.6	108.8	111.4	111.6
Health	103.4	104.0	106.5	108.9	112.2
Transport & communications	103.1	104.9	105.7	108.0	106.1
Culture & teaching	105.5	106.8	108.7	110.0	113.2
Other goods & services	104.2	105.5	106.9	108.2	108.6

Source: Office of the General Comptroller of the Republic
(a) The data used to calculate this index were based on the spending habits of 1,070 families of various income levels. Such information was taken from the "Survey on family living conditions", which took place in Panama city between 1993/94.

RE-EXPORTATION OF THE COLON FREE ZONE
1996-2000 (In thousands of dollars)

Continent, economic zone and destination	1996	1997	1998	1999	2000(P)
TOTAL	*5,491,138*	*6,290,664*	*5,995,267*	*4,949,601*	*5,300,913*
THE AMERICAS	*5,342,532*	*6,131,453*	*5,857,911*	*4,799,394*	*5,139,398*
North American Free Trade Agreement (NAFTA)	**345,684**	**396,995**	**443,658**	**420,525**	**543,460**
Canada	4,829	3,397	2,186	1,648	2,501
United States	280,331	288,633	324,511	272,259	268,472
Mexico (1)	60,524	104,965	116,961	146,618	272,487
Central American Common Market (MCC)	**607,490**	**738,349**	**860,289**	**858,799**	**914,477**
Costa Rica	144,981	182,204	214,884	215,152	233,161
El Salvador	143,495	118,242	138,068	144,812	165,026
Guatemala	128,709	199,104	238,212	215,278	241,256
Honduras	76,338	97,977	128,774	136,454	137,633
Nicaragua	113,967	140,822	140,351	147,103	137,401
Latin American Integration Association (ALADI)	**3,408,204**	**3,953,663**	**3,423,015**	**2,395,928**	**2,684,272**
Chile	192,839	189,754	166,052	129,324	112,354
Mexico (1)	60,524	104,965	116,961	146,618	272,487
Southern Common Market (MERCOSUR)	**803,930**	**736,807**	**639,877**	**317,928**	**327,931**
Argentina	82,928	76,717	85,659	52,738	43,763
Brasil	440,621	397,060	311,520	142,245	164,502
Paraguay	219,056	216,352	185,695	81,259	84,702
Uruguay	61,325	46,678	57,003	41,686	34,964
Andean Group	**2,350,911**	**2,922,137**	**2,500,125**	**1,802,058**	**1,971,500**
Bolivia	45,416	38,768	35,711	22,692	17,875
Colombia (2)	1,512,207	1,708,060	1,371,181	1,035,727	882,654
Ecuador	419,220	463,334	271,409	127,449	198,250
Peru	103,075	102,112	123,967	61,975	71,692
Venezuela	270,993	609,863	697,857	554,215	801,029
Caribbean Community (CARICOM)	**121,502**	**146,741**	**148,120**	**151,534**	**183,024**
Bahamas	6,441	7,205	8,002	9,261	16,751
Barbados	4,689	6,313	6,993	8,742	8,543
Belize	4,936	6,004	6,413	9,808	28,009
Guyana	7,110	7,506	10,868	10,671	13,879
Grenada	246	280	251	492	515
Jamaica	61,771	79,600	73,867	72,828	73,520
Leeward Islands (British) (3)	2,499	2,456	3,634	3,725	4,924
Surinam	12,108	10,295	9,684	7,375	6,313
Trinidad & Tobago	18,074	22,879	22,831	22,402	24,298
Windward Islands (British) (4)	3,628	4,203	5,577	6,230	6,272

RE-EXPORTATION OF THE COLON FREE ZONE
1996-2000 (In thousands of dollars)

Continent, economic zone and destination	1996	1997	1998	1999	2000(P)
Other	**920,177**	**1,000,669**	**1,099,789**	**1,119,229**	**1,086,651**
Canal area	8,148	4,576	2,473	1,217	-
Aruba	35,706	43,294	43,028	39,234	43,072
Bermudas	991	1,224	1,453	1,233	1,752
Cuba	214,379	204,162	257,708	235,966	234,318
Curaçao	27,871	27,983	27,250	29,265	32,666
Haiti	61,276	64,727	66,518	68,512	59,393
PANAMA	378,200	416,927	433,254	438,267	389,019
Dominican Republic	148,312	196,897	216,850	262,897	279,945
Puerto Rico	8,720	6,177	10,036	8,276	8,912
Other countries	36,574	34,702	41,219	34,360	37,574
EUROPE	**42,927**	**52,212**	**27,935**	**36,722**	**21,106**
European Free Trade Association (EFTA)	**1,484**	**898**	**2,832**	**4,441**	**674**
Iceland	249	-	102	7	-
Norway	-	1	-	107	-
Switzerland	1,235	897	2,730	4,327	674
European Union (EU)	**32,317**	**46,886**	**20,814**	**28,504**	**18,665**
Germany	3,898	5,888	2,187	3,194	564
Austria	10	3	1	-	2,234
Belgium/Luxemburg	2,213	5,142	750	7,201	240
Denmark	-	254	140	226	-
Spain	3,092	4,135	4,195	4,188	3,828
Finland	32	672	593	176	5
France	2,277	992	958	474	205
Greece	236	34	29	195	86
Ireland (Eire)	521	573	34	-	2,975
Italy	3,597	934	1,148	2,914	4,239
The Netherlands	14,447	22,075	8,387	6,214	3,260
Portugal	593	4,192	729	790	599
United Kingdom	1,071	1,647	1,663	2,937	336
Sweeden	330	345	-	-	94
The rest of Europe	**9,128**	**4,430**	**4,288**	**3,776**	**1,767**
Czechoslovakia(a)	1,228	80	47	132	(a)
Poland	5	139	39	573	41
The Soviet Union(b)	6,538	1,451	996	36	26
Other countries	1,357	2,759	3,206	3,035	1,700
ASIA	**83,489**	**79,603**	**80,176**	**90,099**	**114,153**
Association of Southeastern Asian Nations (ASEAN)	**12,039**	**15,279**	**15,579**	**23,688**	**23,828**
Philippines	815	2,072	3,207	2,644	4,543
Indonesia	712	496	2,166	3,857	2,823
Malaysia	749	1,014	1,323	1,636	2,477
Singapore	6,121	6,626	5,020	8,458	7,478
Thailand	3,642	5,071	3,863	7,093	6,507

RE-EXPORTATION OF THE COLON FREE ZONE
1996-2000 (In thousands of dollars)

Continent, economic zone and destination	1996	1997	1998	1999	2000(P)
The rest of Asia	**71,450**	**64,325**	**64,599**	**66,411**	**90,325**
South Korea	5,137	5,972	8,772	11,585	21,081
Mainland China	686	419	273	233	3,659
Taiwan	6,084	9,110	7,994	8,568	13,264
Hong Kong	30,120	25,516	19,295	16,844	18,729
India	850	642	304	187	333
Israel	3,240	3,470	2,493	1,370	3,280
Japan	4,376	2,750	2,055	2,215	1,367
Other countries	20,957	16,446	43,413	25,408	28,612
AFRICA	**2,283**	**2,931**	**2,937**	**3,753**	**5,349**
South Africa	174	87	286	371	222
Other countries	2,110	2,845	2,651	3,381	5,127
OCEANIA	**1,332**	**2,785**	**2,968**	**427**	**897**
Australia	824	1,242	1,433	144	554
New Zealand	415	995	1,250	224	343
Other countries	93	548	286	59	-
CONSUMPTION ON BOARD (5)	**18,206**	**21,287**	**22,957**	**18,977**	**19,930**
RETURNS (6)	**368**	**393**	**382**	**229**	**80**

(1) Both were added in order to include each economic zone but only once in the continent and in the total.
(2) Includes data for the islands of San Andrés and Providencia.
(3) Includes the islands of Montserrat, St. Christopher and Nevis, and Antigua & Barbuda.
(4) Includes the islands of Dominica, St. Lucia, St. Vincent and the Grenadines.
(5) This refers to the sale of merchandise for consumption ships and planes.
(6) It refers to the sold merchandise that returns to the Colon Free Zone.
(a) Corresponds to re-exports destined to the Czech Republic and Slovakia.
(b) Corresponds to re-exports destined to Russia.

TEMPERATURE AND PRECIPITATION AVERAGE :1996-2000

Month	Liquid precipitation (milimeters)		Temperature (Celsius)		
	Total	Daily Average	Maximum	Minimum	Mean
Average	*156.1*	*5.0*	*35.5*	*21.4*	*28.5*
January	45.8	1.5	34.5	19.8	27.2
February	10.6	0.4	35.1	20.5	27.8
March	10.8	0.3	35.6	19.4	27.5
April	45.7	1.5	34.8	21.2	28.0
May	206.7	6.7	35.3	22.8	29.1
June	188.8	6.3	35.0	22.6	28.8
July	151.1	4.9	42.5	21.9	32.2
August	206.0	5.4	35.0	23.4	29.2
September	272.9	9.1	34.3	21.7	28.0
October	229.3	7.4	35.0	22.4	28.7
November	300.2	10.0	34.3	21.0	27.7
December	205.2	6.0	34.1	20.6	27.4

The data for each year refer to the monthly average. The maximum and minimum figures for each month refer to the average of such values registered during every day of the month. The mean is the partial sum of the maximum and minimum temperatures.

Source: Meteorological Registry, Civil Aviation Administration

INTERNATIONAL MOVEMENT OF FLIGHTS AND PASSENGERS AT
TOCUMEN INTERNATIONAL AIRPORT: 1994-2000

	1994	1995	1996	1997	1998	1999	2000(P)
Flights (1)	47,893	39,234	45,917	33,057	39,193	37,304	37,254
Arrivals	23,918	19,605	23,149	16,535	19,603	18,652	18,629
Departures	23,975	19,629	22,768	16,522	19,590	18,652	18,625
Passengers	1,313,145	1,385,476	1,508,801	1,727,540	1,793,600	1,705,956	1,933,485

Note: The flight figures for 1994 and 1995 were amended due to changes in the information source.
(1) This refers to passenger, cargo and mail commercial flights.
Source: Statistics and Census Department, Office of the General Comptroller of the Republic

ARRIVAL AND DEPARTURE OF PASSENGERS:
1996-2000

Types of Passengers	PASSENGERS				
	1996	1997	1998 (P)	1999 (P)	2000 (P)
	ARRIVALS				
TOTAL	**644,625**	**660,455**	**687,524**	**711,681**	**719,815**
Visitors	**442,637**	**439,265**	**446,937**	**475,760**	**502,118**
Tourists	430,284	409,167	418,520	449,301	464,299
Excursionists (1)	12,353	30,098	28,417	26,459	37,819
Temporary visitors (2)	1,577	1,420	2,583	1,200	887
Inmigrants (3)	1,613	1,056	1,494	854	1,013
Residents	**177,600**	**199,057**	**212,117**	**220,211**	**215,797**
Panamanians	143,735	161,150	176,751	182,756	180,376
Foreigners	33,865	37,907	35,366	37,455	35,421
Destined to the Canal area (4)	21,198	19,657	24,393	13,656	--
	DEPARTURES				
TOTAL	**626,267**	**669,043**	**695,322**	**712,611**	**723,355 (E)**
Visitants	**394,773**	**436,830**	**438,496**	**442,504**	**482,575**
Residents	**208,912**	**217,603**	**222,038**	**233,970**	**240,780**
Panamanians	171,400	173,505	190,164	200,846	205,819
Foreigners	37,512	44,098	31,874	33,124	349,661
Leaving the Canal area (4)	**22,582**	**14,610**	**34,788**	**36,137**	**--**

Note: In order to unify criteria with the Panama Government Tourist Bureau, the 1997 data includes the classification of "Excursionist", recommended by the World Tourism Organization (WTO), instead of "in transit passengers". This explains the contradictory figures.
(1) This refers to passengers who fail to stay over at least one night in the country.
(2) This refers to passengers who stay in the country from 91 days to one year.
(3) This refers to foreigners applying to stay over one (1) year within the country.
(4) This correspondes to members of the Armed Forces of the United States of America, stationed in military bases in Panama.

Source: Inmigration and Naturalization Department, Ministry of Government and Justice and the Panama Government Tourist Bureau

General Index

MAPA FÍSICO
PHYSICAL MA

MAR CARIBE

Nuevo Chagr
Miguel De La Borda

Punta Gaona
Coclé Del Norte
Guásimo

Belén
Coclesito

GOLFO DE LOS MOSQUITOS

Punta Santa Catalina
Calovébora

Cerro Gaital

CORDILLERA CENTRAL

El Copé
La Pintada
El Valle
Güzman
COCLÉ
Santa Fé
PENONOME
Cerro Tuta
La Yeguada
Coclé
Antón
Río Hato

VERAGUAS

Cañazas
Calobre
Nată

San Francisco
Pocrí
Aguadulce

San Bartolo
El Roble
Bahía de Parita

Las Palmas
SANTIAGO
Divisa
Santa María

El Maria
La Mesa
Potuga
Parita

Jorones
Soná
Atalaya
Monagrillo
Utirá
Montijo
Ocú
CHITRE

Río de
Jesús
Los Santos
La Espigadilla

HERRERA
Los Pozos
Colorada
Guararé
LAS TAB

Las
Minas
Santo Do

Leones
Calabacito
La Mesa
Valle Rico
Valle Riquito

**Golfo de
Montijo**
Cerro Quema
LOS SANTOS
Cañas

Isla
Gobernadora
Isla Cébaco
El
Bebedero
Tongsí

Punta Duarte
Arena
Ave María

Punta Mariato

Isla Jicarón
Punta Ventana

Isla Jicarita

OCÉANO PACÍFICO

California

Río Sixaola

Changuinola

Isla Colón
Bastimentos
BOCAS DEL TORO

Isla Popa

Almirante

Isla Cayo Agua
Península Valiente
Tobobe
Isla Escudo de Veraguas

Punta Róbalo
Punta Tiburón
Punta Icaco

Laguna de Chiriquí
Chiriquí
Grande

COSTA RICA

Cerro Echandi

Cerro Pando

Río Sereno
Cerro Picacho
Cerro Punta

Volcán de Chiriquí
Cerro Horqueta
Fortuna

Volcán
Paja de
Sombrero
Cerro Chorcha

Paso Canoa
Dolega
La Concepción
Gualaca
Soloy

BOCAS DEL TORO

SERRANÍA DEL TABASARÁ

Cerro Santiago
Toabré

Progreso
Boqueron
DAVID
Hato Chami

Divala
CHIRIQUI
Chiriquí

Alanje
San Lorenzo

Pedregal
Guarumal
Horconcitos
San Félix
Tolé

Puerto Armuelles
Las Lajas
San

Isla Sevilla
Remedios
Las Lajas

Bahía de Charco Azul
Isla Boca Brava

Isla Parida

Punta Burica

GOLFO DE CHIRIQUÍ

Bahía de San Lorenzo

Punta Pajaronal

Isla Brincanco
Pixvae

Isla Uvas

Punta Jabalí
La Punta

El Tigre

Isla
Gobernadora

Isla de Coiba

ESCALA 1:1,700,000

18   0   18   36   54 KMS.